CRONKITE'S WAR

CRONKITE'S WAR

His World War II Letters Home

WALTER CRONKITE IV AND MAURICE ISSERMAN

NATIONAL GEOGRAPHIC

WASHINGTON, D.C.

Published by the National Geographic Society
1145 17th Street N.W., Washington, D.C. 20036-4688 U.S.A.

Walter Cronkite's United Press (UP) text excerpts courtesy United Press International (UPI).

Library of Congress Cataloging-in-Publication Data
Cronkite, Walter.
  Cronkite's war : his World War II letters home / Walter Cronkite IV and Maurice Isserman.
    pages cm
  Includes bibliographical references and index.
  ISBN 978-1-4262-1019-8
  1. Cronkite, Walter--Correspondence. 2. Cronkite, Walter--Family. 3. Cronkite, Betsy, -2005--Correspondence. 4. World War, 1939-1945--Journalists--Correspondence. 5. War correspondents--United States--Correspondence. 6. World War, 1939-1945--Aerial operations, American. 7. World War, 1939-1945--Campaigns--Europe. 8. World War, 1939-1945--England--London--Anecdotes. 9. United Press International--Biography. 10. World War, 1939-1945--Personal narratives. 11. Love-letters--United States. I. Isserman, Maurice. II. Cronkite, Walter, IV. III. Title.
  D799.U6C76 2012
  070.4'4994053092--dc23

                    2012045334

CELEBRATING

◀125▶

YEARS

The National Geographic Society is one of the world's largest private nonprofit scientific and educational organizations. Founded in 1888 to "increase and diffuse geographic knowledge," the Society's mission is to inspire people to care about the planet. It reaches more than 400 million people worldwide each month through its official journal, *National Geographic,* and other magazines; National Geographic Channel; television documentaries; music; radio; films; books; DVDs; maps; exhibitions; live events; school publishing programs; interactive media; and merchandise. National Geographic has funded more than 10,000 scientific research, conservation, and exploration projects and supports an education program promoting geographic literacy.

For more information, visit www.nationalgeographic.com.

National Geographic Society
1145 17th Street N.W.
Washington, D.C. 20036-4688 U.S.A.

For information about special discounts for bulk purchases, please contact
National Geographic Books Special Sales: ngspecsales@ngs.org

For rights or permissions inquiries, please contact National Geographic Books Subsidiary Rights: ngbookrights@ngs.org

Interior design: Katie Olsen

Printed in the United States of America

13/QGF-LPH/1

For Betsy Cronkite—my beloved grandmother.
—Walter Cronkite IV

For Walter Cronkite, Jr.—anchorman, CBS Evening News,
1962–1981—who reported the world to me.
—Maurice Isserman

CONTENTS

AUTHOR'S NOTE

The letters in this book have been edited by the authors for improved readability, but no text has been changed.

FOREWORD

★ ★ ★ ★ ★ ★ ★

By the end of the 20th century, Walter Cronkite was one of the most famous Americans of his time. He carried the coveted title "the Most Trusted Man in America," and to generations of younger viewers, he was known as Uncle Walter, the steady and wise man guiding the country through so much tumultuous change from his anchor desk on *CBS Evening News*.

To those of us who shared his profession, he was a role model as a journalist and also as a family man, a father and the husband of the incomparable Betsy, a winsome woman he met in the early stages of his career in Kansas City. To their many friends (and I was proud to be in that company), they were simply "Walter and Betsy," a matched pair with a zest for life—whether it was a sailing vacation, an opening night on Broadway, box seats at the Kentucky Derby, or at a sing-along after a dinner party.

Their sense of adventure started early, for they were married in 1940, on the cusp of World War II, when the future of the free world was to be determined in what some military historians have called "the greatest single event in the history of mankind."

By 1942 Walter was headed for that war as a correspondent for the United Press. The next year he was based in London and covering the war on a daily basis, primarily by reporting on the dangerous bombing missions of the Eighth Air Force.

London, that most elegant of cities, was on a full-time war footing, blacked out at night to discourage German air strikes, living on reduced rations, and trying to accommodate the crush of newcomers who poured into the British capital to launch the counterattack against Nazi Germany.

In this remarkable collection of personal letters from Walter to Betsy, the reader is transported back to the pivotal years of 1943–45, when the push against Hitler's war machine was beginning to have its effect. Betsy was back in New York with their beloved cocker spaniel, Judy, for what would prove to be a long separation.

In the straight-ahead, honest prose he later became famous for as an anchorman, Walter mixed the momentous, the personal, and the ordinary in his dispatches to Betsy, worrying about how to make his meager salary cover room, meals, and wardrobe. War correspondents in those days wore special uniforms, which they had to purchase, and they drew rations such as one big Tootsie Roll, vanilla wafers, cheese niblets, a carton of cigarettes, and a box of razor blades. At one point he let her know that his share of a room was $18 a week, explaining that the price may seem exorbitant (!) but that space was scarce.

Walter's days and nights were long and irregular, and he often told Betsy of his exhaustion, brought on by working through the night to hammer out an account of a bombing raid and then to get it through the censors and onto the wires for transmission to the United Press (UP) newspaper clients in the U.S.

It wasn't all work and no play, however. Walter came to be a drinking pal with Clark Gable, the big Hollywood star who had enlisted and flew combat missions with the Eighth Air Force. He began a lifelong friendship with Andy Rooney, and his UP boss was Harrison Salisbury, a legendary journalist for my generation. A bar was always open somewhere, and it's plain that Uncle Walter enjoyed a nightcap.

His most famous assignment that year was also the most dangerous. The gifted young men who covered the Eighth Air Force persuaded Army brass that they should be able to accompany a bombing mission over Germany. Remember, this was at a time when casualty rates were high because the bombers didn't have adequate close-air support and the German homeland was laced with air defense weapons. Cronkite flew in the Plexiglas nose cone of a B-17 during the raid and later admitted that he manned the .50-caliber machine gun against German fighter planes when they were attacked over the target. His bomber made it back safely, but a plane carrying a *New York Times* reporter was shot down and his body never was recovered.

Cronkite's first-person account of the raid—the first ever written by a journalist along for the ride—received wide play and high praise across the United States, but in his letters to Betsy he remained characteristically matter-of-fact in describing the stack of congratulatory messages he received.

As I read these letters, I longed to see Walter and Betsy again so that I could tell them how much I enjoyed them and how much I admired their unconditional love, which comes through after all these years.

The letters to Betsy also reminded me of how the two of them and all of their friends from that time kept up their enthusiasm for taking life head-on. Think about it: They were front and center for World War II. And yet, when it ended, they were on to the next big story, and the one after that, and the one after that, a gregarious couple from America's heartland who relished all their opportunities and loved each other deeply until the very end of their quintessential American story.

Finally—and I'm sorry, I can't help myself—"That's the way it was."

—TOM BROKAW

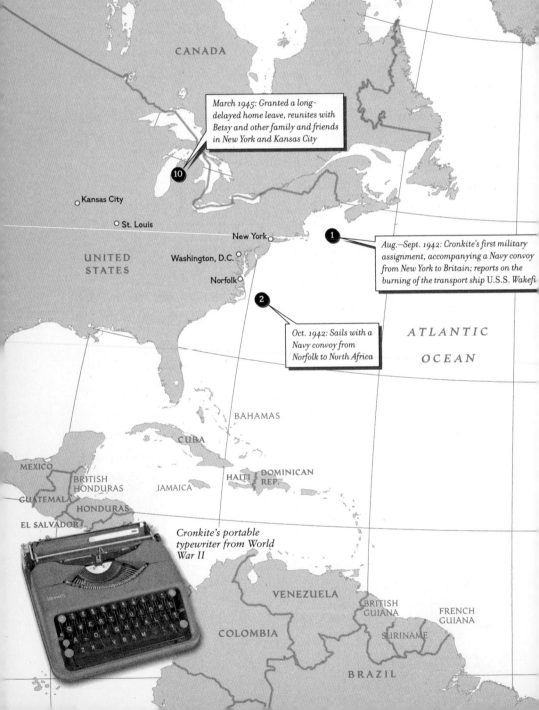

WALTER CRONKITE'S WORLD WAR II ASSIGNMENTS

CANADA

10 — *March 1945: Granted a long-delayed home leave, reunites with Betsy and other family and friends in New York and Kansas City*

○ Kansas City

○ St. Louis

New York ○

UNITED STATES

Washington, D.C. ○

Norfolk ○

1 — *Aug.–Sept. 1942: Cronkite's first military assignment, accompanying a Navy convoy from New York to Britain; reports on the burning of the transport ship U.S.S. Wakefi[eld]*

2 — *Oct. 1942: Sails with a Navy convoy from Norfolk to North Africa*

ATLANTIC OCEAN

BAHAMAS

CUBA

MEXICO

BRITISH HONDURAS   JAMAICA   HAITI   DOMINICAN REP.

GUATEMALA

HONDURAS

EL SALVADOR

Cronkite's portable typewriter from World War II

VENEZUELA

BRITISH GUIANA   FRENCH GUIANA

COLOMBIA   SURINAME

BRAZIL

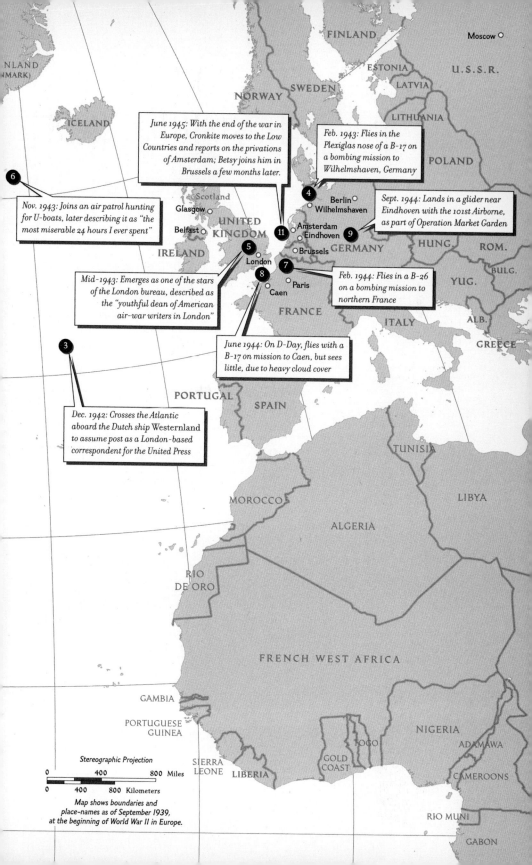

June 1945: With the end of the war in Europe, Cronkite moves to the Low Countries and reports on the privations of Amsterdam; Betsy joins him in Brussels a few months later.

Feb. 1943: Flies in the Plexiglas nose of a B-17 on a bombing mission to Wilhelmshaven, Germany

Nov. 1943: Joins an air patrol hunting for U-boats, later describing it as "the most miserable 24 hours I ever spent"

Sept. 1944: Lands in a glider near Eindhoven with the 101st Airborne, as part of Operation Market Garden

Mid-1943: Emerges as one of the stars of the London bureau, described as the "youthful dean of American air-war writers in London"

Feb. 1944: Flies in a B-26 on a bombing mission to northern France

June 1944: On D-Day, flies with a B-17 on mission to Caen, but sees little, due to heavy cloud cover

Dec. 1942: Crosses the Atlantic aboard the Dutch ship Westernland to assume post as a London-based correspondent for the United Press

Stereographic Projection

0   400   800 Miles
0 400 800 Kilometers

Map shows boundaries and place-names as of September 1939, at the beginning of World War II in Europe.

CHARACTER KEY

Anderson, Dave *New York Times* correspondent who briefly shared an apartment with Cronkite in Brussels in 1944.

Astaire, Adele Entertainer Fred Astaire's older sister. She appeared with him on Broadway in *The Band Wagon* in 1931 but gave up the stage when she married Lord Charles Arthur Francis Cavendish, becoming Lady Cavendish.

Ault, Phil United Press correspondent in London, covering the air war.

Baillie, Hugh President of United Press from 1935 to 1955. A former police reporter, he was known as a martinet and proud of his reputation.

Barhydt, Frank An old friend of Cronkite's.

Beattie, Edward W., Jr. Veteran war correspondent and United Press bureau chief in London. He was captured by the Germans in France in September 1944.

Bennett, Lowell International News Service correspondent in London. He was shot down over Berlin in a U.S. bomber raid in November 1943 and described his captivity in Germany in his book *Parachute to Berlin* (1945).

Berlin, Irving America's favorite songwriter, whose works include "White Christmas" and "God Bless America." His wartime show *This Is the Army* played on Broadway in 1942 and then went on tour to military bases overseas, including England. Berlin appeared in the production, on Broadway and abroad, singing "Oh! How I Hate to Get Up in the Morning." Ronald Reagan starred in the 1943 movie version.

Bigart, Homer *New York Herald Tribune* correspondent and member of the Writing Sixty-Ninth who went on the Wilhelmshaven raid. In 1946 he was awarded a Pulitzer Prize for "distinguished reporting" from the Pacific. He remained with the *Herald Tribune* until 1955, when he switched to the *New York Times,* retiring in 1972.

Boni, Bill Associated Press correspondent who landed with the 82nd Airborne in Operation Market Garden.

Boyle, Harold Vincent "Hal" Associated Press columnist. He won the 1945 Pulitzer Prize for "distinguished war correspondence."

Brandt, Bert Photographer for Planet/Acme, the United Press picture wire service. He covered the D-Day landings.

Catenhauser, Robert W. Kansas-born Army Air Force second lieutenant and glider pilot.

Clark, Ronald British United Press correspondent who helped cover Operation Market Garden and was later assigned to the Brussels bureau.

Colwell, Ward E. Kansas City bureau manager of the United Press in the 1930s.

Cronkite, Helen Fritsche Cronkite's mother.

Daly, John Charles CBS Radio correspondent in London. After the war, he hosted the weekly *What's My Line?* panel game show on CBS from 1950 through 1967.

Daniell, Raymond "Pete" *New York Times* London bureau chief. His book *Civilians Must Fight* (1941) reported on the Battle of Britain.

Davis, Elmer Head of Office of War Information.

Day, Clifford L. "Cliff" United Press London bureau manager.

Dickinson, William Boyd "Bill" United Press correspondent in London who handled the desk rewrites on the air war. A Missourian, he joined the UP in 1930, was assigned to London in 1940 to cover the Battle of Britain, and in 1943 left for a new assignment in the Southwest Pacific reporting on Gen. Douglas MacArthur's campaign. He covered the Japanese surrender on board the U.S.S. *Missouri* in 1945. After the war, he served in editorial and executive positions at the *Philadelphia Bulletin* until his retirement in 1973.

Disher, Leo "Bill" United Press correspondent in London, covering the air war. He later became chief of the UP bureaus in Czechoslovakia and the Balkans.

Downs, William Randall "Bill" A former United Press correspondent and one of the "Murrow Boys" with CBS Radio during the war.

Duff, Robin BBC correspondent famous for covering the Blitz and D-Day.

Dursten, John *New York Herald Tribune* correspondent in London.

Eaker, Ira C. Eighth Air Force commander.

Evans, Joe *Newsweek* London bureau manager.

Falkenburg, Eugenia Lincoln "Jinx" Model, actress, former tennis champion, and socialite who married "Tex" McCreary.

Ferguson, Harry Veteran United Press sportswriter and assistant general news manager.

Frankish, John F. "Jack" United Press correspondent. He arrived in England in spring 1944 and was killed during the Battle of the Bulge, December 23, 1944.

Fritsche, Edward "Uncle Ed" Cronkite's uncle, his mother's only sibling.

Fritsche, Jack Cronkite's cousin and an Army Air Force officer.

Gable, Clark A leading Hollywood actor and the star of *Gone With the Wind* (1939) who enlisted in the Army Air Force in 1942. Promoted to captain, he was assigned to the Eighth Air Force to make a recruiting film for aerial gunners. He flew combat missions as an observer-gunner. Cronkite refers to him in letters to Betsy as "The Face."

Gaskill, Gordon American war correspondent who landed on Omaha Beach on D-Day. He spent Christmas Day 1944 with Cronkite in Luxembourg.

Gellhorn, Martha Veteran war correspondent and Ernest Hemingway's third wife. She spent Christmas Day in 1944 with Cronkite in Luxembourg.

Gerteis, Louis H. Former United Press correspondent who worked for the Office of War Information's foreign news bureau during World War II.

Graebner, Walt *Time*'s London bureau chief. He had reported for *Time* and *Life* on the Battle of Britain, and his book *Their Finest Hour* (co-authored with *Time* correspondent Allan A. Michie) was published in England in 1940 and in the United States the following year. He later reported from the Soviet Union.

Graham, Frederick *New York Times* correspondent in London.

Grigg, Joseph W. A veteran United Press foreign correspondent who covered the start of the war from Germany. After the invasion, he was assigned to Paris and later became UP's Paris bureau chief.

Hales, Samuel Dale United Press correspondent in London, covering the air war and the war in France after the invasion.

Harmon, Dudley Ann One of the rare women war correspondents employed by the United Press in London. She later covered the war in France and the Nuremberg trials.

Hawkins, Eric *New York Herald Tribune* correspondent. Hawkins published the last edition of the Paris *Herald Tribune* in June 1940 as the Nazis approached the city. His memoir, *Hawkins of the "Paris Herald"* (1963), includes a vivid description of wartime London.

Higginbotham, Charles "Bill" United Press correspondent in London, covering the air war.

Hill, Gladwin AP correspondent and member of the Writing Sixty-Ninth who went on the Wilhelmshaven raid. Like Cronkite, he was head of his wire service's air war desk, which made the two of them fierce if friendly rivals, eager to be the one to file a story first. After the war, Hill worked at the *New York Times* from 1946 to 1979, for which he covered the Kennedy assassination and became a pioneer of environmental reporting.

Johnson, Earl J. United Press vice president and general manager in New York.

Judy Cronkite family cocker spaniel.

Kirksey, George Eighth Air Force public relations officer and a former United Press sportswriter.

Knox, Betty *London Evening Standard* reporter, and a former star of vaudeville and the music hall stage.

Krum, Morrow Army public relations officer. He was killed in an air crash in Iceland on May 3, 1943; the same crash killed Lt. Gen. Frank Maxwell Andrews, commander of U.S. forces in the European theater of operations.

Kuh, Frederick United Press correspondent in London, Berlin, Moscow, and Manchuria who became chief London correspondent for Field Publications in 1942. "There was no diplomat Kuh did not know," Harrison Salisbury recalled, "no Foreign Office man he had not dealt with."

Laidlaw, Bill Major in Eighth Air Force public relations.

LeSueur, Larry Joined CBS Radio in 1939 as one of the "Murrow Boys," covering the London Blitz, D-Day, and the liberation of Paris, before winding up in Belgium in December 1944, where Cronkite met him. He left CBS for the Voice of America in 1963.

Lewis, Boyd United Press correspondent covering the fighting in Belgium.

Lockett, Edward B. London bureau chief for *Time* magazine from 1942 to 1944. He later covered the White House for *Time*.

Lower, Elmer Office of War Information field representative and former United Press reporter and bureau chief. He later worked with Cronkite at CBS News and became president of ABC News in 1963 and dean of the University of Missouri School of Journalism in 1982.

Lynch, Charles Canadian reporter working for Reuters who landed on Omaha Beach on D-Day. He later covered the Second British Army with Cronkite.

Manning, Paul CBS Radio correspondent hired by Edward R. Murrow and a member of the Writing Sixty-Ninth who did not fly on the Wilhelmshaven raid. Later in the war he moved to the Mutual Broadcasting System, and after the war he served as a speechwriter for Nelson Rockefeller.

Manring, Bob Sometimes referred to by Cronkite as "nephoo" (nephew), he was the son of Betsy's eldest sister, Lora. Manring was about the same age as Betsy and Walter, and the three were very close. According to family lore, Manring was serving in a "hush-hush" military capacity during the war.

Marchant, Hilde Chief feature reporter for the *Daily Express* and author of *Women and Children Last: A Woman Reporter's Account of the Battle of Britain* (1941) before joining the *London Daily Mirror* as a daily columnist. She was also Bill Dickinson's girlfriend. According to Harrison Salisbury, "She was as widely known as any woman in wartime England."

Maxwell, Allan Betsy Cronkite's brother.

Maxwell, Arthur Betsy Cronkite's father, referred to as "Petty" in the letters.

Maxwell, Betty Betsy Cronkite's sister-in-law, married to Allan Maxwell.

Maxwell, Eva Betsy Cronkite's mother, referred to as "Molo" in letters.

McCreary, John Reagan "Tex" Journalist and public relations specialist who rose to the rank of colonel in the U.S. Army during the war. He married Jinx Falkenburg and later became prominent in Republican Party politics.

McGlincy, Jim United Press correspondent in London, covering the air war, and Cronkite's friend and roommate. He later covered the ground war in France and Belgium.

McLemore, Henry Syndicated columnist for Hearst newspapers.

Middleton, Drew Arrived in London to cover sports for the Associated Press and stayed on to cover the war, becoming the *New York Times* military correspondent in 1942. After the war he reported for the *Times* from Moscow, Berlin, and London.

Miller, Elizabeth "Lee" Condé Nast Publications war correspondent and photographer. Before the war she had been a model and then a fashion photographer. During the war she often worked on assignments with *Life* photographer David E. Scherman. In 1944 she covered the fighting in Normandy and the liberation of Paris. In 1945 she photographed Buchenwald and Dachau concentration camps. Her postwar marriage to English artist Sir Roland Penrose gave her the title Lady Penrose.

Morris, Joe Alex Joined United Press in 1928, became UP foreign editor in 1938, and later was named foreign editor of *New York Herald Tribune*.

Murray, J. Edward "Ed" United Press correspondent in London. After the war he helped found the *Los Angeles Mirror* and was its managing editor from 1948 to 1960.

Murrow, Edward R. Director of the CBS Radio Network in London. With the possible exceptions of Ernie Pyle and Hal Boyle, Murrow was the most famous journalist of World War II and is widely credited with inventing broadcast journalism. He was unsuccessful in his attempts to recruit Cronkite to CBS, but they later became colleagues at the network. In addition to his coverage of the Battle of Britain from London, Murrow is most famous for his early 1950s television series *See It Now,* especially for the episode challenging the credibility of anti-Communist zealot Joseph McCarthy, Senator from Wisconsin.

Musel, Robert "Bob" With the United Press since 1927, he covered the Lindbergh kidnapping case and came to London in 1943 and reported on the air war and later the Battle of the Bulge. He also had a side career as lyricist of popular songs like "Pappa Piccolino." He lived in London until his death in 1999.

Newman, Al *Newsweek* correspondent in London and a fraternity brother of Cronkite's.

Packard, Eleanor and Reynolds Married United Press correspondents who often worked together, covering the Italian invasion of Ethiopia in 1935 and the Spanish Civil War in 1936, and co-authoring *Balcony Empire: Fascist Italy at War* (1942). They were nicknamed "Pack and Peebee" by their fellow journalists.

Parris, John United Press correspondent in London who switched to the Associated Press in 1944. After the war, as columnist and editor at North Carolina's *Asheville Citizen-Times*, he became an expert on the state's mountain culture.

Pinkley, Virgil Senior United Press correspondent in London. He became European business manager of United Press in 1930 and was wounded while covering the desert war in Libya in 1941. After the war he was founding publisher of the *Los Angeles Mirror* and author of *Eisenhower Declassified* (1979).

Poorbaugh, Earl International News Service correspondent.

Post, Robert Perkins *New York Times* correspondent in London who covered the Battle of Britain. A member of the Writing Sixty-Ninth, he was killed in Wilhelmshaven raid.

Ragsdale, Wilmott *Time Life* war correspondent who landed on Omaha Beach on D-Day plus one. He became a journalism professor at the University of Wisconsin–Madison in 1960.

Richards, Bob United Press correspondent in London, covering the air war.

Richardson, Bill Former United Press correspondent and managing editor of the U.S. Army magazine *Yank* in London.

Richardson, Stanley NBC Radio correspondent.

Roberts, Ned United Press correspondent in London, covering the air war.

Roussel, Roy Major in the Eighth Air Force. He was city editor of the *Houston Press* in the 1930s when Cronkite was starting out there as a reporter.

Russell, Ned United Press correspondent in London. After the war he worked for the *New York Herald Tribune*.

Salisbury, Harrison United Press editor, Cronkite's boss in London, and later a *New York Times* foreign correspondent. His chapters on wartime London in his memoir, *A Journey for Our Times* (1983), are filled with colorful anecdotes about Cronkite and many of the other correspondents Cronkite mentioned in his letters to Betsy.

Scherman, David E. *Life* magazine photographer since 1936 who often worked with Condé Nast war correspondent "Lee" Miller. Before the United States entered the war, he had survived the sinking of his ship on the Atlantic by a Nazi surface raider, which was disguised as a merchant vessel. His photographs of the Nazi ship, published in *Life*, helped the Royal Navy track down and sink the raider. He remained at *Life* until the magazine's demise as a weekly in 1972 and edited the best-selling book *The Best of "Life"* (1973).

Schulstad, Mel Major in the Eighth Air Force, decorated B-17 pilot, friend of Cronkite's.

Shadel, Bill CBS Radio reporter and a "Murrow Boy" who covered the D-Day landings, the Battle of the Bulge, and the liberation of Buchenwald concentration camp. He later was a television anchor for ABC News.

Sippy, Josephine Red Cross worker.

Small, Collie United Press correspondent in London. He took over traveling to air bases for Cronkite in mid-1943 and later covered the fighting in France.

Smith, Clayton Major in Eighth Air Force public relations.

Stewart, Jimmy One of Hollywood's best loved actors, for such movies as *Mr. Smith Goes to Washington* (1939), as well as an experienced amateur pilot. He enlisted as a private in the Army Air Corps in 1941 and received his pilots' wings and a commission in 1942. While the Air Force wanted to restrict him to public relations activities, he campaigned for a combat assignment, and was sent to the Eighth Air Force in December 1943. He flew more than 20 combat missions, was twice awarded the Distinguished Flying Cross, and ended the war with the rank of colonel.

Stowe, Leland Pulitzer Prize–winning foreign correspondent. He spent Christmas Day 1944 with Cronkite in Luxembourg.

Stronoch, Sally United Press London bureau secretary.

Tait, Jack *New York Herald Tribune* correspondent.

Taylor, Henry J. Scripps-Howard foreign correspondent. Later U.S. ambassador to Switzerland.

Tighe, Dixie International News Service correspondent in London, "famed for her blunt language and flamboyant life style," according to Nancy Caldwell Sorel's history of women correspondents in World War II, *The Women Who Wrote the War.*

Trammel, Niles President of NBC Radio Network.

Twelftrees, Joan British United Press correspondent.

Wade, William Warren International News Service correspondent who arrived in London in 1941. A member of the Writing Sixty-Ninth, he set off on the Wilhelmshaven raid, but his plane developed engine trouble and turned back. After the war served as bureau chief for Voice of America.

Wagg, Alfred *Chicago Tribune* correspondent in London.

Wallenstein, Marcel *Kansas City Star* correspondent in London.

Walton, Bill *Time* correspondent and a fraternity brother of Cronkite's. He dropped into Normandy with paratroopers.

Wellington, Clarence George "Pete" *Kansas City Star* editor. One of the cub reporters he taught the craft of journalism to was Ernest Hemingway.

Werner, Merle McDougald "Doug" United Press correspondent in London who took over traveling to air bases for Cronkite in mid-1943. He landed on Utah Beach on June 6, 1944, and the dispatch he wrote that day was among the first published eyewitness accounts of the invasion. After the war he covered the Nuremberg war crimes trials with Cronkite. He later joined the U.S. State Department as a press attaché. When he died in 2004 at age 91, he was the last surviving correspondent to have accompanied the D-Day landings.

Whitney, "Jock" John Hay Socially prominent investor serving in the Army Air Force as an intelligence officer. Taken prisoner by the Nazis in southern France in 1944, he escaped from the train carrying him to a POW camp.

Willicombe, Joe International News Service correspondent.

Wolf, Tom Reporter for the Newspaper Enterprise Association (a Scripps-Howard syndicate) and an Acme European bureau manager.

Wyler, William Prominent Hollywood director who won an Oscar for directing 1942's *Mrs. Miniver,* which also won five other Oscars, including one for best picture. In 1943, while a major in the Army Air Force, he made the documentary *Memphis Belle: A Story of a Flying Fortress,* which told the story of the Eighth Air Force's bombing campaign over occupied Europe. His 1946 feature film, *The Best Years of Our Lives,* about veterans returning to civilian life, won him a second Oscar for best director.

THE GIANT I CALLED GRANDDAD

★　★　★　★　★　★　★

In the summer of 2010, a year after my grandfather died, my father and I went to the Lyndon Baines Johnson Library and Museum, which is located on the University of Texas at Austin campus. In collaboration with the Dolph Briscoe Center for American History, it had just opened an exhibition titled "Cronkite: Eyewitness to a Century," encompassing my grandfather's life and career. Among other items, the exhibition featured the uniform he wore while serving as a foreign correspondent during World War II. We also spent several days looking through my grandfather's papers, deposited at the Briscoe Center. I was fascinated as I read his personal correspondence from the war years, especially the scores of letters that he wrote to my grandmother from Europe between 1943 and 1945. They reminded me strongly of the talks about World War II, and military history more generally, that my grandfather and I had shared as I was growing up.

Recently, while watching the HBO series *Band of Brothers,* which features a company of paratroopers from the 101st Airborne during the war,

I marveled at how often the story of Easy Company reminded me of the tales my grandfather told me about his own wartime experiences. He flew over Normandy on D-Day, not long after the paratroopers had jumped behind enemy lines. He landed in a glider in Holland with the 101st Airborne in Operation Market Garden, and afterward he was allowed to wear the 101st Airborne's screaming eagle shoulder patch insignia on his uniform. He survived the bombing of Eindhoven by the Luftwaffe on the night after it had been liberated by the Americans. He went on to cover the Battle of the Bulge, including the relief of the 101st during the siege of Bastogne.

Those are just a few of the great stories that he told me. Co-author Maurice Isserman and I share those and many more in the pages that follow—along with some of my own observations and experience growing up as his grandson, in the hope that they'll contribute to a more comprehensive picture of the man, his life, his family, and his career.

Walter and Betsy Cronkite were both of solid midwestern stock, born and raised in Kansas City, Missouri. The Maxwells, my grandmother's family, were a tough Scots-Irish clan. When she died in 2005, I visited Kansas City for her funeral, and my grandfather took us on a driving tour of their old haunts. He was raised as an only child in a large house in a nice neighborhood. My grandmother, the daughter of a postman, grew up in a very small house with many brothers and sisters. The Maxwells were gun enthusiasts, and my grandmother learned how to shoot as a girl. The family used their basement as a pistol shooting range until the foundation of the house started to crumble from the attrition of years of bullets fired. Her parents scraped together enough money to send her to the University of Missouri for a few semesters, but when the money ran dry, she had to drop out. After she got married, she finished her degree by taking night classes. Interestingly, my grandfather never finished his degree at the University of Texas, and he never felt the need to go back and complete it. But it was important to my grandmother to do so.

Betsy Cronkite also had a professional career in journalism, and so my grandfather's correspondence with her should be read not only as letters to his wife but also as letters to a fellow reporter. She attended the University of Missouri School of Journalism and found a job at Kansas City's KCMO radio station as an advertising writer. In 1936 my grandfather became the station's news announcer. He later said that when he first saw her walk into the office, he was paralyzed by uncharacteristic shyness. The first time they conversed, they were both reading from a script that she had written for a commercial (for the popular Richard Hudnut brand of cosmetics) the station was scheduled to broadcast. After they finished reading the commercial script, my grandfather asked her out to lunch, and they married four years later.

During the early years of the war, my grandmother was working as women's editor of the *Kansas City Journal-Post,* where, among other contributions, she wrote a column providing advice to the lovelorn. In the later years of the war she worked as an editor and writer for Hallmark Cards. She remained an avid reader of newspapers all of her life.

The effect that World War II had on my grandfather was far more profound—and provided the foundation for the rest of his illustrious career. In August 1963 he toured the beaches and cliffs of Normandy with Dwight D. Eisenhower, filming a CBS News special that would air on June 6, 1964, the 20th anniversary of the invasion of Normandy. The former war correspondent who had faced enemy fire to report on the invasion from a bomber overhead walked beside the commander who had led the monumental effort, and the two remembered the thousands of soldiers and sailors who had braved the infernal conditions on the ground that day. Millions of Americans, many of whom were WWII veterans, watched this show on their televisions.

I was fortunate enough to hear my grandfather tell these stories in person many times over the years. World War II had vaulted him into the top ranks of American reporters. His wartime experience had taken him from the landing grounds of North Africa to bombing raids over occupied

Europe, to crash landing in a glider behind enemy lines with the 101st Airborne, and to the Battle of the Bulge and finally to the Nuremberg trials. But it wasn't until I traveled to the University of Texas to examine his archives did I realize what a defining role the war played in his life.

One of my grandfather's favorite war stories took place during the Battle of the Bulge. Somehow he lost his helmet and it rolled into a minefield, and he decided he wasn't going to risk getting it back. He decided he would rather go around bareheaded, which was against regulations. So, who should come driving down the road in a motorcade but Gen. George S. Patton. Old Blood and Guts was a stickler for regulations, especially concerning dress. When he saw my grandfather without his helmet, General Patton ordered the motorcade to come to a screeching halt and, assuming WC was a soldier, got out to yell at him. General Patton was disappointed to find out that the object of his lesson was a correspondent, and he could not punish him.

My grandfather spent all of 1943 stationed in London, covering the U.S. aerial war against Germany. The country had been bombed relentlessly during the German Blitz, and everyone who lived through that time faced shortages of all kinds. My grandfather's preoccupation with finding a decent meal—not surprising given the scarcities of wartime England—left a lasting mark on him. After the war, my grandparents loved going out to dinner with friends. In New York they enjoyed mingling at the top restaurants of the day. When I was young, I remember them frequenting Le Cirque, Aquavit, Le Côte Basque, and Caravelle. In his Christmas letter of 1943, he reminisces about going to the steak house Keens with my grandmother while they were living in New York. They continued to eat at Keens occasionally, and eventually my grandfather had his pipe hung on the wall, alongside pipes belonging to Teddy Roosevelt, Babe Ruth, Albert Einstein, and other notable patrons.

Coffee was also scarce in wartime Britain, but that didn't bother my grandfather, who rarely drank it. My grandmother, in contrast, drank coffee all day long. She always bought Maxwell House coffee, probably because it shared the family name. WC preferred hot chocolate, and he drank milk with anything. In letters home from their time in Moscow, in 1946–48, Grandmother complained that they could never find fresh milk, only powdered. But she would mix it with cocoa or Ovaltine to make it palatable.

When nighttime came, my grandparents, like many of their generation, enjoyed a good drink. Newspapermen were hard drinkers in those days, and some of them, like my grandfather's wartime friend and colleague Jim McGlincy, battled a serious problem with alcohol. In his letters home to my grandmother, WC would note that he wasn't drinking nearly as much as the other reporters he socialized with. Some family history helps explain his need to reassure her on that score. During the First World War, his father—my great-grandfather—became an alcoholic. The family story is that he was fine before he went, but after enduring the horrors of that horrific war, he came out a changed man. Perhaps my grandfather wrote to Betsy to reassure her that he wasn't going to turn out like his own father.

But he wasn't a teetotaler—and neither was my grandmother. At a restaurant, if a waiter informed her that they served only wine and beer, she would leap to her feet and lead the party out the door in search of a more hospitable venue. If my grandparents arrived at a party that didn't have liquor, they wouldn't stay for long.

A shortage of another sort—at first my grandfather hardly had anything to wear—reveals a side of him that many people don't know about. WC placed a great deal of importance on personal appearance. He took the utmost care in his dress and grooming, believing it reflected outwardly the care a man took in his professional and personal life. He made sure the knot of his tie was always perfectly in place, his shirt cuffs were trim, his shoes were shined, etc. After the war he wore tailored Brooks Brothers suits and Hermès ties.

My grandmother, too, was extremely well dressed, always choosing, with help from her personal shopper at Bergdorf's, classic styles. According to my mother, my grandmother loved Adolfo, and my grandfather gave her an Adolfo suit every year. She wore Ferragamo shoes, and her winter coats were lined with fur. She had beautiful red hair that stayed red until she was in her 90s, and she liked emerald green clothes because they complemented her green eyes. For the same reason, my grandfather always gave her jade jewelry. She wore the jade engagement ring he bought for her in Kansas City until the day she died, along with her platinum wedding ring. My grandfather wore his San Jacinto High School ring until the day he died. They were a glamorous couple who enjoyed living well in New York, but they never forgot where they came from. All who knew them well were aware that they remained in personality and values a down-home middle-American couple.

Nowhere is that better reflected than in the humor that appears in so many of their wartime letters. My grandparents till the end of their lives were constantly ribbing each other and sharing jokes. My grandfather's letters to her are full of puns, and he never lost his taste for the art. It's a shame that Betsy's wartime letters to my grandfather didn't survive, because I suspect they would reveal a similar sense of humor. Every time someone told her, "Mrs. Cronkite, please walk this way," she would respond tartly with the old vaudeville line, "If I could walk that way, I wouldn't need talcum powder." And when she walked into some public event, she'd say skeptically, "Ballroom? There's hardly elbow room."

My grandfather was a favorite target of her jokes. He became hard of hearing in his old age, but instead of regarding his infirmity solemnly, my grandmother treated it as just another foible to laugh about. She would silently mouth words at him from across the dinner table, causing him to pop out his hearing aid to check the batteries—to the delight of the grandchildren in attendance. In his memoir, *A Reporter's Life,* my grandfather wrote that he attributed the duration of their marriage to "Betsy's extra-ordinarily keen sense of humor, which saw us over many bumps (mostly of my making), and her tolerance, even support, for the uncertain sched-ule and wanderings of a newsman."

Her humor was one of the things he loved about her. The letters show, however, that he suffered the most at Christmastime; they spent three Christmases apart between 1942 and the end of the war.

He never forgot how deprived he felt during those lonely holidays. In later years, my grandfather was an enthusiastic and sentimental cel-ebrator of Christmas. He always went all-out. The whole family would gather at my grandparents' town house on East 84th Street on Christmas Eve to sing Christmas carols around the piano ("Good King Wences-las" was a favorite), and then we would have a lavish dinner followed by stollen, the traditional German cake, in homage to my grandfather's maternal German ancestry.

On Christmas Day we would open the door to find the living room filled wall-to-wall with presents. My grandfather took a childlike delight in unwrapping presents, and he instituted a custom of elaborately wrap-ping a great many trinkets in order to have as many gifts to open as pos-sible. My grandmother loved filling the stockings with tangerines and marzipan and other penny-shop gifts.

Apart from what my grandfather's wartime letters tell us about his personal life, they reveal a great deal about his professional life. Friends, family, and colleagues alike knew that he was an extremely competitive man who loved to win. The letters reveal many instances of this. Later on, he would proudly tell his grandkids stories of scooping the competition—Chet Huntley and David Brinkley at NBC in the 1960s, and Barbara Wal-ters at ABC in the late 1970s. During summers on Martha's Vineyard, he loved playing board games such as Monopoly, Risk, and Diplomacy.

Unlike many celebrities, WC never grew tired of accepting awards, great or small. He was genuinely thrilled to be honored at the most obscure and humble institutions. His dining room in Martha's Vineyard was furnished with the chairs he had been awarded along with his honorary doctorates.

Competitive as my grandfather was, he didn't care as much about the amount of money he was paid. The letters tell the story of how he was offered the chance to work for CBS Radio by Edward R. Murrow, at a higher salary, but turned it down to stay with the United Press because he liked his job. My grandfather later became well paid by CBS as a reporter and an anchorman, but it was only after he had retired that anchors' salaries skyrocketed. Given a choice of negotiating terms, he would always ask for more time off (especially in the summer) rather than for more money. He even had a joking competition with Johnny Carson to see who could get more time off from his respective network. At the funeral of Dick Salant, president of CBS News, Mike Wallace told the story of going to ask him for a raise, and Salant saying, "So, you think you should get more money than Cronkite gets?" Wallace responded, "Oh, I guess not." So in a way, he held down all the other broadcasters' salaries.

Like many people who grew up during the Depression, WC was thrifty, an inclination reinforced by the scarcity of World War II. I remember he would say, "Use it up and wear it out. Make it do or do without." He would keep a car on the road until it fell apart. Whenever I rode in the backseat of one of his cars with my cousins, we would fight over who would get to sit next to the one window that still rolled down; the window on the other side was permanently stuck.

My grandfather could make do with less because material goods didn't matter to him. What drove him was the zeal to be the best reporter around. He had no illusions, however, about the difference between him and the heroic soldiers he was covering. During the war he took numerous risks as part of his job as a correspondent. But as he made clear to my grandmother, flying in bombers, landing in a glider, and coming under enemy fire were not adventures he enjoyed or intended to repeat if he could avoid it. WC told me wryly that the only time he was ever wounded in the war was during the liberation of Amsterdam: The joyful citizens were throwing tulips bound in wire at their liberators, and one bunch struck him in the cheek and drew blood.

Still, in peacetime he continued to be a risktaker. In the early 1950s he began driving race cars. As his family grew and CBS needed to provide him with life insurance, my grandmother and his bosses at the television station finally convinced him to take up the less dangerous sport of sailing.

Starting in the 1960s, he kept buying bigger and fancier cabin sailboats. The first three were all named *Chipper,* after my father, and his later sailboats were all called *Wyntje,* the name of the first woman living in New Amsterdam in the 17th century who married a Cronkite. (The Cronkites trace our ancestry back to the Dutch settlers of New Amsterdam.) Before the days of GPS, he could figure out his nautical position by charts and dead reckoning. He kept a cool head when sailing, even during several hair-raising storms. He was out sailing with his buddy Mike Ashford in October 1991 in the waters off Martha's Vineyard when they ran into the famous "perfect storm." They made it back through the violent waves to harbor safely, and I remember Ashford, who had been an Air Force bomber pilot, saying it was one of the most terrifying outings of his life.

World War II made my grandfather the man he was. He was already smart, competitive, and driven, but the war made him tough, worldly, and thoughtful. He was catapulted from a promising but obscure wire service reporter in the Midwest to an internationally famous war correspondent. In the early days of the war his greatest ambition was merely an overseas assignment. By the war's close he was discussing with my grandmother which European capital he would be assigned to as United Press bureau chief. When I read these letters between my grandparents, I am reminded of how young they were when they were separated. My grandfather was 25—only a year older than I am now—when he left for the war. People in that generation had to grow up fast, and he handled the chaotic wartime situation adeptly.

I knew Walter and Betsy as grandparents who were always a joy to be around—smart, fast-paced, funny (at times outrageously hilarious). They were also both incredibly kind people who were still very much in love. In reading the letters I can hear their voices still, only refracted through the distance of time. Back then they were two young lovers torn apart by the greatest war the world has ever known.

—WALTER CRONKITE IV

Walter Cronkite, Jr., and grandsons Peter Cronkite and Walter Cronkite IV raising the flag on Martha's Vineyard

CHAPTER ONE

A PRETTY PERSONAL MATTER

★ ★ ★ ★ ★ ★ ★

Tomorrow is our fourth anniversary . . . The first two years seemed to go so quickly, and the last two have dragged so horribly. Two whole years out of our lives. It makes this war with Hitler a pretty personal matter.
—Walter Cronkite to Betsy Cronkite, March 29, 1944

On March 30, 1940, a 23-year-old reporter named Walter Leland Cronkite, Jr., married fellow journalist Mary Elizabeth "Betsy" Maxwell in Grace and Holy Trinity Episcopal Church in Kansas City, Missouri, following a four-year courtship. Their marriage lasted happily for 65 years until her death in 2005. Shortly after the young couple celebrated their second anniversary, Walter Cronkite was credentialed as a war correspondent for the United Press wire service. They spent many weeks apart in the summer and fall of 1942, as Cronkite twice sailed on convoys across submarine-infested waters, first to Britain and then to

North Africa. After a brief reunion in New York City in early December, Cronkite shipped out on an overseas assignment.

This time the two were not reunited until 28 months later. Cronkite consoled himself in the meantime by writing Betsy long, detailed letters, sometimes five in a week, narrating his experiences as a war correspondent, his observations of life in wartime Europe, and his longing for her. For Walter and Betsy Cronkite, as for millions of other young men and women in those years, the war with Hitler was "a pretty personal matter," as well as an event of world-historical importance.

Betsy Cronkite carefully saved her husband's letters, copying many to circulate among family and friends. More than a hundred of his letters from 1943 to 1945 survive and are archived in the Walter Cronkite Papers at the Dolph Briscoe Center for American History at the University of Texas at Austin.

For the rest of his life, during which he served for 19 years as anchorman for *CBS Evening News,* Walter Cronkite reflected on his experiences reporting from Europe on the Second World War. In addition, by producing and narrating numerous television series and specials about the war, Cronkite helped shape, and in the process became thoroughly identified in the American mind with, historical memories of "the good war" and the "greatest generation."

Walter Cronkite, Jr., was born on November 4, 1916, in St. Joseph, Missouri, the son of Walter Leland Cronkite, a dentist, and Helen Fritsche Cronkite. The family moved to Kansas City in 1918, when Walter Cronkite, Sr., returned from his military service in World War I, and then to Houston in 1926. Walter Jr. graduated from San Jacinto High School in 1933, entering the University of Texas at Austin that fall as a journalism major. (His parents divorced soon afterward, and both remarried.)

While a student at the University of Texas, Cronkite cut his teeth as a journalist by working on the campus newspaper, the *Daily Texan,* and taking part-time jobs with a number of local and state newspapers. His favorite and best-paying job was the three hours a day he put in as an assistant to the *Houston Press*'s political correspondent in Austin. As Cronkite wrote to his parents in an early 1935 letter, preserved in the archives at the University of Texas:

The five dollars I collect from the Houston Press *tomorrow for the past week's work is going into a bank fund as is each week's salary. If I can keep said funds in bank, then by the end of school I should have quite a sum accumulated. Possibly this new job with the Press will give me the influence to get some sort of world trip out of Mefo [Marcellus E. "Mefo" Foster, editor of the* Houston Press *from 1927 to 1937]. I would like to sell them on the idea of getting me a job on a boat, then giving me five dollars a week to write experiences as a young man sees the world.*

BORED BY HIS classes and eager to begin making his way in the world of professional journalism, Cronkite dropped out of the university following the spring semester of 1935 and went to work, first in the Austin bureau of the International News Service, and then in the Austin Scripps-Howard bureau, which provided coverage for the chain's newspapers in the state. In the fall of 1935 he moved to Houston to take a full-time job with the *Houston Press*. Over the next few years he moved from job to job, sometimes working for newspapers, sometimes for radio stations, and including one stint in the public relations office of Braniff Airlines. While he was working as an announcer with radio station KCMO in Kansas City in 1936, he met Betsy Maxwell, his future bride. In 1937 he joined the wire service United Press as a reporter, and although he left for other positions, he returned in 1939. He spent the next ten years as a UP reporter, six of them as a foreign correspondent.

As his 1935 letter to his parents suggests, Cronkite was a young man with big dreams. He would get his chance to see the world while still a young reporter, but not in the way he expected.

The United Press assigned Cronkite to the night shift of its Kansas City bureau. He was in the UP office the night of September 1, 1939, when news arrived that Germany was attacking Poland. Within days, Britain and France declared war on Nazi Germany. The war settled into months of watchful waiting on both sides—a period referred to at the time as the "phony war." But the war turned deadly in April 1940 when Hitler launched his blitzkrieg assault on western Europe, conquering Norway, Denmark, the Netherlands, Belgium, and France in short order. British Prime Minister Neville Chamberlain stepped down from office in disgrace in early May 1940. His successor, Winston Churchill, oversaw the evacuation of the British army from the French port at Dunkirk in the first days of June. The Nazis were now undisputed masters of Europe, from central Poland to the English Channel.

In August the Luftwaffe launched a concentrated bombing assault on Britain, in preparation for an invasion across the English Channel. The stiff resistance of the Royal Air Force in the Battle of Britain, however, forced Hitler to postpone his invasion plans. Instead, the following summer the führer vastly increased the scope of the war by invading the Soviet Union.

In the United States, isolationists and internationalists debated how to respond to the threat of Nazi aggression. President Franklin Delano Roosevelt cautiously but steadily increased U.S. aid to Britain (and after June 22, 1941, to the Soviet Union). The Lend-Lease program, enacted in March 1941, authorized shipment of American military supplies to Allied nations. Within months, American destroyers were accompanying merchant vessels carrying supplies to Britain. By the fall, the U.S. Navy was engaged in an undeclared shooting war with German U-boats. On December 7, 1941, on the other side of the globe, the Japanese attacked Pearl Harbor, provoking an American declaration of war the following day. Germany and Italy declared war on the United States in solidarity with their Axis partner Japan, and the United States responded in kind.

In the last months of peace, Cronkite and his wife had enrolled in the newly established Civilian Pilot Training Program, designed to create a pool of trained pilots. Betsy Cronkite got her pilot's license; her husband, it turned out, was color-blind, and was thus disqualified. The disability also meant that Cronkite would not be drafted. But after Pearl Harbor he was eager to get as close to the war as he could, requesting an overseas assignment. His bosses at the United Press, recognizing his potential, transferred him from Kansas City to New York City in May 1942—a first step toward becoming a military correspondent. Shortly after his arrival, he wrote to his mother, Helen Cronkite, to say that he was putting in ten-hour days rewriting the cables that foreign correspondents sent in to the New York office. His own future remained uncertain:

I still have absolutely no conception of what the United Press intends doing with me. Joe Alex Morris, the foreign news editor who had me brought into New York, admits that he is confused by the return of all our correspondents who had been interned in the Axis countries, and he adds that he may not know himself what to do with me for another couple of weeks. I'd still like to go abroad but I like this town so well that I wouldn't mind too much being told to just stay here.

SOMETIME IN THE next few months, Cronkite received the necessary credentials from the U.S. Navy to accompany a convoy across the North Atlantic to Britain. The Battle of the Atlantic was raging, as German

U-boats sank a sickening number of Allied merchant and troop transport convoys and their naval escorts. It was vital to the Allied cause to
secure their lines of supply and reinforcement from the New World to
Britain. Yet Allied air patrols, crucial to the detection and destruction of
marauding packs of U-boats, were unable to operate in mid-ocean, leaving an exposed gap in which the Germans concentrated their attacks.
More than a thousand Allied merchant ships were lost in the North
Atlantic alone in 1942. (Later on in the war, new long-range patrol
planes, equipped with radar and other electronic detection devices,
turned the tide of battle; the number of Allied ships sunk in the North
Atlantic the following year was reduced to just over 300; in 1944, it was
just over 100.)

In the late summer of 1942 Cronkite got his first chance to realize his
youthful dream of seeing the world as a reporter when he was assigned
to accompany Task Force 38, a troop-transport convoy voyaging from
New York to Greenock, Scotland. He traveled aboard the U.S.S. *Arkansas*, a 32-year veteran of the Navy's battleship fleet. The convoy set sail
from New York on August 6, 1942, and reached Greenock on August
17, returning to New York on September 4. Two days later, Cronkite
wrote home to his mother to report on the adventure:

———

*The trip was swell. As perhaps you have learned, I was in the biggest
convoy ever to cross the Atlantic. The only newspaperman on the trip,
I occupied the admiral's cabin on the escorting battleship—private
bedroom, lounge with desk, and private bath, all on the main deck. We
encountered no enemy action and the weather, although extremely cold
in the North Atlantic, was rather calm. The last couple of days on the
way over we ran into some roughness but apparently I'm not subject
to seasickness and I weathered it with no difficulty. We were 10 days in
the British isles during which I saw London, a couple of counties south*

of London, Edinburgh and Glasgow in Scotland. At most of those
spots I stayed in the American officer clubs—all the British Isles cities
are filled with Americans, it seems—and had a gay time. In London I
visited with newspaper friends, some of whom I had known back here,
and toured the usual tourists sites and bombed areas . . .

The trip back was just like a cruise as far as the weather was concerned, in
fact, it was just a little boring. We did get a little action, however, about which
I'm sorry I can't tell you just yet. I've got a pretty good story on my hands
when and if I can fight it through censorship.

———

CRONKITE'S "PRETTY GOOD STORY," which was datelined September 3
and ran in American newspapers on September 9, concerned the burning
of the Navy transport ship U.S.S. *Wakefield,* which Cronkite witnessed
from the deck of the *Arkansas.* The *Wakefield,* formerly the luxury liner
S.S. *Manhattan,* was returning to the United States from England when
it caught fire. All hands and passengers were rescued, although the ship
was reduced to a burned-out hulk. (After extensive repairs in Boston
Harbor, the ship was returned to duty in the spring of 1944.)

"My story, by some miracle, got past the censors," Cronkite wrote
in his 1996 memoir, *A Reporter's Life,* "and made the banner headline
in a lot of American papers. I had lucked into early recognition as a
war correspondent." Cronkite wrote a few other stories during the trip,
including glimpses of wartime life in London. The main story, about the
convoy itself, fell a little flat, as suggested in its lead sentence, "A successful convoy is a boring convoy."

Cronkite's second overseas assignment that fall provided better
material, as he covered the first combat landing of American troops
outside the Pacific theater. President Roosevelt and his military advisers
were eager to engage the Nazis in Europe, hoping to take pressure off
the Red Army, which was bearing the brunt of the fight against Hitler's

armies. But the British adamantly opposed what they regarded as a premature and potentially disastrous landing on the European continent. As an alternative, Churchill proposed an Anglo-American invasion of French North Africa, with landings in Morocco and Algeria, then controlled by the collaborationist Vichy government in France. From there the Allies could move eastward through Tunisia, netting German and Italian forces in North Africa in a pincer attack, coordinated with British forces already stationed in Egypt and Libya. It wasn't quite the full-scale "second front" that Roosevelt and his advisers had hoped for, but at least Americans were fighting the Nazis, which was important as a symbol of American resolve in the European theater.

On October 19, 1942, Cronkite found himself flying in a Navy transport plane from New York to Norfolk, Virginia, to join the convoy loading men and supplies for Operation Torch, the invasion of North Africa. "And now the story begins to unfold!" Cronkite wrote excitedly the next day in a journal he kept during the assignment. "And what a terrific story, what an amazing assignment! This, it begins to appear, is the second front!"

The convoy set sail on October 23, 1942, part of the Northern Attack Group commanded by Gen. George S. Patton, with overall command of the invasion entrusted to Lt. Gen. Dwight D. Eisenhower. Cronkite crossed the Atlantic aboard the battleship U.S.S. *Texas*. His assignment during the invasion was to cover the Navy's role in the operation; other correspondents were assigned to go with the landing forces to the beaches and beyond. Secretly, he planned to jump ship after the initial landing and help cover any ground fighting, although the invasion planners hoped that the Vichy French forces would refrain from firing and switch sides against the Germans.

Cronkite celebrated his 26th birthday, November 4, 1942, en route, four days before the scheduled landings. On November 8, the landing craft headed for shore. The ships did not unleash a preliminary naval bombardment, again hoping that the French would welcome the invasion, but those hopes were disappointed, and three days of costly fighting ensued. Eventually the big guns of the U.S.S. *Texas* were brought to bear on the French lines. Cronkite went ashore with a naval party to assess the effectiveness of the bombardment, which turned out to have missed its intended target, a French ammunition dump.

Cronkite might have stayed onshore, as part of his plan to cover the U.S. ground assault, but he heard that the *Texas* was sailing to Casablanca, where more fighting was expected. Once aboard the ship, he discovered to his dismay that it was heading directly back to the U.S., cutting short his coverage of the invasion. Making the best of a bad situation, he decided he could still claim a scoop by being the first war correspondent to return to the U.S. from North Africa. The problem was that a correspondent from the International News Service was also headed home, aboard a ship scheduled to arrive before the *Texas*. Cronkite stole a march on his rival by hitching a ride on the *Texas*'s catapult-launched observation floatplane when they were within flying distance of Norfolk, Virginia. From there he hitched another ride to New York City. "After the emotional telephone calls to Betsy and my mother in Kansas City," he wrote in *A Reporter's Life*, "I sat down to rewrite my previous stories [which had been radioed from the *Texas* to Allied military headquarters on Gibraltar, but had not been forwarded to the States as planned]. They hit the wires with an editor's note saying that I was the first correspondent back from North Africa and these were the first uncensored stories from that historic landing." Cronkite's report, proudly labeled by the United Press as the "exclusive account of how the Americans took Port Lyautey in a bitter three-day battle," was datelined November 11 and ran in American newspapers two weeks later.

Betsy, who had moved back to Kansas City when her husband left for North Africa, joined her husband in New York City at the end of November, but their time together was brief. One year later, on

December 12, 1943, Cronkite wrote to Betsy to mark the anniversary of their latest separation:

———

Another gloomy Sunday, this time made even lonelier by the fact that it is just a year ago today that I left you on this last, longest trip of all. I knew then, when they said I was going to London, that the easy days of the Navy assignment with frequent returns to the United States were over, but I held a secret hope—almost a belief—that nothing could really keep us apart for long and that somehow we would be together before many more months had passed. Well, now it has been a year and, although some say the end is in sight, it still seems to be a far stretch down the road. Every day of this last year, and every day until we are together again, I miss you more, love you more, and [am] more lonely for you . . . It hasn't been much fun. It won't be fun until we can be together again.

———

THEIR NEXT REUNION was still a long, long time in the future. The letters to Betsy between 1943 and 1945 that are reprinted in the chapters that follow provide a vivid record of the Cronkites' "personal war."

CHAPTER TWO

THE WRITING
SIXTY-NINTH

JANUARY–MAY 1943

In the winter and spring of 1943 Walter Cronkite's life changed forever. When he arrived in London, two days before New Year's Day, he was an obscure United Press correspondent. By March, as he marveled in a letter to Betsy, he found himself a celebrity. He was assigned to cover the fast-expanding air offensive by the U.S. Eighth Air Force against Nazi Germany, the biggest story in the European theater of operations. Less than two months after arriving in England, he risked his life in accompanying a dangerous bombing mission against the U-boat base at Wilhelmshaven, Germany. His letters home chronicle his professional advance as well as the personal side of life as a correspondent in wartime London. The letters also reveal Cronkite's acute unhappiness because of his separation from his wife.

Cronkite shipped out from New York on December 11, 1942, for a hazardous journey across the Atlantic aboard the 25-year-old Dutch

The Writing Sixty-Ninth: From left, Gladwin Hill, William Wade, Robert Post, Walter Cronkite, Homer Bigart, and Paul Manning. Andy Rooney and Denton Scott, the other two members of the group, are not shown.

passenger ship *Westernland*. German U-boats attacked the convoy, sinking several of the slow-going and vulnerable freighters and tankers, but the *Westernland* reached port in Glasgow unscathed. Despite his relief at the safe passage, Cronkite wrote on arrival that the trip aboard the "old crate" was "abominable from every other standpoint."

The British Isles were the staging area for a planned two-pronged Allied assault on Nazi-ruled Europe. The air war had already been launched, and the cross-channel invasion of France was eagerly awaited, though it would not take place for another year and a half. Cronkite was one of the three million Americans, most of them young men in uniform, who made the lone Allied outpost in western Europe their home between January 1942 and June 1944.

Cronkite reminded Betsy in his first letter from Britain that their correspondence would be subject to military censorship, and that consequently she should write on only one side of the paper (lest a censor's scissors inadvertently eliminate information on the other side of the page).

From Glasgow, Cronkite traveled by train to London, arriving on December 30, where he found lodging for his first night in the Savoy Hotel. Located on the Strand in central London, the venerable and luxurious Savoy was a favorite stopping place for American correspondents during the war. It was also known for the comfort of its air-raid shelters. But the hotel was far too expensive for a reporter like Cronkite surviving on a salary and an expense account meted out by the notoriously penny-pinching United Press. Finding permanent lodgings in London was his first priority.

———

12-30-42

This is just a brief note to tell you I'm safe and fairly sound. At the moment I'm in my fiftieth hour without sleep (Oh, perhaps 20 nods but they didn't add up to more than a full hour, I'm sure) and as a result I'm pretty dead on my feet. The trip over was without incident as far as the enemy was concerned but was abominable from every other standpoint, and since arrival on land I've been battling constantly against transportation and housing difficulties. Passage across was just as dirty and uncomfortable as that old crate looked and I'll try to tell you more of that when I can keep the eyelids propped up. Here I've got a room at the Savoy for one night . . . I must vacate by 10 am tomorrow, New Year's Eve. God knows what I'll do then inasmuch as the hotel situation here on New Year's Eve is just as it is at home.

I'm sure I shall get no more kick out of celebrating the advent of a New Year without you than I did out of Christmas. We had a Christmas tree on the ship but it was a pretty cold gruesome business compared with those wonderful holidays at home. Thanks so much for the gifts, Darlingest. Vitamins, cufflinks, chewing gum, etc. and the swell note . . .

I hope a letter is on the way, written on one side of the paper only, so that the censor's scissors don't ruin it.

———

CRONKITE FOUND THAT London was a city under aerial siege. In the first four months of the German bombing campaign, the "Blitz," more than 13,000 of the city's residents had been killed, and nearly 18,000 seriously injured. By May 1941 more than a million of the city's homes had suffered bomb damage, and one-sixth of the population was at least temporarily homeless. Among the iconic images defining the war were London citizens sleeping on the city's Underground subway platforms and St. Paul's Cathedral lit up by the flames of nearby burning buildings.

By the time Cronkite arrived in London, Americans had developed a strong sense of identification with and affection for the city. In large measure this feeling resulted from the reporting by Edward R. Murrow and other war correspondents during the autumn of 1940, the beginning of the Blitz bombing campaign. "In 1940," British historian David Reynolds wrote in *Rich Relations: The American Occupation of Britain, 1942–1945,* his 1995 account of American-British relations during World War II, "Britain's best propagandists were in fact the American media."

"This is London," Murrow began his broadcasts from the embattled city for CBS Radio, and listeners at home sometimes heard the sounds of antiaircraft fire and exploding bombs in the background. The image of Britain popular in much of prewar America—as a land of haughty aristocrats and surly workingmen, an arrogant imperial power undeserving of sympathy or help—was replaced by that of plucky, stoic, and heroic Londoners, carrying on with their lives in the face of a brutal, unending assault. Another American correspondent, *Collier's Weekly* editor Quentin Reynolds, narrated a short documentary/propaganda film about the first five weeks of the *Blitz, London Can Take It!,* which was widely viewed in the United States in 1940–41 and credited with helping sway American popular sympathies toward providing aid to Britain. He described the residents of London as a "people's army" and concluded with an uplifting salute to their spirit and prospects:

> I am a neutral reporter. I have watched the people of London live and die ever since death in its most ghastly garb began to come here as a nightly visitor five weeks ago. I have watched them stand by their homes. I have seen them made homeless. I have seen them moved to new homes. And I can assure you there is no panic, no fear, no despair in London town. There is nothing but determination, confidence, and high courage among the people of Churchill's island.

By the time Cronkite was posted to London, Reynolds's unconvincing pose of neutrality was no longer one required of American reporters. London was the front line in the battle against the common enemy. Wartime Anglophilia, a projection of American patriotism, idealism, and internationalism, was in full flower.

London was not the first, or the only, urban British target of German bombers. Port cities and industrial cities throughout the island were also hit, often with heavy damage and high casualties. All told, more than 60,000 British civilians were killed and hundreds of thousands injured. The country's housing stock was severely damaged. But the impact on its industrial production and military capabilities was far from decisive, and the impact on British civilian morale, from the German perspective, perversely counterproductive. Indeed, the strongest support for the war was found in the bombed cities. By 1942, German air raids on London had receded to the level of occasional nuisance; more bombs were dropped monthly on the city in the winter of 1940–41 than in all of 1942. Still, the occasional bombing raid, combined with the vast stretches of urban rubble left in the wake of the earlier heavy bombing, made a deep impression on American newcomers like Cronkite.

Shock-Troops of the Press

With the U. S. Marines who swarmed from landing boats one dark dawn to storm Guadalcanal was Robert Miller, United Press correspondent. With them he remained for several weeks, gathering news at first hand of their savage, dogged fight to break Japan's grip on the island. His disregard for danger and hardship won from the commander on Guadalcanal, Major-General Alexander Vandegrift, the comment, "Miller is a good Marine."

As the British convoy for the relief of Malta twisted and shot its way through seas white with the wakes of torpedoes and under skies black with enemy dive-

bombers, a lone news correspondent watched the action from the bridge and open flag deck of one all the ships. He was Henry Gorrell, of the United Press, risking his life to get an historic eye-witness story.

Aboard the American cutter that crashed the harbor boom at Oran was Leo Disher, of the United Press. He stayed with the craft until gunfire blasted it to the bottom. In the action, he was wounded fifteen times. Despite this he swam ashore, crawled into the town on his elbows and dictated his story to a fellow correspondent in a French hospital. For his conduct the

U. S. Army awarded to Disher the Order of the Purple Heart.

Such incidents as these reveal the spirit and share of the shock-troops of the press, the war-front correspondents. These incidents are not unique. They have their counterparts among hundreds. Wherever fighting men go, American correspondents go with them to see with their own eyes the actions they report.

Since the war began, the United Press has provided consistently the world's best coverage of the world's biggest news. The courage and skill of its front-line correspondents are in large measure responsible for this achievement.

THE WORLD'S BEST COVERAGE OF THE WORLD'S BIGGEST NEWS   UNITED PRESS

United Press advertisements celebrating the role of reporters in the war effort appeared in popular magazines on the home front during World War II.

During the war, the United Press advertised its reporters as "Shock Troops of the Press," who risked their lives to bring news of America's military exploits from the front lines to the readers back home. One advertisement depicted a civilian correspondent, typewriter in hand, leading armed troops in an assault on an enemy beach, which gave new meaning to the term "adversarial journalism." Toward their own government during the war, however, most American journalists were anything but adversarial. They sometimes chafed under the restrictions of wartime censorship but rarely questioned the larger aims of the U.S. war effort. "We were all on the same side then," Cronkite recalled in his memoir, *A Reporter's Life,* "and most of us newsmen abandoned any thought of impartiality as we reported on the heroism of our boys and the bestiality of the hated Nazis."

Notwithstanding their allegiance to the Allied cause, the United Press reporters covering the war in Europe sought to convey to their readers the realities of the grim and bloody struggle. By 1943 the war was taking the lives of scores and sometimes hundreds of young Americans every week, both on the convoys ferrying men and supplies across the Atlantic and in the air war over Europe.

As in all circumstances, reporters were always on the lookout for a good story that could advance their careers. The journalists who staffed the United Press office in London were ambitious young men who had grown up during the Great Depression; their new assignment was the greatest career opportunity that had ever come their way. "London was the road to my future," Cronkite's fellow United Press reporter Harrison Salisbury wrote frankly in *A Journey for Our Times,* his postwar memoir, "the path to making a name for myself, to propelling myself to fame and fortune."

When Cronkite sailed to London, he expected he would continue to cover the Battle of the Atlantic as before. What he didn't want was a desk position. He hoped, he told Betsy, that the "Navy job" would prove "big enough to keep me out of the office most of the time." Instead, the rapidly expanding U.S. air war over Europe became his main beat. And he made the most of the opportunity. As he wrote in *A Reporter's Life,* "I was lucky enough to be assigned to cover the American and British air forces." The air war was the only war in northwest Europe during that long year of 1943 and the five months of 1944 before the landings in

Walter and Betsy in 1942

Normandy. Stories of aerial warfare shared the headlines at home with the fierce battles fought in North Africa, Italy, and the island-hopping invasions in the Pacific.

Andy Rooney, who as an enlisted man reported the war for the Army newspaper *Stars and Stripes,* later became a CBS colleague of Cronkite's and one of his closest friends. He wrote in *My War,* his 1997 memoir of the war, "Anyone who thinks of Walter Cronkite today as the authoritative father figure of television news would be surprised to know what a tough, competitive scrambler he was in the old *Front Page* tradition of newspaper reporting."

Cronkite's letters recorded his loneliness, far from his wife, but also his friendships with fellow correspondents and others he met in London. He mentioned Fleet Street, the center of the British newspaper industry, in passing, as well as the building where the United Press had its offices during the war. He also mentioned 20 Grosvenor Square, the building that housed the U.S. military's European theater of operations (ETO) headquarters. Grosvenor Square, where the U.S. Embassy was located, was the operational center of what historian David Reynolds has referred to as "the American occupation of Britain." Cronkite complained about the high cost of living, starting with the $13 it cost him to stay overnight at the Savoy Hotel. Adjusted for inflation the bill for his night's lodging would be about $174 in 2012 dollars—not unreasonable given that the sum included drinks and having his clothes pressed and shoes shined. But Cronkite had a thrifty streak, and his meager United Press salary made him feel he had to count every penny.

New Year's Day, 43

I got your wonderful letter this morning . . . I was very down in the dumps until I got it. It is raining and very gloomy here today and last night, such as it was, was a horrible washout. So you see how badly I needed that letter, and it was just what I wanted to hear, the family gossip. (It is good when you are so far away from it) . . .

What hours I'm going to be working and what I'm going to be doing I won't know until Monday when I meet with the Navy bigwigs and find out how much of an assignment the Atlantic Fleet thing is going to be. I'm hoping it will be big enough to keep me out of the office most of the time. I have no desire to sit on the desk writing cables, and if the Navy job is not going to keep me out of the office, I shall put in for some other outside assignment. British [United Press] manager Cliff Day said today however that he was very much interested in getting complete coverage of the Navy, so perhaps I'll get back into my element. Incidentally, the Navy boys here are starting agitation to put Navy correspondents in Navy uniforms, so when I next show up at home I might be in blues. (And I pray that the "Show up at home" will be soon.)

I'm going through my meager funds like they were pennies in an amusement arcade and unless Doug Werner and I get an apartment in a hurry I shall soon be sleeping in one of the Hyde Park air raid shelters. Of course the office is keeping me on an expense account until I find an apartment . . .

Well, I'm into the Savoy Wednesday morning so tired I really was seriously afraid of dropping in my tracks. When I awakened Wednesday night and took my first real look around the room, I was stricken with fright. My God, darling, it was sumptuous. A huge living-bedroom with a couchbed effect, a huge hollywood night table with the phone and other necessities on swinging shelves within reach of the bed, a lamp larger than any street light in NY, 1 wall filled by a gigantic mirror out of which swung a dressing table, 2 closets each large enough for normal bedroom, a bath almost as large as our NY apartment. It was lovely but I was a little glad that the Savoy was only able to accommodate me for one night. I had 2 sets of drinks sent up to the room that night (You can get drinks in your hotel room when the bars are closed, which is most of the time), first for Doug Werner and 2nd for Jack Lovell, RAF Squadron Leader (comparable to a major). I had 2 suits and my overcoat pressed, and I had my shoes shined. The bill for the 24 hrs was $13.00. Wow.

I was kicked out of there as they told me I would be on Thursday (New Years Eve) noon. I was booked into the Grosvenor House, another of London's finest, for Friday and Saturday nights so I decided on a finesse in an attempt to get a bed for Thursday night which, after calling every hotel in London, seemed to be an impossibility. I had that great stack of luggage brought rite here Thursday morning. I had the boy drop it right in front of the desk, and they told the desk they would have to find a place for it. That duffle bag, I believe, turned the trick. Obviously the Grosvenor House could not have it lying around. The frock-coated gentry were sorely perplexed, and the result was finding me a room for the night. It really was only a cell with an adjoining bath, on the top floor (highly undesirable on

*account of air raids which there have been none of for some time) and so
cold that my breath was visible. But it was a bed, and now today I am in a
very nice room again. I probably shall stay here until I find an apartment.
I have no idea what this room is costing but I am sure it will not be on the
Savoy level—indeed it doesn't compare with the Savoy room.*

*Doug Werner, who arrived about three weeks ago, had just about closed
a deal for a single apartment at Crane Court, a little joint right off Fleet
Street and within only a couple of minutes of the office. He is checking
there today to see if we can't get a double apartment and I shall probably
know something about that within the next day or so. Living there will be
very reasonable, I believe, and my living allowance should well take care
of it and any increase in food costs necessary. London apartment owners
are not signing leases these days so Doug and I will still be available to find
something larger with Sam [Hales] when he arrives, although the office has
not received word that he will be en route within a couple of weeks.*

*Wednesday night I ate at the famous Simpson's next door to the Savoy
and had plenty of food—more than I could eat, really. There is a five shilling (one dollar) ceiling on restaurant meals but a service charge is permitted
and at the better spots the service charge sometimes is more than the meal.
Rackets, I suppose, are the same the world over . . .*

*Thursday I spent in a wholly fruitless pursuit of credentials, addi-
tional passport pictures which I needed, and other official business.
Being New Years Eve, 20 Grosvenor Square was not interested in doing
much business. This being New Years Day, although not normally a
holiday here, the American force officers are in no mood for business, so
it will actually be tomorrow or Monday before I get all lined up. Since
I was here last, correspondents accredited to American forces have been
extended additional privileges—all of the privileges, in fact, of any officer, which include trading at the post exchange where candy and peanuts
and American cigarettes and uniforms and all the rest may be obtained
at low, untaxed Army prices. Things are looking up a bit in other words.*

Last night, as I have said, was a washout. Doug and I did our darnd-
est to scrape up excitement with no luck. I wasn't feeling so hot with
absolutely no desire for liquor but I had a couple of wartime Martinis
(No olive, less liquor, no boot, and .70) at Victors Bar here at the hotel,
wandered to a crowded smoky joint called Shepherds Bar in Shepherds
Market where they were out of liquor and serving only beer of which we
had 1 glass each, and then to Piccadilly Circus where we were mauled
by the Times Square type crowd in the blackout. Then to Doug's dingy,
gloomy hotel where we sat in the lounge, had 1 drink from his bottle,
and a spam sandwich, wished each other a happy New Year at midnight,
and went home. Gay, eh? . . .

———

IN THE UNDATED early January letter to Betsy that follows, Cronkite introduced her to two additional United Press colleagues: fellow correspondent Bill Dickinson, who was already covering the air war, and Harrison Salisbury, soon to arrive in London to take over from Joe Alex Morris as UP bureau chief. Salisbury later described the offices they shared in London without nostalgia: "Never had I known a place as cold as the United Press offices in the News of the World plant, a cement-floored factory building," he wrote in *A Journey for Our Times*. "The only heat came from what the English called 'electric fires,' feeble grilles mounted on the ceiling; there was no heat whatever in my bleak office. In my trenchcoat, I huddled over my typewriter, a tiny heater tucked in the knee space of the rolltop desk, and batted out my early morning stories with frozen fingers."

Cronkite's letter features a good example of the "cablese" that crept into his letters. To save space in expensive trans-Atlantic cables, words in news stories were frequently shortened or combined—"United States" was rendered "Unistates." In this case, "Czechoslovakia" becomes the slightly shorter and considerably more whimsical "Czechosloetc."

Cronkite was evidently frustrated that the United Press had not made effective use of him since his arrival in London. In the midst of a great world conflict, his assignment to cover the exchange of notes between Britain and Argentina, he felt, was trivial, irrelevant, and boring—and unlikely to command headlines in American newspapers.

———

[Early January 1943]

Well, here I am at the Park Lane and here I'm afraid I'm likely to remain at least until Sam arrives. Everyone in the office practically is looking for an apartment and all of them want to go in with everyone else but that is as far as the thing goes. They are an impossible bunch to get organized and the more I think it over the more I believe that I'd rather live holed up here in a hotel room by myself than have to tolerate other people around all the time. The difficulty, of course, arises in the expenses. This spot . . . is costing about $3.60 per day and every penny of it is too much. The only advantage is that you can tell the folks at home that people see me outside Buckingham Palace—that's where I live; outside Buckingham Palace and face on the Mall (but my room doesn't).

They are clamping me on the night desk alongside Bill Dickinson, a capable editor . . . who should be able to teach me a lot. Harrison Salisbury is en route to take over from Joe Alex.

I have a rotten cold and cough that I can't seem to shake. I caught them on the boat but had them pretty well under control when I was sent on a story Saturday. With a dozen other newsmen I rode 6 hrs. in an open army truck, then sloshed around at a certain point for a couple more hours, then found out that the story wasn't coming off after all, and rode a drafty train back to London . . . I took it easy Sunday and stayed in bed all day. But that didn't help much. I feel fine but the cough and stopped up nose are bothersome. Let me remind you not to worry about it, though, because it undoubtedly will be cured by the time you get this letter.

I had dinner several nights at the Grosvenor House simply because it was easier to go straight to the hotel from the office in the blackout than to try to find another restaurant . . . [Royal Air Force Squadron Leader Jack] Lovell, who I mentioned in the other letter, joined me 1 night and Surgeon Lt. Mathews another night. It is really a most cosmopolitan joint. Almost every night you see the uniforms of Poland, Netherlands, Czechosloetc, New Zealand, Canada, Fighting French, Norway, Greece, and the babble of tongues is about what you would imagine.

I've written only two stories, really, since I've been here. They were both on the exchange of notes between Argentina and England. For them I had to contact the Argentine embassy, which is just about as impressive as my Park Lane hotel room . . .

I haven't heard from you in six days, but I'm praying for one tomorrow. You probably shall never know how important your letters are . . . Walter

---

CRONKITE MENTIONED THREE additional United Press colleagues in London for the first time in his January 9, 1943, letter to Betsy: Jim McGlincy, Bob Musel, and John Parris. Of the three, McGlincy played the largest role in Cronkite's life during the next year and a half—as friend, roommate, and drinking companion (although Cronkite did not keep up with the hard-drinking McGlincy). He made a passing reference to Webb Miller, a United Press foreign correspondent who had covered Europe since the First World War and died in an accident in the London Underground in 1940.

Food emerged as another preoccupation in his correspondence. He waged a never-ending but largely futile effort to satisfy a young American's appetite and culinary preferences in austere, rationed, wartime Britain.

This is also the first letter in which Cronkite made direct reference to continued if sporadic German (or "Jerry") bombing raids on England, although he downplayed the dangers involved. The blackout imposed on British cities, and rigorously enforced by the authorities, was another aspect of wartime Britain that impressed American newcomers, especially those like Cronkite who had come from cities like New York, where well-lit streets remained the norm even after Pearl Harbor (although the neon advertising in Times Square was sacrificed to the city's wartime dimout).

———

January 9, 1943

I have tonight off after being on the 2 to 10 p.m. shift all week. Those apparently are going to be my hours every day except Saturday, when I'll be working from 9 a.m. until 5 p.m. and Wednesday when I'll be off. I'll work a regular trick Sunday, it seems.

Tonight Jim McGlincy is coming by after a while and we are going over to the Red Cross officers club for dinner, then because it will be too late for a movie (last movie eight pm most places) we shall have beers til the bars close at 11 pm, and then home to bed on account (a) there is nothing else to do in this wartime town, and (b) McGlincy has the eight am showup in the morning. It is six now and the blackout has been on a half hour—eugg!

Which reminds me: I forgot my "torch" last night. Having come to work in daylight I didn't realize I had forgotten it until I got ready to go home. Not having it was serious. In the first place, it was a pitch black night and I stood serious danger of tripping over a curb or running into a wall, or worse, completely losing my way—which isn't a darned bit hard to do even for the oldest Londoners. In the second place, the nearest bus stop to our office is a "request only" stop, which means that you have to hail your bus. In the blackout that is almost totally impossible unless you have your torch to signal with. Furthermore, although it is seldom you can get a cab in Fleet

St. that late at night anyway, if one should have come by I couldn't have caught him so easily without a light. But fortunately I did wangle that. A cab did pass, I whistled, and some how or other we found each other in the pitch blackness. Thus ends the adventure of our rover boys in the blackout.

I'm sure that you have written but the darned mails must be fouled up and I haven't had a single letter since that first one which arrived New Years Day, nine days ago. It is badly worn now and shall be a total loss from constant rereading unless I get another early next week. McGlincy and Bob Musel, incidentally, make me pretty sore. They get stacks of correspondence almost daily apparently from scores of relatives and friends. It does seem a little strange how much a letter means when one is expatriated. Any deviation in delivery dates of our letters is the fault of the mails. (NOT the fault of the MALES, either, God, am I getting a British sensahumor?) . . .

The food is not quite so bad as I remember it last August and there is no trouble in filling the old belly. You can't get a great big juicy steak or fruits or all the milk you want and you can't just drop in a restaurant at odd hours and get a meal (which makes it difficult for night workers) but I haven't noticed any effects of starvation yet—either on me after 2 wks or the general populace after 3 yrs. Also some of the shortages in cigarettes (American), razor blades, soaps, etc. are alleviated for the Americans accredited to the forces here by the Post Exchange, an Army store set up right around the corner from the American headquarters . . .

You have been reading by now that Jerry has been giving the south coast a little taste of blitz every day or so (some of the stories whereof I wrote but not from the scene) but we don't get any action at all and for that I'm now knocking on wood . . .

There is quite a bit of sickness in the office with Joe Alex Morris and Doug Werner both in bed but I believe my cold and cough are loosening up now, thanks to Dr. Framels Old Fashioned Cough Syrup (what in the world over here, including the plumbing isn't old fashioned?) recommended by Miss [Sally] Stronoch who has been secretary in the London

Walter Cronkite's War Department visa

bureau since Webb Miller was in knee pants and who delights in mothering the boys . . . Enclosed is a new identification picture I had to have made for some additional passes here. I look as if one more shot of heroin would put me out—which, come to think of it, would. Tell mother I shall write soon . . . Walter

---

LIFE IN WARTIME London wasn't all plucky and heroic stoicism, as evidenced by the misadventure revealed in Cronkite's next letter to Betsy. During the war a dramatic increase in personal crimes occurred in the city, including robberies, rapes, and murders. Cronkite, in many ways a stereotypical "innocent abroad" during those first weeks in London, had a lot to learn about big city life.

January 10, 1943

This week was horrible—my wallet was stolen. I lost about 10 pounds (sterling—$40.00) as well as all my valuable identification papers—

*passport, War Department passes, Muehlebach and Lexington Hotel
credit cards, etc. But more important, I lost your picture. So, Darling,
will you please airmail me another one immediately . . .*

*Re the wallet: It was the black moroccan one, you know, that I had
so I could carry a passport. It was in my suit coat pocket when I hung
the coat on a rack. When I returned to the rack two hours later, the wallet was gone. Joe Morris was very concerned so we called in Scotland
Yard. I was very disappointed. They didn't show up with peaked, checked
caps and long pipes at all. In fact they looked to be, and apparently are,
right of the same ilk as our Kansas City flatfeet. A very nice and pleasant inspector is working on the case and the Embassy and War Dept are
pressing the investigation greatly concerned, are they, over the loss of the
identity card but it has been six days now and I have heard nothing.*

*It really was my own stupidity for leaving the wallet in my coat. I
usually removed it, but with the passport in it, it was a bulky thing to
put in any other pocket and I was always concerned lest it slip out of my
hip pocket or that I fail to put it back in my coat pocket when I left the
building. In that case it would have been a perfect mark for pickpockets,
who are busy little bees in the blackout.*

*The office loaned me a little money to get through the week on and
I believe that I am going to be able to get along without the lost funds
and without going in the hole . . .*

*Sam [Hales] arrived last night . . . I was in a single room about the
size of a good-sized table top until last night and now Sam and I are
together in a double where we probably will stay until we can find
some sort of flat. Bob Musel has been looking frantically at places
for three weeks and he has made exactly no headway. A couple good
air raids might scare a few people out of town, but on the other hand
might likewise increase the housing shortage. C'est l'guerre! . . .*

*A strange coincidence (My God, I'm beginning to write like London
newspaper headlines): Although all bars close at eleven and I don't get*

off until then, I managed to get home the other night in time to slip into the American Bar downstairs for a quick one before retiring. There I ran into an American flyer who turned out to be from Texas. "Where in Texas" I inquired and "Houston" he answered. Well, to cut the story a bit short, he was in my graduating class at San Jacinto (pronounced Ja-sin-to) and knew everybody I knew—but we had never met. Amazing, isn't it? Now, of course, I don't remember his name. Oh well.

Dearest, they have the most wonderful horses over here. You would love them. Most of them are light colored and they are small—they really don't seem large enough to be doing the heavy duty to which they are required. But the marvelous part is the wonderful sweet expression on their pusses. They are shaggy and a whisp of white hair always hangs over one eye, just like Veronica, and from their elbows down they are feathery, just like Judy.

Speaking of Judy, I miss her so terribly. I damn near cry every time I see another pup, and particularly a cocker although no cocker particularly the large English versions, are as pretty as our Judy . . . Walter

———

BETWEEN THE TWO World Wars, relatively few Americans, besides the wealthy and such famous expatriate writers as Ernest Hemingway and F. Scott Fitzgerald, traveled to Europe. Cronkite's first trip abroad the previous fall had allowed him only a glimpse of wartime England. Betsy had never traveled outside the United States. So Cronkite devoted many pages in his correspondence to travel writing, as in his description in his letter of January 25, 1943, of taking Betsy's "nephoo" Bob Manring on a walking tour of London. Manring, about the same age as the Cronkites, was a close friend. According to Cronkite family lore, he was in London on a "hush-hush" assignment.

The references to "Woolcott" and "Barrymore" were to theater critic and Algonquin Circle wit Alexander Woollcott and to theater and film actor John Barrymore, both of whom had died within the past year.

Cronkite closed this letter asking to be remembered to Mom, Petty, Molo, Betty, and Allan. "Mom" was his own mother, Helen Fritsche Cronkite; "Petty" was a pet name for Betsy's father; "Molo" was a pet name for Betsy's mother; "Betty" was Betty Maxwell, Betsy's sister-in-law; and "Allan" was Allan Maxwell, Betsy's brother.

Even the most carefree letters Cronkite sent to Betsy carried reminders of the war raging around him. At night he would sometimes go up on the rooftop above the United Press offices, where he would watch the not-too-distant glow of fires set by German bombs—dangerous duty even if he made light of his "glamorous" appearance in his "trenchcoat and World War type helmet."

———

January 25, 1943

Our nephoo [Bob Manring] was down this week-end and we had a strictly dull time but were so damned glad to be with someone else of the Maxwell clan that I think we both enjoyed it immensely . . . I had to work Sat. from 3 to 11:00 and Sun. from 5 to 1, and I was unable to get anybody to relieve me of any of those hours—even for a nephoo. However, it didn't work out so badly. Bob arrived at 7:00 Sat. night and I took an hour off for dinner during which we went around to the Wellington Inn on Fleet Street and had a very good twenty cent meal for one dollar and a quarter—and which Bob properly annotated by informing me that his principal beef was that he couldn't get enough food, which, calling on my powerful memory, I readily understood. Even I, who was never much of an eater, you know, complain similarly.

Well, on with the tale. Things got quiet around the office about nine-thirty and I managed to slip away. I found Bob where I told him we would meet—the American Bar at the Park Lane Hotel. (Every pub now has an American Bar. It is getting to be something of a laugh.) He was sober, I was sober, and we remained that way all evening. We had a couple of drinks before the bar closed at eleven, then retired to the lounge where guests only may drink after hours and had a couple more during which some air corps gents whom I had met previously intruded on our reminiscing. Such intrusion probably was a good idea at that point. We were about to cry on each others' shoulders about the sad fate that kept us separated from home and all that means. We told each other time and time again how much we love Virginia and Betsy. And you'd be surprised how many times the Maxwell Thanksgiving—Xmas—Birthday table entered into the conversation . . .

We turned in about 2 o'clock, but at 9 Bob was up bouncing around, dressed and ready to go sightseeing. He hadn't been down here before except for a couple of very, very busy days when he first landed. So [Sam] Hales and I managed to drag ourselves up and we actually got a fairly early start—a fact far contrary to those sightseeing trips that you and I always intended to take in N.Y. We had breakfast downstairs on account it is on the bill with your room rent and there is nothing you can do about it. Breakfast has always been a rather horrible institution, I thought, and these ersatz affairs you get around here are doing nothing to change this belief.

Yesterday was a wonderful warm day and midday the sun came out for a few minutes to brighten up the whole picture. During the morning there was the kind of fog that you have heard of persons becoming lost in. It was of the Scottish moors type, you know—rolling in great banks that blotted out everything including the nephew standing next to you. We opened the window in our room in the morning and it rolled into the room. Fantastic and wonderful, it was. We found our way through the fog to the Army Finance Office where Bob had to pick up some sort of delinquent paycheck, then to the Army Post Exchange for our weekly ration of 1 can of orange juice, 1 can of tomato juice, 1 box each of vanilla wafers, chocolate cookies (very much unlike the wonderful ones my wife makes) and cheese niblets, can of tobacco (or 5 packs of cigarettes American brand or 3 cigars), one bar of soap, 1 pack pipe cleaners, etc. Then we went to the officers' club, which is the best place to eat in town. For 80 cents each you get a fair lunch and for the same price a fair dinner. There is a bar downstairs with fireplace and it is really a rather comfortable spot. Its use is restricted to American officers, under which category, of course, those of us who are accredited newspapermen come.

After lunch we set out and for 4 hours we walked. We walked by Buckingham Palace, which is just across a two-block wide park from the Park Lane, down by the barracks for the Coldstream Guards and other of the King's Own Regiments, through the wonderful park with a lagoon and a thousand species of wild birds including gulls and ducks and pelicans and cranes, down through Admiralty Arch out onto Trafalgar Square, thence down Whitehall street past Scotland Yard and the little alleyway entrance to Downing Street which is blocked off but down which you could see dingy Number 10 with an armed guard outside.

And then we turned sharp left and passed the Houses of Parliament just as Big Ben was rattling off 3 o'clock. We wandered across Westminster Bridge into Lambeth, past a hospital which bombed and gutted and still seems to manage to carry on. Then we took a bus back to Trafalgar and down the Strand past Aldwich Circle (at the Aldwych Theater, by the way, "Arsenic and Old Lace," British version, is playing) and all 6 bustling blocks of it, and up Ludgate Hill by St. Pauls, through the blocks of yawning cellars over which once stood buildings, down past Threadneedle St. and the Bank of England, to Aldgate where we got off the bus. We walked over to the Tower of London and gazed for an hour at it from the outside—at its amazing battlements and the one tiny corner where a German bomb did what thousands of arrows and rock catapults and battering rams never could do. We were there at the wrong time for the tour, and so had to content ourselves with gazing from without and chatting briefly with the Beefeater at the gate—you know, the men in the pictures with the hats that look almost as funny as those in Harzfelds window *and the red coats and knee pants. They are still there (and most of them look like they had endured the Battle of Hastings) but nowadays are supplemented by Tommies complete with steel helmets and rifles.*

Then past a tavern founded in 1500 and which a plaque proudly proclaims that "Queen Elizabeth Honoured"—probably by revoking their license and beheading the bartender for staying open after hours. It looks just as crummy as any other pub. Down Cheapside, the much blitzed market district, we wandered, to Billingsgate, the fish market which smells like it, and The Monument, a Wren structure in Pudding Lane which was erected in 1671 to commemorate the Great Fire whose farthest limit it marks. "It is a fluted Doric column 200' in height. A fine view of London may be obtained from the top gallery, to reach which 312 steps have to be climbed. Admission 3d." That's according to the pre-Blitz guide book. The Monument is now much bepocked with shell fragments and is closed, for which I am glad, considering those 312 steps. And then to the office with only one other incident which I still can't explain. We passed a shattered London alley back among some buildings. All the buildings are gone now but the fire-scorched sign on the crumbling archway still identifies it as "Rose Lane." And here is the mysterious part: A powerful scent of roses, there in the midst of the Hitler-created debris, almost bowls one over as you pass "Rose Lane" ... If that is at all reminiscent of Woolcott, then let us pause this moment in honor of that terrific character. Barrymore, Woolcott—the old masters of repartee seem to be dropping by the wayside, and I can't seem to think offhand who might replace them. Unless it's Rudy Vallee. Or me.

I mentioned earlier these air corps guys with whom Bob and I became entangled Saturday night. I met them the previous Wednesday night, which was my night off. We had a few drinks at the bar and then wandered over to the luxurious flat of 1 of the navy public relation boys here. I made the mistake of telling these guys that I thought I had perfect balance and if it weren't for the old color-blindness would make a terrific flyer. To prove which I had to pull that little stunt of holding one leg straight out in front and kneeling on the other—you know. I did the stunt with great aplomb. But I'm still limping, and this is Monday . . .

This is your birthday and that doesn't help matters a bit. I sent you a cable Saturday which was, of course, a couple of days early but I wanted to take no chances of no-delivery as long as I couldn't send a present. What I would like most of all to send you, however, would be myself . . .

I'm losing a little weight, but it all seems to be at my waistline, and that won't do me any harm. I'm getting too much sleep, which is the night worker's occupational hazard (the bars closing at 11 o'clock, the hour I get off, are contributing to that). I'm having trouble with the laundry which has a button-mangler equal to none elsewhere in the world. It not only mangles; it grabs hold of the button and tears it out by the roots including an inch-square patch of shirt . . .

Incidentally, when you read of these London air raids, don't worry about the kid. Out of 7 or 8 million persons, the percentage killed or injured is mighty small and you actually feel rather isolated from the whole thing. The bombs haven't yet dropped close enough in my neighborhood to make me even realize there was danger afoot, although I must admit that the explosions and the terrific pounding of the anti-aircraft guns, particularly at night when the explosions light the sky, make an impressive show. I have been the "United Press rooftop observer" quoted in most of our dispatches. My rooftop observation post is a tower atop the News of the World (the UP) Bldg, and it is a wonderful vantage point. I look pretty damned glamorous, too, in my trenchcoat and World War type helmet . . .

IN JANUARY 1943, as Cronkite was settling into life in London, Prime Minister Winston Churchill and President Franklin Roosevelt were meeting in Casablanca in North Africa, along with their top military advisers. There they announced that the only acceptable outcome of the war was the unconditional surrender of the Axis powers: Germany, Italy, and Japan. They also laid plans for a coordinated Allied air assault against Germany. Cronkite's assignment to the European air-war beat could not have come at a better time.

In January, 47,325 U.S. Army Air Forces personnel were stationed in Britain. By the following December, that number had mushroomed to 286,264. In a December 1943 United Press dispatch, Cronkite charted the expansion of the wire service's coverage of the air war since his arrival. "Throughout last winter," he wrote, "when the American air effort was as a molehill to its present mountain, I was able to cover the story alone." That meant, among other things, that as the lone UP reporter covering the air war, he spent a lot of time traveling to and from the newly established American air bases. Bad weather that winter meant that on many days the bombers didn't fly. But when a mission was scheduled, Cronkite and reporters from other wire services and newspapers would receive a coded telephone call from Army Air Forces public relations, along the lines of "We're going to have a poker game tonight." They would then know to take an early morning train out to one or another of the American bases scattered throughout the English countryside.

Cronkite often traveled to the Molesworth air base in Cambridgeshire, home to the 303rd Bombardment Group, which had arrived in September 1942 and flown its first mission on November 17 over St. Nazaire. (The men of the 303rd would fly a total of 364 missions by war's end.) The unit became known as the "Hell's Angels," named for one of the B-17s in the group that was the first in the Eighth Air Force to complete 25 bombing missions over Europe.

At bases like Molesworth, the reporters would wait for the bombers to return and then interview the aircrews about how the day's mission had gone. They wrote their dispatches at the base, always careful to note the hometowns and ages of the crew members they quoted. As

Cronkite told Don Carleton in an interview for the oral history *Conversations with Cronkite,* "The first thing you ever asked anybody was 'Where are you from?' That was the very first order of business. The UP was wild for a hometown story. And then almost every day you'd write the lead story and get some of the stuff that belonged, the description of the target, the description of the fighter opposition, the flak, and all that sort of thing, but then you would immediately get off to the sidebar stories. There was always a feature story or two of the mission."

The writing was done under the watchful eyes of military censors to ensure that the reports met the standards of military security (which is why the names and locations of air bases were never mentioned). The reporters would then carry (or later on, when security concerns slightly eased, read over the telephone) the censored dispatches to their London offices, where they would be cabled to wire service and newspaper offices in the United States.

The U.S. Army Air Forces' Eighth Bomber Command (the Eighth Air Force also had fighter and air-support commands) had been flying daylight bombing assaults against targets in occupied Europe since August 1942. The American bombing fleet consisted of B-17 Flying Fortresses and B-24 Liberators, both heavily armed four-engine bombers, capable of reaching targets deep in German territory. What the Eighth Air Force lacked in 1942 and for much of 1943 were fighter planes capable of escorting the bombers for more than a few hundred miles. That didn't matter so much when the bombers were sent out to hit targets along the French or Dutch coast. But in January 1943, just after Cronkite arrived in London, Americans made their first strikes against the German homeland, flying beyond the range of American fighters. American air strategists believed that by having the bombers fly in tight formations, the gunners aboard the B-17s and B-24s could ward off German fighter attacks. "This proved to be wishful thinking," Cronkite wrote in *A Reporter's Life.* "To fly in the Eighth Air Force in those days," his colleague Harrison Salisbury wrote, likewise long after the war, "was to hold a ticket to a funeral. Your own."

Cronkite and his colleagues were not as blunt in their reports during the war. Dark notes would occasionally creep into their dispatches, but the overall emphasis of American reporting was one of steady progress leading to ultimate victory. Cronkite's first bylined dispatch from England, which ran in the *New York World-Telegram* on January 27, under the headline "Beautiful Bombing, U.S. Flyers Boast," reflected that optimistic view:

A FLYING FORTRESS STATION SOMEWHERE IN ENGLAND, Jan. 27.—American crew members of the bombers that carried the aerial war to German soil today said tonight "it's a cinch over Germany." There were few fighters and only light antiaircraft fire, they added.

They believed they had smashed their objectives in Wilhelmshaven, which, coincidentally, was the first target in Germany raided by the Royal Air Force in 1939 . . .

The honor of being the first American bomber over Germany went to the "Banshee." The Banshee's pilot was First Lt. Edward J. Hennessy, 23, of Chicago.

"We didn't see a thing except some flak," Hennessy said. "I guess we just surprised the hell out of them. They sure weren't expecting Americans over there in daytime."

In *Masters of the Air: America's Bomber Boys Who Fought the Air War Against Nazi Germany,* Donald L. Miller wrote of the first Wilhelmshaven raid, "The Germans were caught off guard and there was little opposition, but clouds obscured the target and bomb damage was minimal." Yet even the minimal opposition, as Cronkite reported, shot down three American planes. As Cronkite would personally observe the next time the Americans hit Wilhelmshaven, the Germans would be better prepared.

That mission was described in his February 6, 1943, letter to Betsy. Cronkite excitedly announced a new opportunity that he and several fellow reporters were offered—the chance to go along on a bombing mission over Germany. Cronkite's invitation to join this select group of reporters, which included Gladwin Hill of the Associated Press, William Wade of the International News Service, Robert Post of the *New York Times,* Homer Bigart of the *New York Herald Tribune,* Paul Manning of CBS Radio, Andy Rooney of the Army newspaper *Stars and Stripes,* and Denton Scott of the Army magazine *Yank,* marked a turning point in Cronkite's journalistic fortunes. A wit in Air Force public relations dubbed them the "Writing Sixty-Ninth," after a famous doughboy outfit from the First World War, the Fighting Sixty-Ninth.

The Associated Press and the United Press were engaged in a perpetual competition to file their dispatches first and to provide the most detailed reporting and the most dramatic content, all of which often determined which wire service's story would be featured in newspapers the next day. As heads of their respective air war desks in London, Cronkite of the UP and Gladwin Hill of the AP were thereby rivals as well as friends. Cronkite later told an interviewer that as he completed a story, he would often worry, "Gosh, I wonder what Glad is going to write." After filing their stories, they might meet up at a pub and each would try to wheedle out of the other the details of his story. On one occasion, when Cronkite revealed that he had written a story estimating that 875 bombers were involved in that day's raid over a German city, Hill (according to the story that Cronkite later told, in any case) immediately telephoned his office to raise his own estimate of the bomber fleet to 880. "He'd have more than I had. And whoever said more was going to get his story in the papers back home."

In his February 6 letter, Cronkite also explained to Betsy the advantages of switching their correspondence to "v-mail." V-mail, or victory mail, involved the microfilming of a specially designed combination letter sheet and envelope. It was a process designed by the U.S. Postal Service to save precious cargo space and speed the delivery of wartime correspondence from overseas. The writer would write on a 7 $^7/_8$-inch-wide-by-7 $^3/_8$-inch-long sheet of paper, add the address and postage to the other side, then fold the form and mail it. Before overseas shipment, it would be micro-filmed into a thumbnail-size image. At a receiving station on the other side of the ocean, the thumbnail image would be expanded into a facsimile of the original letter, 4½ by 5½ inches, and sent to the addressee. Cronkite's typed v-mails to Betsy could be no more than 700 words, which is why he often resorted to UP's cablese language to save space.

Cronkite's letter of February 6 was written four days after the German surrender to the Red Army at the Battle of Stalingrad, and two weeks before green American troops in North Africa suffered a humiliating defeat at the hands of crack soldiers from the German Afrika Korps in the Battle of Kasserine Pass.

———

Feb. 6, 1943

I returned to London yesterday after a week away to find that I had hit the jackpot. I had four letters from you . . . It was the first mail I had received since the air mail letter (yours of December 19) that arrived Jan. 1. Was I glad to get it. I was horribly weary, dirty and worn when I called from the hotel here and the office told me that it was there but I immediately hopped a taxi and ran to the office for it. Then I came back here, fighting off the urge to open all the letters in the cab, climbed into the tub and laid there in much more than the required five inches and read my letters. I found it was a good idea to be in the tub because I couldn't help shedding a tear or two as you described Christmas at home.

The letters of yours I got were those mailed Dec. 22, 26, 30 and Jan. 2. They were all, of course, regular mail. I also got . . . an AIR MAIL letter

*of mother's posted Dec. 30. Air mail is strictly a gamble. Some air mail
letters arrive here within 10 days or 2 weeks while others—indeed most—
like mother's are apparently put on the boats and arrive right along with
the other mail. Within the next couple of days I will be able to write you
a v-mail letter in which I will explain how you can v-mail me too. I like
the apparent certainty and speed of v-mail—about 10 days, normally—
but I don't like the impersonal character of a photostated letter or the
prospect of some army officer with whom I might be acquainted or at
least known censoring my outgoing letters. However, because of its speed
I'm going to suggest that we write each other one v-mailer (or more, if
possible) a week and supplement it with one airmail letter a week. How
do you think that would be?*

*I'm so sorry you didn't get to have a tree Christmas. Those prices were
prohibitive but I'll bet if the Cronkites could have been together they would
have figured out something to keep from disappointing Judy and Betsy. I
suppose by now it is a little late for me to tell you that I'm praying for you
on the job situation. You have probably worked something out, and I hope
it is along the publications or radio line . . . If these publishers only knew
what so many of us know about your capabilities they'd be bidding in an
open market for you. I was damned interested to hear of Frank [Barhydt]
going with the OWI [Office of War Information]. I don't suppose you have
heard, but there is a heluva fight brewing between the press services and
the government over OWI. It seems that OWI is trying to sneak in under us
and with a subsidized, controlled service sell or even GIVE American news
to foreign newspapers. That sort of competition, of course, would practically run the UP out of the foreign field, from which it obtains much of its
revenue, and we are watching the thing like the hawks we are. Elmer Davis,
OWI head, has promised that no such competition is planned by OWI but
we aren't convinced. Still I think we'll smash the incipient menace before it
reaches puberty—and then I hold by the belief I've had all along: i.e., that
these war-time agency jobs aren't worth the effort they take to get . . .*

Incidentally, the package has not shown up and when I saw Bob [Manring] two weeks ago his ham likewise had not shown. Or maybe he was just playing it cagey. I got a call last night which missed me and was taken by Sam [Hales] that he will be in town tonight and to get him a hotel room, a damned near impossible order in this war-crowded city on week-ends. But I did manage to wangle it here at the Park Lane, considering my long-time residence here. So he'll be in at six o'clock and I suppose we'll have one of those evenings which pass as a synthetic, homesick version of FUN. Although you know the UP. I just got back from a back-breaking week and now they may want me to come into the office this afternoon to take a trick on the desk. That hangs fire . . .

Now I must interrupt. I have to go over to an Eighth Air Force conference, from which I will return here to talk with you again . . .

It is now Sunday, February 7. The conference developed a story which I had to run into the office to write, file and fight through censorship. Then it was six o'clock and Bob was calling. I was just finishing the story when he called and I was pretty darned tired and wanted to splash a little water on the face. So I came on back to the hotel and we met a half hour later down in the bar. We had a couple of drinks and managed to bribe our way into Maxims, a chop suey joint. We really did have to fork up 2 bucks to get into the place. This city is impossible almost every night, it is so crowded, but on Saturday nights with the tremendous influx of Americans, Canadians and British on leave it is positively unlivable and unless you have long-standing reservations dating back to the revolutionary war days (I wonder if that one'll get by censorship) you can get into the greasiest spoon only by bribing the head waiter. Believe you me, when I get home I'm going to be a past master at the art of oiling palms . . .

We returned to the Park Lane and, being residents here, were permitted to sit in the lounge and have a couple of drinks before turning in. That is one way they get around the eleven o'clock closing law here— residents of hotels may sit in the lounge of their respective (although not

*always respectful) hotels and drink until the waiters go home. We cried
in our beer over being away from home and reviewed happier days of
the past, my quoting all the while quite liberally from your letters. It was
damned nice being with one of the family again. His ham arrived last
week and he is saving it until I can get up to his post which I hope to
do next weekend if all works out well. He is billeted with an old English
family who are going to further cook the ham for him, and if I know
most English cooking they will manage to ruin it, probably smothering
it in brussel sprouts.*

*Did you know that brussel sprouts are the new backbone of the Brit-
ish Empire? No kidding. You get them every meal, even including breakfast at which time they fry them. I still like them but my love is waning
and—don't know how long it can last under the strain. I seem to be getting enough food—I eat most meals at the American officers club where
the supply is more plentiful and a little better prepared than most other
places—but I still lost weight and my suits now look a little as if they had
been tailored for my father . . . This working in the London bureau is
very much like Washington or any other similar job, you know; constant
running here and there to interview this character or that, dashing into
the office and grinding out stories regardless of the hour and forgetting
completely to eat.*

*And now, before I get interrupted again, I must tell you about the last
week. Probably you shall know about it through the newspapers and
perhaps even Time and Newsweek or Editor and Publisher, long before
this letter ever arrives. I'm going to write my story later today or early
tomorrow and it will be released in Tuesday morning newspapers. For
the past week six other correspondents and I have been under full army
regime going to school from seven-thirty in the morning until ten-thirty
at night learning how to take our places as the tenth member of a Flying Fortress crew. We've been assigned by our papers to the Eighth Air
Force. We're going to live on the airdromes with them and, occasionally,*

when the story warrants, we're going along on their raids with them. The story involves a certain amount of risk but it's a terrific opportunity . . .

Along were Gladwin Hill of AP, William Wade of INS, Robert Post of the NY Times (Gerry Harrington's friend—you might write that bit of news to Gerry), Homer Bigart of New York Herald Tribune, Paul Manning of CBS, and two service paper correspondents—one from Yank [Denton Scott] and the other from Stars and Stripes [Andy Rooney]. We're now called by the Air Corps boys, for no particular reason, the "Writing Sixty-Ninth" and we're just like a bunch of kids about the assignment. We have our own secret handshake which is not dirty but involves a military secret. Remind me to show you when I get home.

We left here in a contingent on an early train Monday morning, which in typical Cronkite style I damned near missed by failing to get a cab at the last minute out in front of the hotel. We were told to bring along our helmets and gas masks and I'm sure I cut a very military figure in service pants, galoshes, mackinaw and helmet and gas mask slung over shoulder. I felt pretty war-like too racing through Paddington Station to catch that train. We were met at the depot at the other end by an army truck—our first in a very long series of rides by army truck for the next week. It took us first to a nearby air station where we were to have taken tests in pressure chamber to determine our adaptability to high altitude flying. There was some hitch there however and we played ping pong all morning, finally being ushered into the air station dining hall for lunch—and a very good one, shared by the personnel of the station which is now mostly American but still contains some RAFers. Then back into our army truck for a forty minute ride to the Combat Crew Replacement Center which was to be our home for a week . . .

Well, about the school. We spent a week being routed off our ultra-hard mattresses in our officers' barracks by bugle each morning, hastening through dressing (which you know was a chore for me), out into the blackout and into our truck for a cold ride the mile and a half from the barracks area to the mess hall, then a walk back to the classroom, then usually a mid-morning ride by truck again to the airfield or some other dispersed area, then the truck again back to mess for lunch, an afternoon repeat in classroom, dinner in the mess and usually time for one drink but no more, then back to classroom, and finally back to the barracks by 10:30 or so. That went on for a week while we learned first aid, aircraft identification, use of oxygen equipment, how to bail out and how to get out of a ditched plane into a rubber dinghy in case you should go down in the channel or the North Sea. We learned some secret matters too which it is forbidden to mention but which sometime I shall be able to tell you about. We made one high altitude flight, climbing to 25000' where the temperature is more than 45 degrees below, centigrade. I felt like a real aviator in heavy flying suit and oxygen mask. Some pictures were taken of us in our garb which I will send along as soon as the army gives us some copies. On the flight I had the good fortune of being in the bombardiers compartment with its glass enclosure. It was a real thrill taking off in that spot.—Watching the ground roar past you as those 4 great motors throbbed, and then the ground pulling away. All the way up to that great altitude I was able to get a beautiful picture of the whole proceeding through that glass nose. My only effect from the flight was a light popping in my left ear which still persists slightly. We took 4 very tough examinations before "graduation." I passed one with second highest grade in the class—a 98 on aircraft identification, made the second highest grade also on one of the secret tests, barely eked by a third test and flunked a fourth, but I passed the course as a whole and now have a letter from General [Ira C.] Eaker saying I'm accredited to Eighth Air Force and have passed a course qualifying me to make operational flights. Also we were given highest honor by other airmen and requested to remove the wire stays from our hats, which is the identifying mark of the air force. Also we're going to wear on our sleeves the Eighth Air Corps shoulder patch—the star with wings . . .

Oh, yes, I forgot to tell you. Also taking the course with us were the members of the Eighth Air Corps film unit. They were led by Major William Wyler, the Hollywood director who produced Mrs. Miniver *and other such well knowns. The other 5 members of his crew mostly were famous Hollywood cameramen except one—Tex McCreary. McCreary is that horrible guy who did newsreel commentaries for the newsreel theatres in NY. Remember? The guy who sat on the edge of a desk and shouted at you in a loud, raucous voice and obviously didn't know what he was talking about. Well, despite the fact he used to be married to Arthur Brisbane's daughter and now is engaged to Jinx Falkenburg and is Wyler's sidekick—he still is loud and raucous and doesn't know what he's talking about and is pretty universally disliked. By coincidence you might also remember that the last time we went to a newsreel theater we saw him in a commentary which was loudly proclaimed as his last before joining the armed services. Wyler wasn't much better, although I have heard that he really isn't such a bad guy, but he was throwing his weight around with the group of lieutenants (including McCreary) he had with him and was one of the loudest voices in our barracks where— yes, even Wyler lived. He had one great gag. In each of the final exams he managed to get a phone call about 15 minutes after the exam started and have to leave the classroom. When he came back 15 minutes later he scribbled madly in order to get down all the answers that he had just looked up before he forgot them. We had it rigged up that Glad Hill was going to have me paged from one classroom as "Major Cronkite" but somehow the gag fell through, although I'm still known and probably will be forever with the Writing Sixty-Ninth as "The Major" . . . Tex McCreary did pull one good gag. We were boning one night on aircraft identification and were on one particular plane with Wade giving out the identifying features. "It has a V-cutout tail, a humped back, retractable landing equipment, and a prominent air scoop on the belly," he said. "Sir," McCreary answered, "You're speaking of the woman I love."*

Cronkite with fellow war correspondents, circa 1943

Whereupon Wyler had to put in his two-bits worth by stating that Jinx wouldn't like that.

One other funny incident. (Laughter-in anticipation.) One of the boys awakened the middle of one night to go to the little boys room. He stumbled over a chair and awakened one of the other gents. The 2 of them chatting in whispered tones awakened a third party. Before anyone knew exactly what had happened we all were awake, the lights were on, and we were getting dressed, somehow thinking it was time to get up. Some of the boys were even shaved by the time the misfortune was discovered . . .

———

IN 1942 THE Glenn Miller Orchestra and the Andrews Sisters each had hit recordings of "Don't Sit Under the Apple Tree (With Anyone Else But Me)," a song pledging and demanding sexual fidelity despite a couple's wartime separation. A recurrent theme in Cronkite's letters throughout 1943 and 1944 is the hope that he could soon arrange to bring Betsy to London to sit the war out with him under their own personal apple tree.

Cronkite wasn't alone among American newsmen in London in having left a spouse at home, but not all of his colleagues were eager to be reunited, as he discovered when he encountered reporter Bill Richardson in the company of a woman not his wife, recounted in his letter of February 14, 1943. CBS's Edward R. Murrow, another married man, carried on what his biographers Stanley Cloud and Lynne Olson describe as a "passionate affair" with Pamela Churchill, estranged spouse of Randolph Churchill, son of the prime minister. UP correspondent Harrison Salisbury was another unhappily married man for whom wartime separation felt like liberation. "Sex hung in the London air like the fog," he recalled in his memoir, "its scent permeating every corner . . . I began to sleep with girls, sometimes because I was fond of them, sometimes because we found ourselves together at the end of an evening." In drawing Betsy's attention in an amused way to the infidelities of other married men in London, Cronkite was obviously confident that his own wife would harbor no suspicions of unfaithfulness on his part.

The letter that follows makes reference to Tom Wolf of the NEA—the Newspaper Enterprise Association, a Scripps-Howard syndicate.

———

February 14, 1943

This isn't much like the Valentines Days of the past . . . I've thought constantly of you and Judy all day, as I seem to every day. I've even got out my big oom-paul pipe that you gave me last Valentines day. But that wasn't enough of a substitute for being at home . . . I missed the Sunday lounging all day, never getting around to eating, finally dashing over to Molo's for one of those great big dinners, and then maybe a show or some Tonk . . .

Instead this Sunday I slept until noon (what, come to think of it, is "instead" about that) finally got up, bathed and washed my hair leaving too much soap in it so it now stands out like a Communist party badge, and began the tortuous process of going downstairs. Don't think that isn't tortuous, too. With typical British impracticality, there are 3 lifts in the Park Lane, and none of them have interconnecting signal systems. They are about a half-block apart, it seems, so you run from one to the other pressing buttons while nothing happens. The signal system telling you what floor they are on also has been on the blink since the blitz, so that doesn't give you any hint as to which, if any, of them are running. Then when one finally does arrive at your floor, which in my pitiful case is the top, you are invariably at the other end. By the time you have run down the hall to catch the elevator that is there, it isn't. The boy—who, of course, is 95 and hence undraftable—has looked out and not finding you standing right there ready to hop in, started down again. Then you start the whole business over again.

Well, in the elevator this morning I ran into Bill Richardson, who used to be with the UP in NY and now is managing editor of Yank, the army magazine. He was with a girl he introduced as Ricky Richardson, which meant nothing to me but who later turned out to be a rather famous English model—sort of the London edition of Jinx Falkenburg. She'd make a good Mr. Hyde to Jinx' Dr. Jekyll. But that is beside the point. We stopped in the lounge downstairs for a morning drink and since he introduced her as [illegible] Richardson [illegible] wedding ring, I assumed that she was his wife, and made some such asinine remark as "I didn't know you were married" or "When did this happen" or something like that, which turned out to be a little embarrassing, since both are married but not to each other, etc. Thus did a typical day begin.

They were on their way to a picture show, probably "Casablanca" but I wasn't interested in a show so we parted company. I was just going out the hotel door to find a spot where I could still get lunch at that hour—it was then about 2 o'clock—when Tom Wolf, who recently came over for NEA, came in. He said he was looking for me, thought I might like to go to a concert. He had had lunch, but agreed we would have time to stop into a snack bar (which would be the equivalent of our hamburger joint, if they had hamburgers over here. It is a joint where you can get spam and cheese sandwiches and a cup of tea . . .) Over the tea we began to equivocate about the concert. You guessed it. We ended up by going to see "Casablanca" instead of the National Symphony Orchestra. Did you see the picture? It was really swell. I wasn't expecting much, but it turned out to be an all-star cast and really great. Bogart and Rains and support- ing characters whose names I never remember but always like.

It is the 3rd picture I have seen here. First, I seem to get so very very little time off and second the shows cost so much. We sat in the last row of the balcony today after having stood in the queue for a half hour and the seats cost us 5/6 five shillings six pence, or $1.10. For choice seats you queue up too, but they cost 10/6—$2.10. Last week I saw "In Which we serve" which, like today's movie, was worth the price of admission—if you have it . . .

Piccadilly Circus truly looks like a World Congress of Uniforms these days. Every nationality but German and Italian (thank God) are represented either by their national uniform or in the case of some of the refugee governments with British uniforms and shoulder patches explaining their national heritage. You see kilts of the Highland Regi- ments and the six-footers of the Grenadier Guards. And you see an occasional well-dressed Scottish civilian, or maybe even English, in good-looking tweeds. I shall never get used to kilts and never shall adopt them although I must admit that some of the plaids are beauti- ful. I will say, however, that my knees could not be nearly as unlovely as some I've seen around here . . .

I got two more letters from you last week and now I have high hopes of getting them on a fairly regular basis from here on out. They told of your interview with Wellington and your getting out on your own in that desperate search for features, which I suppose you know is the absolute *hardest part of all newspapering. I hope by now you have gotten on, because you deserve it and I know that the Star could use you. Just like you said, though, these exchange of letters seem to take so long that any advice I could give now would arrive much too late to help. And anyway, you are far the cleverer and advice from me would be purely superfluous. You know I'm praying and wishing you the best of luck.*

I had quite a day Thursday in running into old friends. First of all Roy Roussel, my old city editor on the Houston Press, telephoned and without identifying himself gave me hell for missing the Home Edition with that tax assessment story. I admit complete bafflement until he identified himself. He had just read in Stars and Stripes a squib to the effect that I was at this air corps training school and immediately looked me up. By that time, however, he only had a few more hours leave in London—he is a captain in the air corps—so we only had time for breakfast together, but we spent that hour and a half jawing over the old Houston Press crowd and I enjoyed it immensely . . .

Then that same noon I was back at the officers club for lunch and thought I recognized a major standing over in a corner talking with another officer. I walked by him a couple of times staring and he stared back. Then I gathered up my nerve and asked if he wasn't Tilden Wright, which he was and gave the recognition signal by saying, "And you're Cronkite." He was a frat brother at UT and visited me in Houston in 1935 on his way to West Point. He's a pilot but is stuck in some sort of administrative job and very unhappy about it all.

Strange that I should meet those 2 the same day when I haven't met anyone else I knew from the really old days since I've been here. I haven't seen Roussel since 1936 and Wright since that day in 1935 . . .

I must go now . . . Even more men are being sent over from home and that doesn't add up to my getting back very soon. I'm thinking constantly of you . . .

ALTHOUGH DATED MARCH 8, 1943, from the context, and the reference to the "big story" he was about to embark upon, Cronkite's letter to Betsy that follows was clearly written prior to the February 26 Wilhelmshaven raid, an experience he would describe in a subsequent letter also dated March 8.

———

March 8, 1943

If this v-mail trails off into paragraphs of expletives, blame it all on that old anathema of mine—fire-building. I'm at this Fortress base some-where in England and I'm living in one of the cells of a long, wooden, one-story barracks building. Bigart of the Herald-Tribune *shares this room with me, and the other rooms of the building are shared by pilots and administrative officers. It really isn't too uncomfortable—except for this smoking, pot-bellied, coal stove that Bigart and I try to keep going. Bigart could no more qualify for the fire-building merit badge than I could and we are sweating so much by the time we almost get a fire going that we no longer need the damned thing. It seems that we spend more than half our time chopping kindling, gathering up coal, or slaving (and worrying) over that darned fire. It is much more understandable to me now why the British officers have their own batmen. The officers could never get around to fighting a war if they had to build and main-tain fires themselves.*

Bigart and I are at this base waiting for the "go" signal on that big story. Yesterday we drew our flying equipment—almost a day-long job. We got the works: heavy, leather, fur-lined jackets, pants and overshoes, flying coveralls, fur-lined cap, goggles, oxygen masks, Mae Wests. We are all set to go now and are just waiting for the word. There is no need, however, for you to worry inasmuch as by the time you get this it will be all over, the story written and published.

We have written two stories since we have been here and the rest of the time, with the exception of the fire-building, we loaf at the officers club, go to the movies in the gymnasium, and gather background material by bulling with the pilots and crews. We planned to shoot some skeet this afternoon but that was canceled for one of the many Army reasons that I never seem to understand. So, instead, Homer and I bicycled about five miles to the country surrounding the base. The principal means of transportation in these airdrome areas is bicycling and Homer and I were fortunate enough to draw a couple of them. This has been one of England's mildest winters and this afternoon was almost spring-like. Right outside the airbase we hit a small hill which led down into a valley and a tiny, old English town. The houses were built next to the road. They had thatched roofs and dirty curtains in the windows and old men tending the tiny gardens. In one an old gnome-like woman stood in the doorway which was barely large enough to allow her four-foot frame to pass and she leaned, so help me, on an old-fashioned, home-made broom like the witches ride on Halloween cards. The Crossed Keys Inn, the village pub, was, according to the sign hanging outside, "Established in this building in 1800." Of course, it wasn't open, the hour being four o'clock and pub hours being between eleven and three and five and ten-thirty. (The damned fire's going out. Nuts!) We hope to visit the pub some night and sample British village opinion.

I talked to the office by telephone today and they said I had a letter from you. They are sending it up tomorrow by army courier . . . Walter

---

AMERICAN REPORTERS HAD been pushing for permission to go along on bombing raids since the early days of the war. In January 1943, *New York Times* correspondent Jamie MacDonald, a Scotsman, flew in a Royal Air Force Lancaster bomber on a raid on Berlin, and that same month *Life* photographer Margaret Bourke-White flew in a

Cronkite in flying gear, circa 1943

B-17 raid on a German airfield in Tunis. The Eighth Air Force, always publicity-conscious, decided to allow reporters a firsthand look at its air fleet's prowess in carrying the war to the German homeland. Eight reporters, six civilians, and two military were chosen to undergo a week's training the first week in February to prepare them to accompany a bombing mission. William Wyler would go on to direct the documentary *Memphis Belle*, chronicling the 25 missions flown by a B-17 crew in the air war.

On February 26, six of the eight members of the Writing Sixty-Ninth, including Cronkite, boarded bombers and took off for an attack on a target in Germany—only the second such attack by the Eighth Air Force. The strike force consisted of 76 B-17s and 17 B-24s; all the correspondents except for Bob Post of the *New York Times* flew on the B-17s. The original target for the mission, an aircraft factory in Bremen, was covered by dense clouds, so the bombers were diverted to Wilhelmshaven, their secondary target.

Cronkite flew in a B-17 named *S-for-Sugar* and commanded by Maj. Glenn E. Hagenbuch, commanding officer of the 427th Bomb Squadron, 303rd Bomb Group, based at Molesworth. The other crew members included co-pilot Lt. John C. Barker, navigator Lt. Walter M. Soha, bombardier Lt. Albert W. Dieffenbach, engineer Technical Sgt. Charles E. Zipfel, radioman Staff Sgt. Clarence S. Coomes, and gunners Staff Sgt. Durward L. Hinds, Staff Sgt. George W. Henderson, Staff Sgt. Jack Belk, and Sgt. Edward Z. Harmon. The American planes came under heavy aerial and ground antiaircraft fire; German fighter planes introduced a new tactic, air-to-air bombing of the attacking bombers. Cronkite's plane was attacked by German fighters, as well as antiaircraft fire. He flew in the Plexiglas nose of the B-17, manning a gun.

Seven of the planes on the raid were shot down, including the B-24 Liberator carrying Bob Post. He had fatalistically told a friend the day before that he thought he would die on the raid, and his intuition proved correct. He was the 12th American war correspondent killed during the war, one of 37 all told who would lose their lives before it was over, and the second from the *New York Times*. One hundred and twelve other war correspondents were wounded, for a total of 149 casualties. The

U.S. government accredited only 1,646 reporters for overseas posting, so approximately one in every 11 American war correspondents was a casualty by war's end. The most famous correspondent to die in the war was Ernie Pyle, of the Scripps-Howard newspapers, who was killed by a sniper on Iwo Jima in April 1945.

Harrison Salisbury was waiting at Molesworth to greet Cronkite and the other correspondents when they returned from the raid, although he had opposed the assignment. "It had been set up before I arrived in London," Salisbury recalled. "I was not happy about it, but a dozen elephants could not have kept Walter out of the B-17." He was struck by Cronkite's uncharacteristically grim appearance and the lack of his usual wisecracks. Salisbury, in his version, accompanied Cronkite to a windowless room set aside for the correspondents at the base and stood over him as he wrote the story of the raid. Cronkite's letter to Betsy provides a different, and probably more accurate, account—that the two of them drove to London, where the story was written under the watchful eyes of military censors at the Ministry of Information. In either case, Salisbury recalled that Cronkite "was wound up like a top." It didn't help that people kept coming in with reports on the missing Bob Post. Salisbury also recalled suggesting the story's lead paragraph to Cronkite: "American Flying Fortresses have just come back from an assignment to hell—a hell 26,000 feet above the earth . . . ," but Cronkite never acknowledged his help, if indeed that's the origin of the line. That was the kind of lead, in any case, that UP reporters were trained to use. Early in the war, UP president Hugh Baillie sent out a cable to his European news manager with these instructions: "Tell those guys out there to get the smell of warm blood into their copy. Tell them to quit writing like retired generals and military analysts, and to write about people killing each other."

With their own correspondent a fatality of the raid, the *New York Times* ran Cronkite's account on the front page, one of only three times that Cronkite's byline would appear in the *Times* during the war.

HELL 26,000 FEET UP

By Walter Cronkite

United Press Correspondent

AT A UNITED STATES FLYING FORTRESS BASE in England, Saturday, February 27 (UP)—American Flying Fortresses have just come back from an assignment to hell—a hell 26,000 feet above the earth, a hell of burning tracer bullets and bursting gunfire, of crippled Fortresses and burning German fighter planes, of parachuting men and others not so lucky. I have just returned with a Flying Fortress crew from Wilhelmshaven.

We fought off Hitler's fighters and dodged his guns. The Fortress I rode in came out without damage, but we had the element of luck on our side.

Other formations caught the blast of fighter blows and we watched Fortresses and Liberators plucked out of the formations around us.

We gave the ship repair yards and other installations at the great German submarine and naval base on the North Sea a most severe pasting. As we swept beyond the target and back over the North Sea from which we came we saw great pillars of smoke over the target areas.

Six of us represented the American news services, newspapers and radio—"The Writing Sixty-ninth"—after undergoing special high altitude flight training. A seventh correspondent could not go because of illness and the plane taking another had to turn back because of technical difficulties.

Actually the impressions of a first bombing mission are a hodgepodge of disconnected scenes like a poorly edited home movie—bombs falling past you from the formation above, a crippled bomber with smoke pouring from one motor limping along thousands of feet below, a tiny speck in the sky that becomes an enemy fighter, a Focke-Wulf peeling off above you somewhere and plummeting down, shooting its way through the formation; your bombardier pushing a button as calmly as if he were turning on a hall light, to send our bombs on the way.

Our bombardier was First Lieutenant Albert W. Diefenbach, 26, of Washington, D.C. His job began at that thrilling moment when the bomb bay doors swung open on the lead ship and on down the lines to us.

That signaled that we were beginning the bomb run. Then we swept over Wilhelmshaven. There were broken clouds but through them there appeared a toy village below which was really a major seaport and I thought:

"Down there right now people are scurrying for shelters—which means interrupting work on vital submarines and ships and dockyards."

Lieutenant Diefenbach's left hand went out to the switch panel alongside him and almost imperceptibly he touched a button and said calmly over the communications system:

"Bombs away."

That was it. Our mission was accomplished—our bombs were on their way to Hitler.

What Cronkite couldn't tell his readers was that he had been firing a machine gun at approaching enemy fighters during the raid (a violation of the Geneva Conventions, since he was a civilian and not a military crew member); on returning to England, he could barely exit the plane, because he found himself, as he would write in *A Reporter's Life,* "up to my hips in spent .50-caliber shells."

This was not the last time that Cronkite would come under fire during the war. Afterward, however, he was always careful to distinguish his own experiences from those of the fighting men he covered. "Personally, I feel I was an overweening coward in the war," Cronkite told an interviewer from *Playboy* magazine in 1973. "I was scared to death all the time. I did everything possible to avoid getting into combat. Except the ultimate thing of not doing it. I did it. But the truth is that I did every-thing only once. It didn't take any great courage to do it once. If you go back and do it a second time—knowing how bad it is, that's courage."

After the war Cronkite obtained a copy of the Eighth Air Force's offi-cial record for the bombing raid on Wilhelmshaven. It rated the bomb-ing results as "fair to good" and also provided a detailed account of American losses:

> Of the B-17s, 12 returned early and 5 are missing. Of the B-24s, 6 returned early, 2 are missing and 3 failed to bomb. In addition, one B-24 crash-landed at Ludham . . . In the B-17 crews, 11 were wounded, and 52 are missing. In the B-24 crews 3 were wounded and 21 are missing. Total: 14 wounded, 73 missing.

Veterans of the strategic bombing campaign often commented on the odd juxtapositions in their day-to-day routine: terror and bloodshed in the early morning hours when they flew their missions, followed by the comfort and relaxation afforded them once they returned home safe to their air bases. Cronkite's March 8 letter similarly veers from an account of combat to recounting a meal he subsequently shared in Lon-don with Harrison Salisbury, Bill Dickinson, and Dickinson's girlfriend, London *Daily Mirror* reporter Hilde Marchant, at Jack's Club, a jour-nalists' hangout. Salisbury, in his own memoir of wartime London, also recalled fondly an evening he spent there drinking with Cronkite. His tale is interesting for what it reveals about Cronkite's taste for pranks as well as his professional ambition:

> Why it was called Jack's no one knew . . . War transformed it into an inner sanctum of the American press corps . . . Sandy was the pro-prietor of the establishment . . . No one knew how [he] managed it, but Sandy had access to sides of beef, racks of lamb and, although he

didn't like to mention it, excellent horse-meat steaks. You didn't order at Jack's club, you ate what Sandy cooked . . .

Every news desk in London had Sandy's telephone number. If you were at Sandy's, there wasn't much chance you would be scooped. Your competitors were there too. One night a call came in for an INS man who wasn't there. Cronkite took the call and on a whim said: "He's not here. I think he's gone out to the airport to meet General Marshall [U.S. Army Chief of Staff George C. Marshall, based in Washington, D.C.]." We all laughed. "That'll give them some bad moments," Walter said. Twenty minutes later the telephone rang for another absent newsman. In ten minutes there was another call. Then a call to one of our number. His desk had heard that General Marshall was arriving. We had a big laugh. But then the telephone rang yet again. Walter said, "You know, this isn't so funny. Maybe Marshall is coming to town." And he dutifully got on the telephone to check the false rumor he had himself started.

The March 8 date of the following letter, as with the previous one, probably refers to the day when Cronkite finally mailed it. In addition, this letter seems to have been written in stages over a period of several days, possibly beginning the day after the Wilhelmshaven raid. The Henry McLemore mentioned in the letter was a syndicated columnist for the Hearst newspaper chain. Earl J. Johnson was the United Press New York bureau manager, and Hugh Baillie was president of United Press.

———

March 8, 1943

By now, of course, you know about the flight over Wilhelmshaven. That came this morning after my last letter was written to you. Since then I really have been jumping. We returned from the flight about three-thirty that afternoon. Harrison Salisbury was at the airdrome to meet me, we rushed off in a car toward London and then things really began spinning. I sat down at a typewriter about 11:30 that night and began writing my story. I finished it at 1:30 in the morning while John Daly was breathing down my neck and shouting that we had to get to work soon on the radio script and Salisbury was shouting at Daly that we had to get the UP story out first, and meanwhile I was trying to work with some impetus I'll admit from Salisbury who kept saying: "That's right down the old groove, Cronkite—now you're cooking."

Out from the office Daly and I finally rushed over to BBC where CBS maintains their office and studio. We ground out a script and rushed it over to censorship with only about forty-five minutes to go before broadcast time stateward which was 3:45 A.M. here. The cab driver taking the copy to the Ministry of Information for censoring stopped to get coffee along the way, and when he did arrive the British censor couldn't find the American army censor to check the copy, and by that time only ten minutes remained until broadcast time. One minute before broadcast time—even as Daly was setting up the circuit to NY and they were doing the hold "Hello, New York, Hello, New York. London calling, New York, London calling . . ." censorship called and said the script was okay. Then, as you probably know, we were on for about 3 minutes and the circuit got so bad that they were forced to cut us off. A half hour later NBC got through with an absolutely clear circuit—just to show how those things go . . .

. . . I was horribly tired last night. We had been routed out at [censored], for our briefing and spot of breakfast before taking off for Germany, and then [censored] hours in a bomber at high altitude, living on pure oxygen, standing up most of the time with 60 lbs. of heavy fur flying equipment and parachute on your back, and the general exertion of shooting guns and moving about keeping out of other people's way, is very tiring.

So I fell into bed at 5:30 Saturday morning. At 10 I was routed out again by the office. They said that the Army had agreed to release the story of Bob Post being lost on the flight, and would I hurry down to the office and do a piece on him. Which I did. It was 1:30 in the afternoon when I finished that and Salisbury said he wanted to take me to lunch at the Savoy. Bill Dickinson of the desk and his fiancée, Hilde Marchant of the Daily Mirror, joined us and we had a wonderful lunch on the Savoy (glassed-in) Terrace overlooking Waterloo Bridge and the Thames with the Houses of Parliament and Big Ben not so far away. But I was still so very tired that right after lunch I went back to the hotel and re-collapsed. I was awak-ened at 6:30 by Salisbury calling. He and Dickinson and Hilde were still together, now at Jack's Club, a newspaper hangout where the food is good (at least better than elsewhere) and people play gin-rummy after dinner and sit around a roaring fire. They wanted me to join them for dinner. (Now, you see, I had again become one of those momentary heroes of the United Press. It was just like returning from one of the fleet assignments, you know, except that it wasn't delicious like before because you weren't there.)

I joined them and after dinner they insisted that we go to Covent Gar-den and watch the boys and girls of the armed services jitterbug. Covent Garden used to be the opera house of Royalty. The Duke of Bedford's box is still maintained, locked and intact, for his use supposedly after the war. And so is the royal box. But presently this elaborate place with great chandeliers and tier after tier of seats is a dance hall. The floor has been built over the pit and it accommodates hundreds upon hundreds of ATS and WAAFS and WRENS and Land Girls and soldiers and sailors and marines. And, boy, has jitterbugging hit this land! Wow! Hilde has done several stories on the place so the management greets her with open arms and ushered us to a box where we could see all. I really began feeling old when I realized that at last I had come to a place to WATCH people dance.

Bill was beginning to feel a little organized at that point so we ended up at the Cocoanut Grove, a night club. Salisbury, Marchant, Dickinson and Cronkite celebrated Cronkite's safe return, and, as usual, everybody got drunk but Cronkite.

Again Sunday I was jerked out of bed early by the office with another cable from NY containing a story idea. I had to go down and do that business which took too many hours. I finally got through in time to edge into the officers' club just under the deadline for lunch. Who should I meet there but John Fahey, a lieutenant off the Arkansas. For a moment I was overjoyed with the idea that the Arky was somewhere in these waters, but it turned out he had been detached from her and was attending some sort of school over here. So we had lunch and an afternoon round of drinks, together.

By that time, however, I was famous. No kidding. Every Sunday newspaper in London, and there must be a dozen of them including the famed Times, *front-paged under great glaring headlines my story of the Wilhelmshaven raid. And, strangely enough, everybody from bootblack up in the British Isles reads not only their favorite newspaper from front to back but pays particular close attention to by-lines. So at the hotel snooty elevator boys who hadn't bothered saying hello before began ingratiating manners, the teller at the bank where I cash my check bowed and scraped, the telephone at the hotel rang all day with congratulations some from persons I knew and more often not. Ben Lyons called and Jock Whitney and Mr. Gooch of the Snow Hill police station who looked for my wallet and never found it. Honestly, it was the damndest performance I've ever undergone.*

But best of all, my darling, better than anything and a greater thrill than the ride itself was the following cable from Earl Johnson: "Cronkite WARMEST CONGRATULATIONS SAFE RETURN STOP YOUR STORY VASTLY SUPERIOR OTHERS STOP YOU HAVE GIVEN AMERICAN PUBLIC FIRST BEST UNVARNISHED ACCOUNT WHAT ITS LIKE STOP FINE STIMULANT COUNTRYWIDE STOP ALL HERE JOIN ME IN ADMIRATION YOUR UNDERTAKING YOUR WORKMANSHIP." [Hugh] Baillie, too sent a message. "Congratulations, your story best of all," it said, simply but nicely.

I also got a nice cable from Mother, which I wish you would call and thank her for. I'll write her this week, I'm sure. The whole episode, of course, had the typical Cronkitiana touch, however, thanks to my wonder wife. This stack of cables was awaiting me Sunday when I got to the office. I started through them, getting mother's first, then Baillie's, then Johnson's, then to the last one, which I figured must be from you. I was right. It said: "V-mail impossible without APO number. Love. Betsy." . . .

Well, to explain my delinquency in writing, the office has now decided that I'm an expert on affairs aeronautic. So Monday I got bounced out of bed at 8:30 and pushed onto a train to return to "my" airfield (the "my" touch is strictly Margaret and Betsy) to do a follow-up story. Henry McLemore was on the train. We'd met previously but since then we've become chummy as hell, sharing meals and, because of his proclivity along that line, too damned many drinks . . . Tuesday morning I'm routed out at 7:30 by the army. "A good idea to get back to your station," they say mysteriously. So I go through that horrible train ride again, only to reach the field and find that there isn't any story after all. Back to town that night, miserable and unhappy. Wednesday I'm allowed to sleep almost until noon when I have to go to the American Correspondent Association luncheon at the Savoy. That afternoon I rush to army headquarters for a meeting on whether or not the Air Corps correspondents are going to get to live in London or will have to move outside of town with a headquarters company . . .

In the midst of all that hectic activity last week, I moved. I moved from the Park Lane next door to the Atheneum Court, a much more modern building and considering that I'm sharing a tiny room with Tom Wolf of NEA, a little cheaper than the Park Lane . . . The only advantage is that if I am out of town most of the time on the air assignment, he will collect from me for room rent only a nominal holding fee rather than the full share. Incidentally, for this room we each pay $18.00 a week—and

that is not exorbitant considering other rents in this war town. Can you
imagine that? . . .

More right away . . . Walter

———

IN HIS LETTER of March 14, 1943, Cronkite recounted the tale of his dinner
with Gen. Ira C. Eaker, a key figure in the emerging U.S. air war in Europe.
General Eaker headed the Eighth Bomber Command from the spring of
1942 until December of that year, when he was briefly transferred to the
North African campaign. In February 1943 he returned to Britain to command the U.S. Eighth Air Force. General Eaker personally led the first U.S.
bomber attack on August 17, 1942, a successful raid on the rail junction
at Rouen, from which all of his planes returned to base unscathed. Both
the American and British air forces subscribed to the doctrine of strategic
bombing, the belief that air power could play a decisive role in winning
wars by attacking the enemy behind the front lines of battle, destroying
factories, railroads, shipyards, and other installations necessary to waging
modern war, and in doing so both deny the enemy military vital materiel
resources and undermine the morale of the enemy civilian populations.

The Royal Air Force had been conducting night raids against such
targets in Germany since 1940. Night bombing cut down on "precision"—instead of aiming their bombs at a single target, the British
would blanket an entire area. But the American air force commanders, including General Eaker, thought that a wasteful approach, and
ordered American bombers to carry out their raids during the daytime.
Carefully placed bombs, so their thinking went, would knock out key
enemy resources while minimizing collateral civilian casualties. When
President Roosevelt and Prime Minister Churchill met in Casablanca in
January 1943, they decided to support General Eaker's plan for round-
the-clock bombing of Germany in a "Combined Bombing Offensive,"
with the Americans attacking by day and the British by night.

Cronkite's recitation of the treats he acquired on a trip to the American military PX, including "1 big tootsie roll, 1 box of candied jellies, 2 (British) chocolate bars, 2 pkg gum," etc. may sound a little obsessive, but since 1942 British subjects had been rationed to eight ounces of sweets or chocolates every month—which amounted to a little over a single standard-size chocolate bar a week. By virtue of being an American with post exchange privileges, Cronkite was in a far better position—not to mention that Betsy was sending him packages with off-ration treats. Not surprisingly, British schoolchildren got into the habit of cadging surplus American sweets with greetings like "Any gum, chum?"

––––––

March 14, 1943

. . . This air force assignment turns out to be one of the most vicious things I've ever done from the standpoint of complete envelopment of time. But let me outline briefly the week's activities, which, come to think of it, I'm afraid are going to greatly resemble those set forth in last week's letter.

Sunday night, as I think I mentioned, I had a date to have dinner with General Eaker, the Eighth Air Force commander. After posting your letter downstairs and carefully polishing my buttons and shining my shoes and pinning on my green brassard with the big white "C," I hopped a cab over to Lt. Col. Jock Whitney's flat on Grosvenor Square about 6 blocks from here. (He's Public Relations Officer of the 8th Air Force now and a swell guy. Fairly young and not ostentatious and we "Walt" and "Jock" each other all over the place.) Jock's sharing a flat with Tommy Hitchcock, the famous polo player, but Tommy wasn't in Sunday so Jock and I dashed down a cocktail in this swank apartment whose walls are of some beautiful light wood in natural finish. Then into Eaker's private car (Army drab with corporal chauffeur, of course) which was awaiting us and whisked out to the Eaker billet which is outside of town.

It turned out that this interview which I had requested had turned into a dinner party, wasn't going to be anything private. Beside Whitney, Cronkite, and Eaker, there was Jimmy Parton, the general's aide who used to be a big-shot on Time Magazine and a Colonel Ordway of the General's staff, a couple of other colonels who in my usual fashion I have forgotten, and an RAF air commodore—rank equal to that of brigadier-general. We mixed our own bourbon at the general's bar and smoked the general's cigars and had a whale of a swell chat before dinner in front of a great fireplace roaring not with wood but with coal which is used in most fireplaces over here because the purpose is not beauty but utility. Incidentally, that bourbon was gorgeous tasting stuff. Bourbon is even more scarce than eggs over here, and of course the shortage is felt much more deeply by good bourbon drinkers. And the scotch here is not of the quality we are used to at home. It is of a quality definitely inferior and horribly tiresome. We had a typical Sunday night dinner with cold cuts but with hot bread—corn bread, believe it or not. Naturally, though the corn bread was a disappointment, and only served to make me horribly homesick for Betsy and Judy and good food . . .

Eaker filled me in with all the inside information on the air force— much of which I couldn't repeat here and the rest of which you have either read in the papers or would not be interested in in any event. He made it horribly difficult for me by saying "You know what is confidential and what isn't and I'm telling you the whole story here just for background and for your own information." So I had a whale of a story in my lap and no way of knowing what I could do with it. That led to complications, complications that still haven't been ironed out. The next morning I started the whole story, intending to take it to Jock and let him refer it to the general to cut out the parts which were secret and confidential. But that is getting ahead of my chronology.

We left the general's about 10:30 and the car dropped me here at the Atheneum Court. I went next door to the Park Lane Hotel, though, and filled Salisbury in on the whole conversation—an accepted procedure, the reason why bureau managers over here know so much. It was one o'clock by the time we finished chatting and I came back home and tumbled into the hay.

Monday: I upped early and officewarded. I was just finishing the Eaker interview piece when the phone rang. It was 11:30 then and the 8th Air Force spokesman gave me the code suggesting that it would be a good idea if I caught the noon train from St. Pancras station for Blank, the depot nearest my airdrome. So I was off. The Force that day went to Rennes and Rouen and I had a pretty fair story. I got back to London in time to write my story just in time for release with the communiqué . . .

Tuesday: I slept until about 9:30 trying to recoup a little strength. Then I dashed into the office and put the finishing touches on the Eaker piece and rushed out to the army office to confer with Jock on it. We conferred and conferred and conferred and conferred. We had lunch and resumed conferring. Jock didn't like the piece a damned bit and didn't think the general would . . . Then went back into the office and conferred with Salisbury and together we reworked the piece (Salisbury having liked the original version, thank goodness), and I dashed back out to the army office. But Jock was gone. So I conferred with a couple other guys and by then it was 7 o'clock. One of them, Capt. Hal Leyshon who used to be a NY newspaperman and more recently a Miami publicity man, finally gave up the ghost and said I better put it up to Whitney again the next day which I knew I was going to have to do anyway. Meanwhile, however, Frederick Kuh of the Chicago Sun had come out with an exclusive Eaker's interview, putting all the more pressure on me, to get mine out with the "true" story of the 8th Air Force's battle for daylight bombing. As prearranged I met Salisbury at Sandy's for dinner and we debated the thing some more there. At this point I was certain that the story wasn't worth the effort. We left Sandy's about eleven, and . . . of course, couldn't get a cab and walked home again. Again I collapsed.

Wednesday: the phone rang this morning at eight and by eight-fifteen, an all-time record for me, you will admit, I was in a cab en route to Kings Cross station for a sortie up to a fighter station. I got that story, which is as yet unprintable or even unmentionable and is just on a "hold for release" basis, and got back here at 10:30 PM again with only 1 meal under the old belly—the noon lunch at the fighter station which was done in elegant fashion to the accompaniment of beer.

Thursday: tonight we of the Writing 69th are scheduled to have dinner with Eaker and I'm particularly anxious to get my story whipped into shape so Jock can take it out early to the general and he will have a chance to make corrections and return it to me before I leave there tonight. This involves another horrible day of conferences, writing 2 versions into cablese and then dictating in plain English to Jock . . . The dinner this time was just the newspapermen, Ordway, Whitney, Parton, and the general. The newsmen were Gladwin Hill, AP, William Wade, INS, Homer Bigart, Herald-Trib, Ray Daniell, Times, Stanley Richardson, NBC, and Ed Murrow, CBS. As usual, there we were at the fountain-head of all the information all of us wanted to know, and what did we talk about? Newspapering, of course, and all the usual boners we'd all heard a million times. But it amused the general and Ordway, so I suppose we accomplished something. And we did have a good meal and some more of that Bourbon.

Friday and Saturday: Those lump together under the heading, "See Monday and Wednesday" . . .

Today I finally caught up on a little sleep, arising about 11. Sam [Hales] and I had lunch together at the officers club (chili—made from spam—and spaghetti which wasn't bad . . .) then went by the PX to pick up our weekly rations, and then over to Hyde Park to listen to the orators, this being another lovely sunny day. We returned here about 3 o'clock and he stayed another half hour or so chatting and thus delaying my getting to this letter. My ration at the PX this week was 1 box of Zu-Zus, vanilla wafers, and cheese niblets, 1 big tootsie roll, 1 box of candied jellies, 2

(British) chocolate bars, 2 pkg gum, 1 schick razor clip (20 blades), 1 bar lifebuoy soap, 2 penny boxes matches, 1 carton cigarettes and 4 cigars. Total cost was nine shillings—$1.80—not bad at half the price.

Sam and I had forgotten to take our musette bags so we had all our rations stuck into a single bag which was bulging out the top a little like Santa Claus's typical sack. With that under my arm, we wandered over to the orators, many of whom pick on Anglo-American imperialism for their Sunday harangue. I was certain that they'd spot me in uniform with this sack of rationed goodies and point me out as a typical example of the worst from their text. So Sam and I tried to pass the sack back and forth, but I always seemed to be left holding it. Fortunately none of the speakers spotted it . . .

Coming down on the train last night I sat in the 3rd class carriage and opposite a not-so-pretty-as-Judy-but-nice cocker. We exchanged a few words and I told the pup about my doggie a long way away and the pup seemed to understand and we had a good time. The owner exchanged a few words with me and that was that. Except that when the owner and cocker started to get off, the owner said: "Come on, Judy, here's where we get off." I damned near cried . . .

So now my space is up for the moment. I hope this schedule slackens so I can write daily this week. Meanwhile please keep the letters coming to me. Despite this whirl of activity I'm terribly lonely for you and Judy and our things . . . Walter.

———

A GAP EXISTS in the surviving letters from mid-March to early May. Nothing in the letters from May indicates any reason why Cronkite would have stopped writing in the interim, so probably the missing letters either never arrived or were misplaced after Betsy received them. A number of bylined Cronkite dispatches appeared in the meantime, including one in which he reported on the introduction of the P-47 Thunderbolt fighter, which made its combat debut over Europe in March 1943—probably the "hold for release" story he mentioned to Betsy in his letter of March 14. The Thunderbolt, Cronkite wrote in a dispatch that ran in the *New York World-Telegram* on April 15, "may alter the whole picture of aerial warfare in this theater" because it was capable of accompanying the bombers into Germany. This view was overly optimistic. Most Allied bombing missions into Germany continued to fly unescorted, with the results an appalling attrition rate. By May 1943, after ten months of bombing, the Eighth Air Force had lost 188 heavy bombers and 2,000 crew members. Heavier losses were to come. According to Donald L. Miller, author of *Masters of the Air, America's Bomber Boys Who Fought the Air War Against Germany,* "Approximately seventy-three percent of the combat fliers who had arrived in England in the summer and fall of 1942 failed to complete their tour of duty [of 25 missions]. Fifty-seven percent were killed or missing in action, and another 16 percent had been either seriously wounded, killed in crashes in England, or permanently grounded by a serious physical or mental disability."

8 C   Oakland Tribune, Thursday, June 1, 1944

DON WAS REAL 'MAN'S' SOLDIER

*   *   *   *   *   *   *   *   *   *

War Reporter Writes Memorial Day Eulogy

By WALTER CRONKITE

LONDON, May 30.—(Delayed)—(U.P.—This is a pretty personal note for Mr. and Mrs. Stockton, Los Angeles, U.S.A. I don't know their initials and the last street address I had for them was 756 South Broadway. But if the editor uses this, they might see it—and I'd like them to get this message:

promised to go out to Brookwood Cemetery and visit his grave this Memorial Day.

But the war—the one that cut that grand full life of his short at 22 years—interfered in carrying out that simple little gesture of tribute.

It interfered because I write the air war, and today as I write this

Cronkite's eulogy for B-17 pilot Don Stockton was reprinted in 1944.

Cronkite and other air-war correspondents knew all too well that the young men they interviewed for their stories were not likely to survive many missions. When Harrison Salisbury arrived in London, Cronkite gave him some advice. "'Don't make friends with the kids,' Walter had told me. 'Don't get to know them too well. It's just too much when they are lost, and most of them, you know, will be.'" Cronkite himself was particularly affected by the death of 21-year-old pilot Donald E. Stockton, killed on a bombing mission over Kiel in May 1943. Stockton had piloted a B-17 named *Bad Check* in the February Wilhelmshaven raid, but his bomber had turned back with mechanical difficulties before reaching the target. The flight to Kiel was his 25th and intended-to-be-final bombing mission.

Cronkite's May 9, 1943, letter to Betsy opened with his comment on the May 3 crash of an American Liberator bomber over Iceland that killed Lt. Gen. Frank Maxwell Andrews, the highest ranking American military officer to die in the war to that point. Morrow Krum, who also died in the crash, was an Army public relations officer.

———

May 9, 1943

Hello, my darlingest,

Here I am just back from another trip made in lousy weather and generally unhappy circumstances. This has been a horrible week all the way around. You read in the papers, of course, that Morrow Krum was killed in the plane with General [Frank Maxwell] Andrews. The deaths of Andrews and [Lt. Col. Fred A.] Chapman and [Brig. Gen. Charles M.] Barth were a blow to all of us and, undoubtedly, to the war effort—but Morrow's death was that of one who had become a very close friend and one very much needed in court when problems arose among the war correspondents. Strong men wept openly around headquarters Tuesday when it was learned he was on that plane. It came only a couple weeks after he got his full colonelcy and while headquarters still was filled with predictions that he might even get a star on his shoulder before the peace.

Then Wednesday I made a trip to a fighter base and found to my horror that my best friend up there had failed to return from the last sweep. He was "Pappy" Lutz from Fulton, Missouri—one of the nicest guys I've met in a heluva long time. Pappy bailed out, his chute didn't fully open, and Deacon Hively and Vic France who circled him down saw him hit the water, disappear, and reappear a minute later. But he didn't answer their waves and just floated there. Air-sea rescue never found him.

This is all a little gloomy, I guess, but it has been a gloomy week and this is a gloomy Mother's Day. I suppose all this is just a tiny foretaste of what is to come when we, some day, praise the Lord, move across the channel.

I have really had the blues this week. I haven't had a good story in weeks and the present period of inactivity is boring on my nerves. The air force assignment keeps me going fifteen and sixteen hours a day on lousy trains and lousier trucks and isn't very productive after all that work. It is pretty discouraging. Added to all that I got scooped this week, along with Glad Hill of AP, thank goodness, by Earl Poorbaugh of INS who stumbled onto the fact that [Clark] Gable had made an unscheduled operational flight in a Fortress.

Most of all I've had the blues because it is so long since I've been with you and Judy and there isn't any silver lining yet in that cloud. It was helped considerably this week, though, by your short letter of March 24 with the three pictures of Judy, two of which included you. They are wonderful shorts, darling. A couple of dog experts already have seen them and, what we already knew, have pronounced Judy the most beautiful cocker they've ever seen—and that from Brittishcocker specialists. They were absolutely amazed at her features, and they had seen nothing to equal it. One even asked if there were any chance of her coming over soon and gave me his card because he said he wanted to be sure to have a look at her if she ever came to England. It is true: you absolutely do not see long ears and flowing features like that over here. Of course, you don't see anything like Judy anywhere except when you see Judy. She looked so sweet and so intelligent. In fact she looked just a little angry—as if she knew Daddy was going to see the picture and she wanted to show her displeasure at his absence. I love you, honey, and I'll write more later. Forever, Walter

———

THE AIR WAR was glamorous, at least to those who read about it on the home front, and those in charge of the Eighth Air Force made sure to enhance that glamour for their own purposes. They were thinking about not only the war but also the postwar future of the Army Air Forces. As Harrison Salisbury recalled in his war memoir: "The Eighth Air Force was a high octane outfit. It was run by ambitious men and backed by an ambitious command in Washington. It had set up a large public relations staff—men from newspapers, publicity firms, advertising agencies—and made use of Hollywood celebrities . . . The important thing, as the Eighth Air Force saw it in 1943, was to establish a presence, to prove a doctrine, to stake out a position in public consciousness." Hollywood star Clark Gable, who enlisted in the Army Air Force in August 1942, was recruited by Gen. Henry Harley "Hap" Arnold merely to make a training film for aerial gunners, but he wound up flying a number of dangerous combat missions. Although Cronkite speaks of attempts by public relations officers to shield Gable from unwanted attention by reporters, Eighth Air Force brass welcomed the publicity he brought. They worried, however, about the consequences of his being shot down, and were relieved to transfer him back to the States to complete his film. Field Marshall Hermann Göring, who also appreciated public relations, offered his fliers a substantial reward if they brought Gable down, which they were never able to collect. For young Midwesterner Walter Cronkite, encounters with a Hollywood icon like Gable (and the chance to write home to his wife about them) were probably heady stuff, notwithstanding his casual recounting of their conversations. Gable pops up repeatedly in Cronkite's letters home over the next few months.

———

May 18, 1943

Just back again from another trip. I went out early last week to cover what we figured was going to be a stepped-up air offensive against Naziland and have just returned to town for a change of clothing, a quick conference with [Harrison] Salisbury and a letter to you after picking up my mail . . .

I'm having a heluva time these days with Clark Gable. I think I told you that I had a clear beat with an exclusive on his arrival in this area and that finally even the public relations office was calling me to find out where he was. Well, since then pandemonium has broken loose. The poor guy when he talked to me that first day said he was rather sorry I'd stumbled into him because he wanted to be just another officer and do his part in the war effort and he knew that a lot of reporters around all the time were going to hinder him in that ambition. When the pub relations men heard that they clamped down the screws and now nobody gets near the guy—except by accident. So I spend half my time now trying to create an accident for myself and prevent one for the AP or INS . . .

———

As THE NEXT two letters to Betsy (May 22 and May 26, 1943) suggest, Cronkite had reached a turning point in his career with the United Press. Since the Wilhelmshaven raid, he had emerged as one of the stars of the London bureau. With the expansion of the air war, Cronkite found himself increasingly tied to the London offices. While he still did some traveling to air bases in the countryside, more often he sent out others to do the day-to-day work of interviewing aircrews returning from missions over Europe, while he wrote the "experter" accounts that presented the big picture of the air war to American readers.

Other journalists were taking notice of Cronkite's abilities, including Edward R. Murrow of CBS Radio, who invited him to make a guest appearance as a commentator on the network. Not every print journalist proved adept in meeting the requirements of the new medium of broadcast journalism. But Murrow was a good talent spotter.

———

May 22, 1943

It seems so long since I've been able to sit down and write you a full-size letter to tell you all the things I've been doing and thinking. I thought that perhaps this was the day and it yet might turn out to be. But at the moment I'm grasping time for this V-mailer and then shall supplement it with a regular air mailer letter later if possible.

I know that you have gathered that I have been busier than the proverbial bee for the last week and a half. It is gratifying to watch the air force really swing into action and start plastering the enemy—but it is damned tiring on this almost-round-the-clock basis. I've been on the go constantly for almost two weeks. I mean that my musette bag has been packed and I've been on the air force shuttle from base to base to headquarters to base to base to headquarters ad infinitum. The job has now reached the stage that [Harrison] Salisbury and I knew it would eventually when one man no longer is adequate to handle it. So in the midst of all this activity we've tried to put into effect our long-drawn plans whereby I remain at headquarters to coordinate the whole story while others go out into the field under my direction . . . Also I have other problems—things to sandwich in among all this work. Ed Murrow last week tossed into my lap a twelve-minute spot whereupon he wanted me to broadcast a story of the air force to the National Association of Book Publishers convention. I worked like hell on the script for that one. (It would have been a lovely plug for my favorite author.) Then, at the last minute, the broadcast was cancelled. It wouldn't have netted any money but would have been valuable. Then the Blue Network spot, also fruitless, came along and took up considerable time. It originated here at 4:50 A.M., of course. Thanks to your cable, I assume we made it okay. I was so glad to hear that Molo is better, and hope you aren't just trying to relieve my worries. I'm anxious now for another letter saying that she is up and around again . . .

By the end of May 1943, the fifth month since Cronkite's arrival in London, the Allies had won two important victories. The first took place in North Africa, where enemy resistance ended on May 13. The green American army that had gone to war against the Germans in November 1942 had now proven its mettle. And on May 26, German navy commander Karl Dönitz withdrew his U-boats from the North Atlantic, where they had been suffering irreplaceable losses. The moment was approaching when the Allies would carry the war back to the European continent.

In his letter dated May 26, 1943, Cronkite mentioned receiving a copy of *Military News*, featuring a picture of its editor, "Mrs. Krinkit," i.e., Betsy Cronkite, who in 1943–44 worked for the Hallmark greeting card company, editing a newsletter for Hallmark employees in the military. The now rarely heard slang term "darb," common from the 1920s through the 1950s, which Cronkite used to describe a picture of his wife, suggests an item of superior quality.

May 26, 1943

I would like so much to have you here. Because of the apparent possibility that I might be bouncing on off to war fronts where it is impossible to take you, I had almost abandoned the idea, at least temporarily . . . It looks as if, for a while, at least, I'm not going to be travelling so continuously. Air force activity is now stepped up to the extent that I'm going to be here at headquarters most of the time with others out in the field. But it seems that I told you all this in the last V-mailer. I'm writing this at press headquarters of the air force . . .

I've become more convinced than ever that you will be joining me here before I ever return there, and we might be here for some years. (BY "here" I mean Europe, not necessarily England.) . . .

I have seen a few movies lately at air bases. I saw "Yankee Doodle Dandy" again and liked it as much as the first time, perhaps because it is now rich in memories of you and Jackson Heights . . .

I see Sam [Hales] a little more frequently now that I'm getting into town more often. He is covering the Latin American embassies now and the other afternoon he and [Harrison] Salisbury and I went to the Argentine cocktail party. I was invited because one of the attachés is dying to make a bomber trip and he wanted to hear my story. I carried on a long conversation with the air attaché and neither one of us understood a single one of the other's words. Mighty interesting . . .

Did I tell you in a v-mail that your first copy of Military News finally arrived last week? It was swell, darling, particularly the picture on page two of the Mrs. Krinkit or whatever her name is—the gal who is editing same. What a darb! And to think she should have a brain too. Halls certainly digs them up, doesn't it? It was good. I've been wondering if since you have been working there you still get the old kick out of thumbing through the greeting cards, each and every one, in every downtown store including the, horrors, five and ten. Do you, or is the old kick gone now that you are so close to the trees or the forest or whatever it is? . . .

CHAPTER THREE

THE YOUTHFUL DEAN OF AMERICAN AIR-WAR WRITERS

JUNE–DECEMBER 1943

By the second half of 1943, Walter Cronkite was not simply report-ing the war; he had also become a part of the story of the war. In May the weekly syndicated radio series *Soldiers of the Press,* which fea-tured dramatized 15-minute vignettes based on the reporting of United Press correspondents, brought to American listeners an adapted ver-sion of a Cronkite dispatch about a U.S. bomber named *Dry Martini* (with an actor with a pronounced New York tough-guy accent read-ing Cronkite's lines). In November the popular magazine *Look* ran an expanded account by Cronkite of his dangerous flight to Wilhelmshaven under the headline "My Favorite War Story," including a photo of Cronkite looking dashing in his military correspondent uniform. And in December, the United Press sent out a dispatch to its subscribing newspapers under Cronkite's byline, along with an editorial note intro-ducing the author as the "youthful dean of American air-war writers in

London." Cronkite's story began with a colorful description of the daily routine of his subordinates in the London UP office, Collie Small and Doug Werner. The portrait clearly drew as well on his own experiences traveling to American air bases like Molesworth:

> Standing up in crowded trains, crawling over fog-shrouded roads in bouncing jeeps, riding bicycles over muddy lanes, American correspondents in Britain covering the air war are working night and day to keep pace with the mounting round-the-clock Allied aerial offensive . . . These correspondents are "musette bag and typewriter" soldiers. The musette bag slung over their shoulder contains their shaving kit, a towel, a bar of soap—with luck—a clean shirt. That and their portable typewriters are "home."

As for his own role as newly christened dean of the air-war writers, Cronkite wrote:

> In London, I am constantly kept busy assessing the facts, interviewing those "in the know" at the Air Ministry and 8th Air Force headquarters, and seeking to interpret the developing air war, as well to call future plays so that Small, Werner and myself can be at the scene when the big story breaks.

Although there was as yet no such thing as a network television news show and, of course, no such person as an "anchorman," Cronkite's experience as dean of air-war writers provided good preparation for his later career as managing editor of *CBS Evening News*.

From modest beginnings the previous summer, the American air war in Europe grew in 1943–44 into a leviathan. By the end of 1943 there were 66 U.S. air bases in Britain. It reached peak strength, just before D-Day, in June 1944, when more than 426,000 U.S. airmen were stationed in Britain. Others were stationed in the Mediterranean and, after D-Day, in France. In 1944–45 the combined total American and British air forces in Europe consisted of 1.3 million men flying or servicing an armada of 28,000 combat planes. Before the war was over, American and British bombers had dropped 2,700,000 tons of bombs on Nazi targets. In Germany, in addition to the damage done to military targets, war industries, and transportation systems, more than three million housing units were destroyed, 300,000 civilians were killed, and 780,000 were wounded. As the U.S. Strategic Bombing Survey investigators concluded in 1946, "The principal German cities have been largely reduced to hollow walls and piles of rubble . . . These are the scars across the face of the enemy, the preface to the victory that followed."

Cronkite measured the growth of the U.S. air war during its first year of operations in a dispatch that went out on the UP wire on June 10, 1943, noting that the Army Air Forces in Britain had doubled in size since March, and would double again by September. To illustrate the strategic implications of this vast expansion in destructive power, Cronkite quoted comments at a recent press conference by Gen. Ira C. Eaker, commander of the American Army Air Forces in the UK theater:

"The great factor, of course—and it will be the determining factor in a way—lies in the fact that we can replace our losses and the enemy cannot replace his," General Eaker said at a press conference. "Our air force is on the build-up and his is on the wane. He has reached the peak, if, indeed, he has not passed it."

The war wasn't over, but Cronkite's thoughts were increasingly focused on the postwar era. In his June 20, 1943, letter to Betsy, he noted that United Press president Hugh Baillie was coming to London on an inspection tour. Cronkite hoped to find out from his boss a hint of his peacetime prospects with the UP. "Then maybe we can lay a few plans," he wrote.

The London UP bureau was honeycombed with talented young men, all hoping to profit from Hugh Baillie's patronage, Harrison Salisbury among them. While Cronkite escorted Baillie on a tour of air bases, Salisbury was given the onerous, but also potentially advantageous, assignment of finding the great man suitable lodgings, entertainment, and dining opportunities while he was in London and making his appointments with government and military officials. "Baillie must have the best," Salisbury recalled in his postwar memoir *A Journey for Our Times:*

> He must stay in the best suite in the Savoy. He must meet Churchill and Eden, the air marshals, the U.S. brass . . . I must take him to dinner every night at the best restaurants and he must be seated at the best tables. There wasn't much at the theater, but he must have the best seats at the best shows.

Salisbury did all that and more, and Baillie promised to promote him to UP European news manager. That prospect left him "walking on air" for several days, until he discovered that the promised promotion went instead to rival Virgil Pinkley. Thereafter, he and Pinkley "were strange dogs, sniffing and growling at each other," until October 1943 when, to the relief of both, Salisbury was reassigned to cover the war in Russia. (In the long run, that proved a good career move for Salisbury, who shifted after the war to a high-profile position with the *New York Times* as its Soviet expert and won the Pulitzer Prize for his reporting from Moscow in 1955.)

———

June 20, 1943

Just got back from another trip up-country to find another wonderful assortment of mail from you—V-mailers and regulars . . . When I get an accumulation like that I carefully stack them in the order in which they were written and then read from top of stack to bottom . . . About the future . . . I ought to have a more definite idea this very week. Hugh Baillie is here and beginning tomorrow morning he and I are going out touring air bases. He wants to see the American Air Force in action and I am the guy to show him, he figures. So we will be together four or five days at least and during that time there will be many opportunities for long talks. I should get a pretty clear idea of the post-war future then, whether or not I'll be staying over here, if so how long, whether it will be a nomad existence for years or only months after the armistice, etc. Then, maybe we can lay a few plans. More later . . . Walter

---

IN HIS LETTER written around July 10/11, 1943, Cronkite returned again to the question of when and how Betsy might join him in England. He was now convinced that given the extent and depth of his "contacts with the Eighth Air Force," it was "highly improbable" that he would "be covering anything else war-long." That meant, he thought, if Betsy came over, they would not be separated again by his being sent off to another assignment.

Roy Howard was president of the Scripps-Howard newspaper chain. Prior to that he had been president of the United Press, which is probably the reason that Cronkite was going to take him on a tour of air bases, before plans changed.

The Dorchester Hotel on Park Lane in Mayfair, overlooking Hyde Park, was considered one of the safer places in London to ride out an air raid because of its sturdy construction. Gen. Dwight Eisenhower was among its regular guests. The other London location Cronkite mentioned in the letter, Kinnerton Street, off which lead numerous 19th-century mews, is in the Belgravia section.

[No date, July 10/11, 1943?]

It is now ten o'clock in the morning, a slightly coolish, rainy morning, and I'm sitting here waiting for and hoping for my clean laundry so I can pack my musette bag and make the one-thirty train up-country. [Jim] McGlincy is on vacation so he still is sleeping soundly in the bedroom with only occasional grumbles about the typewriter. I'm using his portable, by the way, inasmuch as my poor old battered and shattered machine now sounds all the world like a faulty linotype and awakens the dead— meaning the brass hats who inhabit the Dorchester across the street.

I came back late Monday from my listening post up north . . . I reached the flat about ten-thirty or a quarter of eleven (it was still daylight, of course—we have almost a midnight sun these mid-summer days with the northern sky always alight) to find that McGlincy had uncovered the bottle of Port I'd been hoarding and had finished it off in solo. I didn't even get a sip of it. It was some Portuguese wine that I had been lucky enough to get hold of through one of the officers' messes at an airbase. Oh, well.

I've been taking it somewhat easy the last couple of days to make up, in part, for the impossible 126 hour weeks I've been putting in recently. Although with the responsibility of directing this air force coverage I can't ever really relax from constant vigilance . . .

Managed to crowd in a little relaxation the last couple of nights. Tuesday night Joe Evans, head of the Newsweek bureau here, invited me to dinner at his girl's house and we had a devil of a nice evening. She lives up Kinnerton Mews off Wilton Place in a little artists' colony I didn't even know existed. I say "artists colony." What it is is a "successful artists, writers and actors' colony." The place is about two blocks long with one alley-way of houses running for another block off it at right angles. The little, old-world houses, packed up against each other, have been modernly redecorated inside, and they have little gardens in back. It is a little world in its own. The houses rent for around forty dollars a week furnished, slightly out of line according to our old standards but not so much more than much cheesier places in war-time London. The area is just a couple of blocks off Knightsbridge and a big business area in the West End. The big point, is, honey, that it is one of the places for us to look when you join me over here.

I'm so anxious to get you over here, darling. I find that I'm beginning to like the place and I want you to join me in it as soon as possible. I don't know that we'll be stationed here after the war. It might be Paris or Berlin or Antwerp or some such capital other than London, but I know we're going to have fun wherever we are. And Judy will too. Here in England everyone takes their dog everywhere. Dogs are allowed on the busses and the subways and in practically all of the hotels. The only places they aren't allowed, it seems, are the Post Offices, but we can buy Judy's stamps for her and let her mail her own letters in outside boxes.

Since my talk with Baillie the other day I've been thinking over again the possibility of getting you over here even before the war ends. My contacts with the Eighth Air Force are such now that it seems highly improbable I'll be covering anything else war-long. It also seems improbable that I'll be outside England but for a very short time immediately preceding the armistice. So the most frightening prospect of all about getting you here now has somewhat diminished. That prospect was that you might no sooner get here than I would be ordered on to other theaters of war to which you couldn't accompany me, and thus you would be stranded here without either the family or me. I think the submarine menace has so abated that the danger there is negligible. There is only one other serious consideration remaining. I'm not at all sure that if we could get you over here now we could also get Judy. We might not be able to bring her along until after the war and that would <u>a long hard trip</u> for her alone . . .

Your letter also mentioned that Betty urges you to take frequent pictures of Judy, as often as the film shortage will allow. Would you mind

asking Betty to urge Judy to take pictures of you, too, as often as pos-
sible? I'd love as many pictures of both of you as I can get. Despite this
tremendous activity and that constant scurrying about and, I'll admit,
the interesting things to do and people to meet, I get awfully lone-
some for you and that little dog. It seems so very long since we've been
together. Everything I see and everything I do lacks the final joy of inter-
est it would contain if you were with me . . .

I had a very Sunday Schoolish night last night. I worked at the office
from about four to six, having gotten into town (after standing two hours
on a train) at three and having rushed home to change out of wet uniform
into comfortable, dry civilian clothes. At six McGlincy and I went around
to the King and Keys in Fleet street, had a couple of drinks with [Betty]
Knox and Salisbury and Jack Tait of the NY Herald-Tribune. I came back
out to the Deanery Club right away to meet a couple of fighter pilots
to whom I'd promised a drink. That wound up with my taking them to
dinner—a near four bucks down the hatch. They had to do a broadcast so
I told them adieu, went down to the bar for another drink and ran into a
crowd of fliers and assorted personnel en route to the Red Cross Charles
Street Club for the usual Saturday night dance. I went along and had a
heluva good time—playing table tennis. I played for about three hours
taking on all comers and managing to win all the games. Then up stepped
a challenger who I thought looked familiar. He played a heluva game of
ping-pong but I managed to eke out a win there too. Then he and I went
down to the snack bar and had a soft drink (the Red Cross being what it is)
and a long chat. It was our very own little Robert [Manring]. He'd gotten
to town in the late evening and been unable to find me. I was pretty darned
tired and there wasn't anything to do at that horrible hour of eleven o'clock
when he finished playing, so I came on home here and he went down to the
Red Cross Reindeer Club where he'd booked a room . . .

We are thinking seriously of taking a few days off together and going
down to the south of England where we might be able to absorb a little

sunshine. That vacation matter has become urgent now. If Bob could arrange his time off for that same period we could have an inexpensive few days on the coast (although there is no bathing on account of defense works).

Here is how the war is brought home to you these days over here. Up at the air headquarters where I've been hanging my hat most of these days I frequently wander around to the crossroads pub with Corporal Jim McNeil of the publicity staff. Those boys have been in that neighborhood for almost a year and they take an active part in the pub's political and economic discussions. We were having a quick beer there and I noticed a rather decent-looking middle-aged woman wearing dark glasses fumbling around finding the glass of beer on the table in front of her. McNeil then tells me that she is a village tragedy. She had just returned from the hospital where they told her her eyes had been destroyed and she would never see again. She had been on a one-week holiday at a resort town where just one or two German sneak raiders whipped over, dropped a couple of bombs on churches and schools, and whipped home. She caught too much of the blast of one of those bombs.

I've got to go now, I've got to pack a few clean clothes available, do my best to sew a "War Correspondent" patch onto my field jacket, and be off to Waterloo Station. Tell little Judy I miss her too, and give my best to all the family. Walter.

CRONKITE'S BEAT REMAINED the air war, the main story for correspondents based in England. Elsewhere in Europe, the Allies advanced on the Nazi homeland. The last German and Italian troops fighting in North Africa surrendered in May. On July 9–10 American and British forces invaded Sicily. At the same time, the Red Army was blunting and then reversing the last German offensive on the eastern front, in the Battle of Kursk, the largest and most decisive tank battle in the history of warfare. At the start of September the British and Americans landed in Italy, leading in short order to Mussolini's downfall, Italy's surrender, and Germany's occupation of its former Axis ally.

Only scattered Cronkite letters to Betsy survive for that summer. Since nothing indicates that he stopped writing, most of the letters he sent from June through August were probably lost en route or misplaced after they were received. Also lost to memory is any record of where Cronkite took his evidently unsatisfactory summer vacation in July, though it may have been the "few days on the coast" he mentioned in his letter of July 10/11.

July 20, 1943

. . . The vacation so far stinks, as I knew it would. It is raining and thus there is no golf, even if I could find someone to play with. I told you I played Sunday with McGlincy, didn't I? It had been threatening to rain all Sunday morning and suddenly the sun burst through just long enough to sell us on the idea of going out. And, of course, as soon as we set foot on the first tee the rain started again. It was sporadic, though, and somehow we got through eleven holes . . . This is a lousy letter but that's sort of the way I'm feeling today what with a vacation and no Betsy or Judy . . . Walter

IN HIS LETTER of August 3, 1943, Cronkite announced his intention to write every single day, so his letters would amount to a diary of his war experiences. Eight months after arriving in England, he still pined for his wife's company and mused nostalgically on their last weeks together in the fall of 1942.

Since the "long letter" he alludes to did not survive, there is no way to know how Cronkite wound up as a guest at the London home of

Lord and Lady Jersey. As he explained in his follow-up letter of August 4, Countess Jersey was, prior to her 1937 marriage to George Child-Villiers, ninth Earl of Jersey, a minor Hollywood actress named Virginia Cherrill, and briefly married to Cary Grant. Her most famous role in the movies was as a blind flower girl in Charlie Chaplin's 1931 feature, *City Lights*.

———

August 3, 1943

It is rather appropriate that this daily diary should begin today. It was just a year ago today, honey, that we had lunch in that rather nice restaurant in the Maritime Building and I told you goodbye and watched you walk up the street toward the subway. And then I fooled away those previous minutes that we could have had together while I waited for the boat that was to take me with Captain Bryant out into the bay for the first in this series of assignments. And that night the ship lay in the bay and I thought of you only a few miles away in Jackson Heights and I couldn't do any-thing about it. That had been a hectic day, hadn't it?—picking up the uni-form, trying to get a makeshift arm band, rushing to the dock.

So much water has passed under the bridge since then. That wonder-ful reunion in New York when you hit the apartment at almost the same minute I did after I'd been so disappointed when I didn't get an answer on my phone call from Staten Island. Those swell weeks in New York and then the Moroccan invasion. I missed you so on those trips . . . Then back to Norfolk and frantic unsuccessful efforts to telephone you from there that Thanksgiving night, finally reaching you by phone from the Washington railroad station, and your crying because you hadn't heard a word from me, the first information I had that none of my African stories had got through.

Then there was the whole day and a half I had to wait before you stopped off the plane in New York, and how happy I was. Wonderful days then in New York. But not enough of them . . .

It suddenly occurs to me that this will reach you perhaps before a long letter I mailed yesterday. So a word of explanation: I'm really going to keep a steady flow of letters to you now, darling. They will be in the form of a diary, and if you keep them we'll have some kind of record of the war.

The long letter brought us up to Sunday, August 1, 1943. That afternoon I went, under circumstances explained in the longer letter, out to the Earl of Jersey's. Lady Throckmorton, a Mrs. Keene, a famous Polish artist by the name of Telpowski (approximation) and of course, Lord and Lady Jersey were there. It is a modest house they live in now while the armed services occupy their Isle of Jersey and other properties, but it faces on Richmond Common, there are two dogs, a huge Police and a tiny Sealyham, and it's very pleasant. Most of the dozens of servants they used to have are now in the Army so Lord and Lady Jersey pop up and down doing their own serving. I was only there a few hours but it was most enjoyable. More about it tomorrow. Tell Judy and all the folks hello . . . Walter

---

CRONKITE MADE A passing reference to the Ploesti air raid in his letter of August 4, 1943. That raid had taken place three days earlier, launched from an air base in Libya and targeting oil refineries in Ploesti, Romania, that were vital to the German war effort. The Mediterranean-based Ninth Air Force carried out the attack, supported by three groups of B-24s from the Eighth Air Force. The refineries were heavily defended, and American losses were correspondingly grim: 53 B-24 Liberators and their crews were shot down in the attack.

Most of Cronkite's August 4 letter, and the follow-up on August 5, concerned lighter matters, including the unceasing social whirl of London's journalists. Betty Knox, whose imminent hospitalization was the occasion for a memorable Bank Holiday night out, was a reporter for the *London Evening Standard*. American-born, she had been a vaudeville and British musical hall star in the 1930s. In 1941 she retired from the stage and took up a career in journalism.

Elizabeth "Lee" Miller, *Vogue* correspondent, covered the fighting in Normandy in 1944 and the liberation of Paris, and photographed Buchenwald and Dachau concentration camps in 1945.

The reference to a "certain pair of redheads with whom I'm in love" in the August 5 letter is to redheaded Betsy and reddish-furred Judy, the cocker spaniel.

———

[No date, August 4, 1943?]

I'm having a little trouble catching up with this diary. It seems that I left off as of Sunday evening. (It is now Wednesday, of course.) I was at Lady Jersey's, as I recall. Did I mention in that V-mailer yesterday that she is Virginia Cherrill, formerly of the movies, Cary Grant's first wife, etc.? I don't think I did, although the fact is in a regular letter now supposedly en route by air mail. Well, we had cold salmon salad for dinner with cold beer, a strictly American habit that I suppose Lady J. has imparted to Lord J. Then we thumbed through the Jerseys' intriguing volumes of scrap book including a lot of her intimate pictures of Hollywood personalities, mostly C. Grant, of course, and pictures of the Jerseys and Throckmortons on yachts and at clubs and in forests with feet properly planted on dead elephants and tigers and stuff. Lord J. and I talked about animal breeding. You know how much I know about that! And then back home on the subway.

Monday was about as dull as it is possible for a holiday to be when you are away from the one person that would make a holiday fun. (It was the first Monday in August, a so-called Bank Holiday here comparable to our Labor Day, of which there is none in England. That is sort of a commentary on Democracy and Capitalism and Stuff, isn't it? England has a "Bank Holiday" we have a "Labor Day.") I broke off the vacation in the morning to do a background piece at the office on the Ploesti oil field raid by the Liberators from the Middle East because I knew some of the participants and quite a bit about the way the thing was planned. I had lunch at the officers' club and returned home where I spent part of the afternoon cleaning up my part of the flat. As usual I had my dresser cluttered with notes and old newspapers and magazines and pure, unadulterated scrap. Monday night things picked up a little bit. Betty Knox is going to the hospital this week (today, come to think of it) and so was throwing a Dutch Treat party for herself. I met her, [Harrison] Salisbury and [Bill] Dickinson at the King and Keys pub next to the Daily Telegraph building in Fleet Street, we had a drink there with Jack Tait and Eric Hawkins of the New York Herald-Trib and Doug Werner of our office, and the K.S.D. [Knox-Salisbury-Dickinson] and W.C. [Walter Cronkite] wound our way up to the Savoy Hotel where we were to meet some more people. This adventure of winding our way cost me a shilling, in my own adventuresome, inimitable way. Dickinson was trying to hail a cab in front of the King and Keys and I stepped up and tendered him a shilling saying, 'You will get us the next one, won't you?' He did, and took the shilling! At the Savoy we met Dave Scherman, Life photographer, Lee Miller of Vogue (Vogue's war correspondent—gad!) and some gal I didn't know named Kathleen McCaughlan who I found out only the next day is an editorial writer for the London Times and formerly was a Liberal party whip in Parliament and Clement Attlee's secretary. I'm running out of space again. More tomorrow . . . Walter

---

August 5, 1943

Hello, Honey. It's eleven A.M. of this Thursday morning which until half hour ago had been rainy and now is complete with sunshine and not a cloud in the sky. Whatta climate!

I left off yesterday with our little party reaching the Savoy to meet [Dave] Scherman and his small group. Well, we sat at a corner table of the American Bar. [Bill] Dickinson sat at one end of the semi-circular bench and I sat at the other and [Betty] Knox said it looked like a minstrel show, so you can guess where that went. But Dickinson wasn't nearly the wonderful stooge for corny gags that Sweeney was, and I can promise you that it was no fun playing to an audience that didn't include a certain pair of redheads with whom I'm in love.

We had one drink at the Savoy waiting for Joe Evans, bureau manager for Newsweek here, and his date and they finally telephoned and said they would meet us at the White Tower, a Greek restaurant off Tottenham Court Road near the Ministry of Information. So the whole gang piled into a couple of taxis and went to the White Tower and sat at a table outside in front of the place where the urchins in that somewhat bombed tenement district could lean over the rail and breathe into your food. I had a veal chop which was delicious and with a couple of drinks only cost four dollars. [Harrison] Salisbury and Dickinson drank muska, a Greek liquor, and ended up tottering on the curb gazing up the street which runs into the White Tower, Dickinson arguing that it was a sad street, and Salisbury arguing that it was a very common street with no ability to stir any emotions at all. It was just turning dark when we left to wander up to Tottenham Court Road and spend a half hour hailing already engaged taxis until we finally snared a couple. Only when we got in the cab did we learn that Dickinson was still carrying a glass of whisky from the White Tower. I should point out that Daddy was sober, as usual—and I'm not kidding. I've got a heluva reputation around Fleet Street as a man who holds his liquor, whereas the truth of the matter is that no one seems to notice that I have one drink to everybody else's two . . . more on sheet #2 August 5, 1943. Walter

As CRONKITE'S FAME grew, so did his prospects. On the second sheet of his letter of August 5, 1943, Cronkite mentions an "offer from CBS news." Edward R. Murrow, the head of CBS Radio's office in London, had asked Cronkite if he would consider transferring to Moscow to cover the war on the Russian front for CBS. Murrow offered Cronkite the dazzling salary of $125 a week, nearly double the $67 he was then getting from the United Press. Cronkite expressed interest, but was wooed back when UP bureau chief Harrison Salisbury and UP president Hugh Baillie offered him $82.50 a week to stay in London. Whether he was swayed by the appeal of being one of the highest paid UP foreign correspondents, a preference for wire-service work over radio, or a desire to remain in London, where he hoped Betsy might be able to join him eventually, Cronkite decided to decline the CBS offer. Murrow was astonished, apparently believing that any journalist would jump at the chance to become one of "Murrow's Boys," the talented group of young men he had recruited to report the war for CBS. Despite Cronkite's assurance to Betsy that he and Murrow "departed the best of friends," Murrow never fully forgave Cronkite for turning him down, even after the two became colleagues at CBS Television in the 1950s. However, in retrospect, Murrow's promise that "CBS would be around again in the future" certainly had a prophetic ring. Also, during the war Cronkite made several radio broadcasts for CBS, sharing his air-war expertise.

Meanwhile, Cronkite displayed his gift for punditry in the opening paragraph.

August 5, 1943   sheet number two.

[Bob] *Vining is a heluva nice guy who used to be one of the top-kick public relations men with American Telephone and Telegraph. He's got that professional handshaker business down to a T (an ATandT).*

That's a Belluva note. Just a phoney. Or maybe I've got my wires crossed. The point is, without the puns, that Vining really makes you feel good. He grasps your right elbow with his left hand and pumps, but as he pumps he tells you and anybody else who is around, what a terrific job you are doing, how that last story was a "beautiful thing" etc. etc. etc.

[Joe] Stehlen is a nice guy too but a little 'browned off' (RAF for "sore") because the Air Force says he is too old to fly now, won't give him a job of the importance for which he thinks his experience qualifies him, and instead is involved in running the speakers' bureau.

After lunch I had a long chat with Lt. Harry Cody, a former N.Y. stock broker now also in Air Force public relations. Then I got down to more important things. I went to see Ed Murrow to settle the newest CBS offer . . . I told him that the amount he offered was not enough to lure me away from UP . . . We parted the best of friends with his saying that CBS would be around again in the future and that meantime he might call on me to do a few shows. From there I went down to Hobson's, a uniform outfitters in Lexington street, off Piccadilly, to get some fancier War Correspondents patches than the regular issue ones and an extra pocket button to replace the one lost off my uniform coat. Then on down to the office where I told Salisbury I was going to stay with UP . . . Walter

---

IN HIS LETTER of August 11, 1943, Cronkite complained of a lack of progress on "the book." No manuscript has survived, but it seems likely that Cronkite had made a false start on a co-authored account of the air war: In a subsequent letter in February 1944, Cronkite referred to a book that he and Jim McGlincy had begun some time before, by then "molding in the drawer for lack of time to finish it." Several other war correspondents had already had best-selling books published by this time, including International News Service correspondent Richard

Tregaskis's *Guadalcanal Diary*, published earlier in 1943, slated to become a Hollywood movie.

After Cronkite announced his intention at the start of August to write a "daily diary," his letters to Betsy began to take on a more "writerly" tone, as if practicing for the book he intended to compose. The August 11 letter, for example, featured clouds "constipated with rain," "weather-worn knobs of green land," "tiny cottages with tiny doors," etc. Cronkite soon returned to his usual relaxed and intimate tone with his wife, and in a letter to Betsy on New Year's Day 1944 emphasized that his letters were "to YOU and not diary pages as I crudely suggested last fall."

———

Wednesday, August 11, 1943

Darlingest Betsy,

Another day and another dollar or two. This is a gloomy day with the skies unable to make up their minds about the whole thing. They look like they're constipated with rain, but nothing happens. I know just how they feel. I'm still at the headquarters from which I wrote yesterday, but this evening I'm riding in the courier's reconnaissance car across half of England to another spot. That will be a miserable trip. If it doesn't rain it will be gloomy; and if it rains, it will be gloomier. Furthermore it is cold—almost cold enough for a topcoat, which, indeed, some of the guards on outside duty are wearing. I wonder how many degrees over a hundred it is in Kansas City right now . . .

The English countryside was pretty this morning, the half light under the overhanging clouds. It brought out in sharp relief the rolling hills and weather-worn knobs of green land, spreading trees, stone walls and hedgerows. And sticking up here and there along the horizon the stone steeples of the churches which dot this countryside every few miles so that often four or five of them are visible from a single hilltop. I've ridden over so many hundreds of miles of narrow English back roads in the last several months I no longer see most of it with a tourist's eye but I still marvel at most things: the thatch roofs, the tiny cottages with their tiny doors through which even Eva would have to stoop (and I wonder if the ceilings are any higher inside), the little villages every few miles along any road with their pubs and little stone shops. Right now my trips through are on business only. You see I'm waiting for you before going exploring, so what we find is going to be as new to me as to you. I love you, darling. I had a picture taken today that I'll send along. Walter

---

IN HIS LETTER of August 12, 1943, Cronkite referred to raids on the Ruhr that day. On August 12 two separate Eighth Air Force missions attacked Ruhr targets: 183 B-17s bombed synthetic oil installations at Bochum, Gelsenkirchen, and Recklinghausen, while 147 B-17s bombed factories in Bonn. During the two missions, 25 B-17s were shot down.

Cronkite was preparing himself for his upcoming meeting with United Press president Hugh Baillie with a rueful self-mockery.

Thursday, August 12, 1943

My darling wife:

This really should be dated Friday, August 13, for it is now five minutes past one in the morning, I'm as limp as an old towel and I have no voice . . .

This is likely to be a very fuzzy letter, and I'm so tired, darling, that I'm sure you won't blame me too much if I cut it short around the middle somewhere. As you have read by now, the Fortresses today went to the Ruhr—and Cronkite went to town. I was up at seven-thirty to begin the daily ride on the merry-go-round, but I think that today I caught the brass ring for three free rides. First, I got an exclusive interview with the general who led the raid. Second, I had an exclusive (until the lousy public relations set-up made a handout out of it) on the fact that Gable had gone today. And third, I had a good exclusive feature yarn on a couple of hero crews. It has taken every minute of the seventeen and one-half hours I put on the job today to cover three 'dromes, one headquarters. I had a good breakfast of powdered eggs prepared with onions and cheese to almost taste like something, no lunch except doughnuts and coffee with returning crew members, and a filling dinner. Each meal I ate in a different spot, the last 100 miles from the first. Altogether I guess I covered some 150 miles today, made nine long distance calls (no little feat in this country today), and called in three 500 to 750 word stories (and dictating those babies, repeating a dozen times each name and hometown address, is herculean).

Furthermore, I had some slight hope of getting back to the Big City on a late train tonight but now find my return delayed at least one day and perhaps more . . .

Baillie, Pinkley, et retinue have arrived back on the scene, I'm informed, and all of us young-men-getting-ahead are getting our osculatory muscles back in shape. I'm missing your letters while out on this trip. I worship you, darling. Tell Judy I love her too. Walter

---

"THE FACE" MENTIONED in Cronkite's August 13, 1943, letter was Clark Gable. "Walter's word" was Cronkite marriage code for "shit." Frank Adams was an old Cronkite friend from Austin days, a Navy publicist during the war. The "Deanery" was the apartment building where Cronkite shared a flat with Jim McGlincy, on Deanery Street in the Mayfair section of London.

Friday, August 13, 1943

Darlingest Betsy:

  Well, my daily diary thing is working out just swell. I got back to town this afternoon and went first to headquarters to pick up my APO mail and all I found in my box was two letters to you and one to a R.C. Spears of Dallas, Texas, all returned for postage. I'm remailing them along with this letter tomorrow, but it means a delay of at least a day or two. The letter to Spears is about his son who was lost in the Moroccan landing. Spears said he had learned from the managing editor of the New York Times that I was the only reporter at that landing on that particular beach and that perhaps I could give him some information. I was unable to, unfortunately.

  My luck of Thursday continued today. I got an exclusive interview with Gable this morning to round out the blanket coverage of yesterday's show. Larry Winship, managing editor of the Boston Globe who is one of the visiting firemen brought over here by the British Ministry of Information to see how well the British are getting along (and, incidentally, prepare us for abrogation of any war debts by showing how much reverse lease-lend there is), was tagging along on my heels but I don't believe he sent a story. We went to Gable's barracks and lounged around for an hour just swapping yarns with The Face and John Lee Mahan, top Hollywood scripter who is working with him on this training film he's shooting. It turns out Gable permitted the interview because he believes I've been fairer to him in previous stories than some other press service and newspaper people, and also he and Mahan were impressed by a little remark I dropped at the trumped up interview they had with him for the massed British press some weeks ago. At that time, it seems, I said: "What is all this Walter's word." I made the remark to Bill Smith, pro up at Gable's

*base, who promptly told The Face. That is what he had thought of
the whole proceedings . . .*

I love you, honey. Much more later. Always, Walter

———

JACK FRITSCHE, MENTIONED in Cronkite's letter of August 19, 1943,
was Cronkite's cousin (his mother's brother's son) and an Eighth Air
Force officer.

———

Thursday, August 19, 1943

*. . . Tuesday night the hired car that takes late shift workers home from
the office arrived just as I finished my letter to you—and not a moment
too soon, either. I never have been so tired. I was close to collapse, and
I'd just had a terrific fight with the deskman about the way he was trying to save cable tolls and cutting all the good color stuff out of the air
war story. Wednesday morning I slept until eleven when I hopped up and
rattled out an "experter" on the shuttle raid and called it into the office,
then got involved in a half dozen long distance calls dispersing our legmen
force for the day's activities, if any. I had lunch with [Jim] McGlincy at the
officer's mess, and a soup bowl haircut (the only kind obtainable in this
benighted land) at the Park Lane Hotel. Barbers, here . . . are no different than those at home. They tell you how the war should be conducted,
interspersing their comments with lengthy sales arguments on singeing,
shampoos, etc. But prices are certainly an improvement over New York
seventy-five centers. Two shillings here—forty cents. Then into the office
where I was corralled by [Hugh] Baillie for an afternoon of errands.
I had a pretty good time, though. I was arranging his Clipper passage
home. First to the Air Force to wangle a better priority number, then to
Pan American for tickets and a chat with Jack Kelly, their local manager
who has damned interesting stories of the early war days in Lisbon when*

the refugees were queued in front of the Pan American office there and Kelly's principal job was to keep them from smashing his plate glass windows. Then to the British Overseas Airways Corporation for the ticket to Foynes. Eleven hundred bucks for the round-trip ticket—wow! Start saving that money, darling. Baillie was pleased with the office boy service I rendered, and congratulated me again on the CBS decision. McGlincy and I then had a drink at El Vino's in Fleet street with Bill Dickinson and his gal, Hilde Marchant, Daily Mirror (London) columnist. Mack and I then grabbed a "hamburger" in a Leicester Square joint decorated with bad imitations of Wimpy and went to see Striptease Lady at the Odeon, having a couple of their less expensive seats—six shillings ($1.20). Then home where we had a couple more sandwiches and turned in. Today I raced around catching an early train and am now back in my up-country base where I'll probably be for a couple of days before returning to London. On the way up from the rail station to this base, by the way, we passed an entrancing pub—the "Wait for the Waggon". . . Walter

———

LT. JAMES NIX, mentioned in Cronkite's letter of August 20, 1943, was a B-17 pilot with the 303rd Bomb Group who was shot down on a "milk run" over Holland on August 19. Following wartime convention, Cronkite's UP dispatches on the air war almost invariably tried to hit a positive note, but in his letters to Betsy he felt free to express his dismay and sorrow over the ever mounting casualties in the Eighth Air Force.

———

August 20, 1943, Friday

I'm over at another headquarters now, surrounded by competition. Gladwin Hill of the AP is here and we're bunking together, it looks as if, for a couple of days. Yesterday I covered a mission whereon I lost

another good friend, this time Lt. Jimmy Nix with whom I was sched-
uled to fly on one trip some time ago but which never came off. He was
on what was to have been his last operational trip. The boys in the other
ships believe they saw ten 'chutes come out of Jimmy's plane which at
that time was a couple of miles back out over the channel on the way
home. But they also saw a Focke-Wulf go down and circle the chutes
and they have some fear that the Nazi might have been shooting at our
boys. It seems almost phenomenal the number of good friends that have
come and gone in the eight months I've been covering the Air Force . . .

FROM THE FRONT page of the *New York World-Telegram:*

BLOCKBUSTERS SMASH LARGE PART OF BERLIN

47 Are Lost; War Now is in 5th Year

By Walter Cronkite

United Press Staff Correspondent

LONDON, Sept. 1—British four-engined bombers, hundreds strong, smashed another huge section of Berlin into blazing ruins last night in a 45-minute blockbuster and incendiary assault that marked the end of the fourth year of the war . . .

Waves of allied planes also swept across the English southeast coast in daylight today to carry a non-stop Anglo-American aerial offensive against Hitler's European fortress into its second day.

American Flying Fortresses attacked an airfield at Amiens-Glisy in northwestern France last evening to climax yesterday's raids . . .

Staff Sgt. Chris Giassullo of 2931 Yates Ave., the Bronx, tail gunner on the Fortress Charley Horse, said the American bombs "tore the runway to hell," while Flight Officer E.E. Clark of Pasadena, Cal., pilot of the same Fortress, reported the bombers "smacked the target on the nose."

Sergeant Giassullo, 22, a tail gunner, is a son of Mr. and Mrs. Anthony Giassullo, 2931 Yates Ave., the Bronx. Before the war he worked in a butcher shop.

The August 31, 1943, Royal Air Force raid on Berlin involved 613 heavy Lancaster bombers and nine Mosquitos (the latter bomber so named for being fast and light). As Cronkite reported, 47 aircraft were lost on the raid. The August and September raids on Berlin were merely a foretaste of the all-out offensive the RAF would carry out in November and December 1943, sending as many as 764 bombers on a single night's raid. Thousands of Berliners were killed and tens of thousands were made homeless. But British losses in planes and aircrew were unsustainable, and the 1943 RAF bombing offensive against the city was regarded as a failure.

In the summer and fall of 1943 Cronkite's dispatches increasingly carried "LONDON" as their place of origin rather than "A FLYING FORTRESS STATION SOMEWHERE IN ENGLAND" or the like. As Cronkite noted in his September 11, 1943, letter, his superiors wanted him to concentrate on turning out "air experters," like his September 1 dispatch about RAF attacks on Berlin. His heart was in the field, but until the invasion of the continent the next spring opened up new opportunities, he was increasingly tied down to the "desk job" that he had told Betsy in his very first letter from England he was determined not to settle for.

———

Sept. 11, 1943

. . . I've been staying in town this week doing comparatively easy work at the office, thus getting plenty of rest, and eating regularly. I've averaged about 10 hours sleep a night, and that helps. I feel fine. Exactly

what the status is going to be around the office I don't know yet. That is, we're pondering right now whether I'm to stick around town and do the air experters, or get back out in the field and continue with the leg work. I like the latter business best . . . There are a couple of flights coming up that I want to go along on, but the office seems to have taken a definite line forbidding further operational trips, so it looks as if I'm grounded.

I'm of course itching for some action, but it doesn't look as if I'm going to be permitted to get in any. I'll probably just go along writing these air stories warlong, which gets a bit dull personally . . .

I really need both shirts and sox, honey, if you could send them in the next package. That is, civilian stuff, of course. Thanks to you and the presence of the PX I'm plentifully fixed for uniform stuff. I could also use some regular underwear. I'm stocked with enough longies for the winter months, but there are many days when plain shirts and shorts are more comfortable.

Also with the coming of winter some more Nestles Instant Chocolate would sure be welcome, if it is still available. Darling, I know that such things must be getting pretty short there, if not absolutely disappearing, and you understand, I hope, that I positively forbid your using any of your rations, or going to any extra searches, to fill up my packages. All in all, we get along pretty well over here, and nobody is suffering . . .

There is only one kind of tobacco on which I'm really short here, and that is good pipe tobacco, such as my favorite Bond Street. The PX has it for a couple of weeks every three or four months . . .

A picture is enclosed for you, taken by an Army photographer at a base evacuation hospital where I was picking up a story about the boy also in the picture. He had been wounded in the tail (of his Fortress) but stuck by the gun until all the enemy had ceased . . .

Tell little Judy and all the family that I miss them too . . . Walter

————

ON SEPTEMBER 27, 1943, the *New York World-Telegram* carried a dispatch from Cronkite headlined "Fortresses Rip Emden U-Boat Base, 'Pathfinder' Method Used for First Time." It began:

> LONDON, Sept. 27—Flying Fortresses dropped 1000 tons of bombs on the U-boat base at Emden today in the heaviest American raid of the war on a single target, and started a new pattern of all-weather attacks—"area bombing"—on the Nazi European fortress . . . In delivering the massive weight of high explosive bombs and incendiaries to a fountainhead of the resumed U-boat war, the Fortresses for the first time used the RAF Pathfinder method of setting up the target.
>
> One group of Forts went on ahead of the main formations, found the area marked for destruction and ringed it with flares. Heretofore the Fortresses have "pin-pointed" targets—that is, dumped their bombs at a specific factory or airfield after lining up the target in the bombsights.

Cronkite's story did not reveal that the B-17s in the newly created 482nd Bombardment Group, known as Pathfinders, were equipped with an air-to-ground radar system that the British had been using since 1940 for their night attacks. The Americans would soon employ an improved version of the British system, which would enable bomber raids even when northern Europe was covered in the usual heavy cloud layer of the winter months. Cronkite's UP colleague Collie Small had gotten wind of the Eighth Air Force's decision to employ the Pathfinder technique, and when Cronkite learned that Pathfinders had led the way to Emden, he was determined to break the story. Military censors at first killed it. Cronkite recounted what happened next in *A Reporter's Life:* "I appealed to the chief U.S. censor [and] pointed out that the Germans at Emden sure as the devil knew that there was complete cloud cover through which those bombs tumbled." The censor finally agreed to clear the story. But when it appeared in the newspapers the next day, Gen. Ira C. Eaker of the Eighth Air Force was "apoplectic with rage," according to Cronkite. "I had violated security. I had ruined the Allied air strategy, possibly lost the war to the Germans. My war correspondent credentials were to be lifted. I was to be sent home in disgrace." General Eaker eventually calmed down and let the matter drop. Cronkite concluded that the entire flap had been "politically inspired"—that General Eaker had failed to brief the White House on the new strategy in advance and wanted to prove the effectiveness of the Pathfinders before revealing to either official Washington or the general public what essentially meant the end of the U.S. commitment to precision, or "pin-point," bombing.

In his letter of October 17, 1943, Cronkite again complained about being tied down in London, seeing neither a rapid end to the war nor any opportunity for a more exciting assignment until the invasion. He once again urged Betsy to consider joining him in England, perhaps if she could arrange it as a women's news correspondent for the *Kansas City Star,* her former employer. Marcel Wallenstein, mentioned in the letter, was the *Kansas City Star* correspondent in London. The "pinks" that went so well with Cronkite's new green shirt probably refers to the Army officer's trousers that went with the "greens" of the jacket of the Army officer's (and war correspondent's) winter semi-dress uniform.

Sunday, October 17, 1943

My darlingest wife:

I got back from another week with the RAF yesterday to find two packages and a bundle of mail waiting for me. What a wonderful "home-coming" after a pretty unsatisfactory week. The contents of the packages were just what I wanted and needed. The green shirt is perfect, and I'm wearing it today. Personally, I think they are handsome as hell with pinks but maybe it is my old color-blindness. I was tickled to get the hats, shirts and sox and extra handkerchief. Although the lined Stetson will have to be cleaned and blocked, the allegedly crushable light felt hat I wore last night in the rain because it looked the part and I now call it my "go-to-hell-fog-hat." The pipe cleaners and American chocolate looked like gifts from a lost world. The soap was welcome, too, although at this particular moment the PX is stocking American-brand soaps. How long that will last I don't know, though, and I'm glad to build up a reserve . . .

Week before last, I think I told you, I was up watching the RAF on its night missions. Last week I spent with RAF fighters, intruders, interceptors and train-busters. I ran across a lot of Canadians, some Americans, French, Belgium, Dutch, Australians. They are a heluva good lot. These single-seater single-engined pilots are of entirely different temperament than the bomber boys. They are more like the carefree, devil-may-care stuff we used to see in the movies of World War I aces. I suppose that is because they don't shoulder the responsibility for the lives of nine or so other men every time they lift their wheels.

The fogs set in last week. Almost all week there was solid overcast, clearing perhaps for a few minutes in the late afternoon, but closing back in again at night. Friday I made my first trip south of London since I have been here and I was very anxious to see the Sussex, Surrey, Kent and Hampshire countryside, but the fog was like a blackout curtain drawn along the train windows and it was all you could do to make out the telephone poles ten feet from the tracks. So I just sat in the first-class carriage I was sharing with an RAF officer and argued with him about pasteurization, inoculation and circumcision. He didn't believe in any of them. Dope! I went all the way down within a couple of miles of the south coast not far from Plymouth. The day cleared a little and by yesterday when I started home I could finally see the countryside. Whereas the trip down had taken an hour and a half, I was mistakenly put on a local on the way back and had to change three times, each time on a colder platform, and the whole journey took three and a half hours.

Also I was a little disappointed in the country. It is, compared to the rest of England, extremely flat and looks much more like most of our mid-western scenery. However, compared to the rest of England it is very clean, almost immaculate. The houses seem more modern. In other words, it comes a lot closer to the American idea than anything north of London. For scenic beauty, picturesque towns, intriguing old England, we'll have to go north, though, honey, when you finally get over here . . .

I hate to be pessimistic about things, but I see absolutely no hope of a cessation of hostilities within another twelve months. You've read the statements by both military leaders here and at home that indicate there won't be a second front until spring. That leaves the only chance of ending the war before summer up to either the Russians or aerial bombardment, and while if I were a Heinie I wouldn't want to face either, I don't think either is likely to cause Hitler or cohorts to throw up their hands in the next several months. Likewise I don't see the slightest hope of my getting into any more active theater at least until the second front opens, and, unless there is some drastic reshuffling of assignments before then, even at that time I'll be here more than I'll be there by the very nature of my air coverage.

So I wondered how you feel now about coming over. I'm so lonely for you and it seems almost unbearable to look forward to another long siege of months apart. I may be awfully selfish in even suggesting that you come. I don't know that it would be entirely pleasant over here. The blackout in winter, closing down at five o'clock and lifting at eight, is no fun. Living conditions are pretty punk. Fireplaces smoke. "Geezers"— hot-water heaters (honest, that's what they call them) have to be lighted every time you want a drop. Pull-chain plumbing, of which there is no other, only works half the time and then with such gasps it gives you nervous disorders. If you go out at night and stay later than last bus or last tube around eleven o'clock, you pray for a taxi but bloody well end up hiking. And the newspaper crowd here is no different than any other. All they do is rush from office to pub to appointment to Ministry of Information to pub to office. I'm shuttling up and down country most of the time and hours are pretty uncertain.

All I can offer against that is (1) we'd be together again, which seems pretty darned important at this stage, and (2) everybody here would love you and, except for the family, I don't think even if I were out of town you'd be lonely.

Well, I suppose this sounds like all you have to do is cable "Yes" to cinch the deal. Unfortunately it isn't that simple. As a matter of fact, I don't have a single idea in mind—that is a definite one—on how to get you here. BUT if you were interested, with your back ground and training, I'm sure there is a publication somewhere that would be damned glad to have a London correspondent for whom they wouldn't have to pay a small fortune, for whom, in fact, they would only have to give proper certification to the War Department, pay or arrange for transportation over, and then space rates thereafter. Actually what in hell is wrong with the Star. They've got [Marcel] Wallenstein here, sure, but he has been a resident of London so long perhaps he has lost a lot of the common touch of Kansas City. Besides there are ten-thousand women's angles here, and women's angles to a lot of otherwise male stories—Kansas City males, too. And don't think you couldn't do it. Why you can beat the pants off a half dozen of these females running around here, and off a lot of the men.

Why don't you gather up in your arms a lot of good-ole fashioned gumption and go down and plop it on [Pete] Wellington's desk. The argument is terrific, I think. Look, all he has to do is certify you to Washington as a Kansas City Star employee who they want to send to London as a war correspondent . . .

Let me know if you decide to do it, honey, and I'll put on the pressure through this end. I think I should see Wallenstein if the thing is going to be tried, and I should write a letter to Wellington putting the cards on the table—that is, that primarily we are using him mostly to get you over here, but that incidentally it was going to be damned advantageous to him because your sole function was going to be digging up women's and Kansas City angles, with which you were darned familiar because after all you had just come from Kansas City, while Wallenstein is tangled up, as they know, in a dozen different enterprises besides the Kansas City Star.

There is another advantage to this system. And that is that if you hold war correspondent's credentials and are really doing a job for the Star, if I should be sent into Europe in the wake of the second fronters, you probably could follow in short order—at least with more certainty than you could if you were with the Red Cross.

I've got to rush now, honey . . . I love you, you know, and miss you terribly. Tell little Judy and all the family howdy for me. Forever, Walter

---

IT WAS NOT even Halloween, and Cronkite was already dreading another Christmas spent away from Betsy and Judy, as his letter of October 24, 1943, revealed. That hardly made him unusual. The Irving Berlin song "White Christmas," first performed on a radio broadcast Christmas Day 1941 by Bing Crosby, returned to the top of the Billboard charts whenever Christmas rolled around during the war years, joined in December 1943 with another chart-topper by Crosby, "I'll Be Home for Christmas."

Also of note in the October 24 letter: another Clark Gable (aka "The Man With The Ears") sighting reported by Cronkite.

Sunday, Oct. 24, 1943   picture enclosed

My darlingest one:

Christmas comes but once a year—and this year it has come in October. I got back from another trip Wednesday to find one package awaiting me at the APO. Thursday I got Betty's package at the office. Friday I got another package at the APO. I have taken off the outer wrappings of them all in case they had been damaged or contained perishables, but I haven't peeked in any. I couldn't help reading a couple of the cards, though, and they brought with a flash like a block-buster how terribly, terribly lonely this Christmas is going to be. I spent just an hour sitting in my big chair with the packages on my lap and gazing through the opposite wall remembering our first Christmas together and all the subsequent ones—Judy and her fir-tree allergy, and getting locked out with all our presents inside.

The most horrible thing about this one, aside of course from being so far away from you, is that I feel so cheap about the presents I'm sending you. A couple of little trinkets is all, unless I get some sudden flash of genius and can uncover something of value. Everything is so terribly shoddy here, honey. The prices are so high and the coupon values so impossible. I think you will like what I am sending—but it seems so meager. You know how I used to like to get you a lot of things so you'd have lots of packages to open. And this year—nothing very much. It is heartbreaking. But we'll make it up next Christmas and all the Christmases to come.

I'm taking all my packages and dumping them in my big zippered parachute bag (U.S. Aviator's Bag, Kit, Mark II) to be opened Christmas day. I'm going to open them Christmas day regardless of doing as the Romans do. You know about those fool Romans—Boxing Day and all that. The only thing that worries me is the fruit cake. (I peeked on that one because I was sure it was edible and, hence, perhaps perishable.) Will it keep until Christmas? It doesn't have a "Don't Open Until" tag on it and the advice I get around here is to "dig in" but I strongly suspect that is because of a lot of avaricious people like [Jim] McGlincy and [Bill] Dickinson and [Ed] Beattie. Come to think of it, I'm pretending to be an awfully strong-minded guy, asking you if I should wait to open it. It looks so delicious, and so American, and so Kansas City—a lot of things that I miss an awfully lot. Thanks a thousand-fold, darling.

Thank God there are no Christmas trees available here. I'm afraid McGlincy and I would break down and get one, and that would make the holiday as terrible as anything can be imagined. I'm hoping for a very, very busy day in the office or on assignment. It seems the only way.

I've had a pretty good week, spending three nights with Jack [Fritsche]. Monday I went up to his section of the woods, but didn't get to his base proper until Tuesday . . . There was a heluva storm that night, seemingly threatening to blow away the Nissen huts or at least drown them in the downpour. Jack and I sloshed through the air base mud, the rain and the wind to get back to his quarters, and I damned near ruined my pinks and shoes, but the beer helped alleviate any suffering accrued therein. Jack didn't have an extra bunk in his room, of course, so I slept in the neighboring officers' quarters next door . . .

Wednesday I talked Jack into taking a couple of days leave and accompanying me to London. He had been down a couple of times previously but on each occasion I was out of town. It is a three-hour train ride from his base to London, but, of course, the train took four hours. We got here late in the afternoon with your husband still decked out in one layer of pinks and three layers of mud. The bath I took and the clean clothes (civvies) I donned were plenty welcome. McGlincy was in bed with a cold, I found, so Jack and I shared a couple of drinks with him while I dressed and he and Jack got along famously. I was sorry Jim couldn't accompany us . . . We went down to Sandy's to eat. I treated Jack to one of those steaks I've described, and he was properly impressed. The Man With The Ears [Clark Gable] came in later with Elizabeth Allen, the British movie star he's been squiring around and joined us for a quick drink—but he apparently had other things on his mind. He whispered a small scoop into my ear, and I assume that the world was pleased to learn the next morning that He was on the way home . . .

Oh, incidentally, I had a heluva experience Tuesday on my way from our base over to Jack's. I ordered transportation from the motor pool and got a command car and GI driver. It was raining pitchforks and the country road was slick as glass. But this driver, I thought, handled the car magnificently. He did slide into ditches a couple of times, and he barely missed a couple of oncoming trucks and lorries, but considering the condition of the road—well, he did all right.

Then he turns to me and says: "You know, this is quite a thrill for me to drive <u>YOU</u>, sir." And I swell up with pride and think, "well, the old Cronkite name is getting around a bit, after all." Then he adds, "Yessir, this is quite a thrill. I've never driven a car before."

And sure enough, he hadn't. Some mistake in the motor pool. It is mistakes like that that lose wars—and correspondents, worse thought.

And now lots of business: First of all, you should be getting an extra check for $150 from the UP or Look magazine any day now. I don't know what it is for, frankly. All I know is that a cable arrived in the accounting department last week that New York accounts had $150 from Look for me and where should they send it, London or Kansas City. I advised them Kansas City. I assume that either they sold them a batch of my stories from which to make a piece, or else it may be some re-sale rights on the African stories. Or, horrors, maybe it is some mistake. At any rate, at present standing New York seems to be sending you some extra dough. And that brings up another point: Honey, please don't skimp to build up that bank balance. I feel that perhaps you are, but I don't want it that way. I want you to be as comfortable and happy as is possible under the circumstances, and whatever sum it takes to do that you certainly should feel free to use . . .

Walter

IN HIS LETTER of October 31, 1943, Cronkite referred to a song called "Paper Doll," which was the biggest hit of the popular Mills Brothers, a jazz-pop quartet of four African-American brothers. Originally written in 1915, the song held the number-one slot on the *Billboard* singles chart for 15 weeks, selling over ten million records. One of the song's lyrics, "I'll tell you boys, it's tough to be alone," must have resonated with Cronkite.

In the closing lines of the letter, Cronkite mentioned that he had obtained an exclusive interview with "General Kepner of fighter command." The story ran three weeks later in American newspapers. On November 19, the *New York World-Telegram* printed a dispatch from Cronkite that began:

> LONDON, Nov. 19—Maj. Gen. William E. Kepner, chief of the Eighth
> Air Force fighter command, said today that the German air force had
> been defeated "at every turn" and the Nazis no longer were capable of
> building enough fighters to stop the Allied bombing offensive.

The Eighth Bomber Command suffered heavy losses in the summer and fall of 1943 in its daily "precision bombing" attacks on German targets, most disastrously in two raids on the ball-bearing factories in Schweinfurt. In the first raid, on August 17, which hit nearby Regensburg as well, the Americans lost 147 of the 376 bombers dispatched; in the second raid, October 14, 291 bombers were sent out and 60 of those failed to return. Despite these losses, as Cronkite reported in November, the air war over Europe was finally beginning to tip to the Allies' advantage. Germany was losing experienced fighter pilots and aircraft at an alarming and irreplaceable rate. German air strategists decided to pull much of their fighter force out of northern France and back to Germany, which proved a major advantage to Allied invasion forces the following spring. Harry Ferguson, in this letter, was a veteran UP sportswriter and an assistant general news manager for the wire service.

Sunday, October 31, 1943

I've just written a V-mailer to Dad with a very clever introduction. I said: "The calendar says that this is Halloween. So I thought I'd come around and ring your doorbell." Could I ring yours too, honey. As a matter of fact, I'd like a trick or treat from you. I'd like to rattle your windows, and stick a pin in your doorbell.

(The air raid sirens just went off—in fact, are still going. What an unearthly sound that is. They went last night and the planes didn't even get into the outskirts. Everybody just sits them out nowadays because things so seldom happen. I'm knocking on wood, and going on writing. If the guns begin going I'll probably leave you for a second to stick my head out the window. I'm with air raids like I used to be with fires—remember?)

I made two short trips out of town this week, but I returned from both of them within the same day, so I've to all intents and purposes been in town all week, a phenomena which I hope grows commonplace. I've been working my head off in the office and running around town to the Air Ministry and other news sources, but it is welcome relief to be able to sleep in your own bed every night. Three nights I worked this week and the other three I took off.

On two of the nights off I went to the movies, the first I've seen in almost a month. One of them was "Stage Door Canteen" which I saw with Bill Dickinson. It was a good entertainment but certainly not a great movie. One nostalgic touch, which was almost too much to stand, was the frequent playing of "Goodnight, Sweetheart," as the Canteen closed for the night. It reminded me of the wonderful dances we've had together in our seven years. The other was the Fred Astaire-Joan Leslie thing, the title of which I'm afraid I've forgotten. It was the usual good, light Astaire with one terrific number—"Set 'Em Up, Joe" or something like

*that. I hope you see it. The third night off I attended an American Corre-
spondents' Association cocktail party for Irving Berlin. Berlin played the
piano and everybody sang old Berlin numbers. They are still terrific numbers, but Berlin plays a piano with ten chords learned in ten easy lessons,
and his singing matches his playing . . .*

*Speaking of good numbers, have you heard the Mills Brothers record-
ing of "Paper Doll?" It, for my money, will go down with the old popular classics such as "Melancholy Baby," "My Gal Sal," and the rest. It is
wonderful. The bar downstairs has had it about two days and already
the grooves are wearing out. If I had a record-player I think I'd have it
on all day long.*

*I've just returned to the letter after standing in the blacked-out window
of my bedroom watching the raid. They put up a heluva barrage tonight
but the shells were bursting above the overcast and the show was spoiled.
The guns nearby fired, jarring my eye teeth. I could hear the plane and
watch the searchlights tracking it, apparently through the clouds. Then
when the searchlights apparently had it almost directly overhead the guns
went. The flashes of the guns made every detail of the buildings around
stand out, including the men standing on the Dorchester roof. If the plane
dropped anything I couldn't distinguish the bomb burst from the shell
fire. Then these guns nearby quit and the next battery on up the road took
up the fire, and so it went clear across London. And when the guns miles
away were firing, their flash still lit the skyline. You can hear the whistle of
the shells going up, and then the toy-like bursts far overhead. Just now the
"all clear" went and in a few hours Berlin Radio will be on the air with
an account of the flattening of London. Those liars. Why, even the busses
keep on running, people keep on hailing cabs, and the bicycling night-
workers peddle their way on homeward . . .*

*Incidentally, Bill Dickinson probably will be in Kansas City for the
Christmas season. He is getting home leave after two years over here and,
of course, is heading straight for Independence (Mo.) to be with his two*

children. They live there with his parents. His father is a rather prominent lawyer in Jackson County. Bill's wife, you may remember, jumped out of a New York hotel window the winter before Bill came overseas. He is a very nice guy and is looking forward to taking you to dinner. "Betsy and I are going to the Muehlebach," he keeps rubbing in. I know you'll like him. I hope he'll tell you all the censorable things I can't tell you about where I live, where I travel to, how far I walk to headquarters and the officers' mess, and about Fabulous McGlincy and the London gang. I'm almost as enthusiastic about his meeting with you and telling you all those things as if I were going to be there myself. And, of course, not the least of my enthusiasm is that when he gets back here he'll confirm for all these skeptics how lovely and wonderful you really are. They still think I got that picture of you from a package of cigarettes. . .

Jim and I may be launched as columnists. We dreamed up the idea of writing a combined weekly military-political-gossip column under a joint Pearson-Allen sort of by-line. We wrote our first one yesterday and submitted it to [Virgil] Pinkley. He snatched at it and wrote a fancy cable to [Earl] Johnson in New York telling him to put all possible promotion steam under it. After that kick-off, though, our story got all balled up in transmission and was delayed so late on the Saturday night wire in New York that I'm afraid it probably didn't have a chance for much play this week. Next week we hope to get it in a day early, which should help. We probably will run into stiff censorship problems with it, however, and whether we can make it go or not I don't know.

I got a congratulatory cable this week from Harry Ferguson, acting foreign editor, on an interview (exclusive) with General [William E.] Kepner of fighter command.

It is twelve o'clock, honey, and I'm after my beauty sleep. Please know that I miss you every minute and am terribly lonely for you and that slightly fluffier red-head. Forever and ever, your adoring husband, Walter

FOLLOWING THE DEATH of *New York Times* correspondent Bob Post on the February Wilhelmshaven raid, Air Force publicists lost enthusiasm for the idea of sending war correspondents on combat missions, at least when anyone was likely to be shooting at them. Cronkite's ride on an air patrol hunting for U-boats in the North Atlantic, a flight that he recounted in his letter of November 16, 1943, was his first time in an airplane since Wilhelmshaven. In *A Reporter's Life,* Cronkite described the flight as "the most miserable twenty-four hours I ever spent . . . It was cold; the sandwiches were soggy and the coffee frigid. We dropped bombs on one suspected submarine that turned out to be a whale."

The reference to "my old ship" was to the battleship U.S.S. *Arkansas,* on which Cronkite had sailed in late summer 1942 accompanying a convoy to Scotland, and which, still on convoy duty, was in port in Northern Ireland in November 1943.

The photo that Betsy sent to Cronkite carried the inscription "Just call me Irium." "Irium," according to Pepsodent advertisements, was the mystery ingredient in the toothpaste that whitened teeth.

———

Tuesday, Nov. 16, 1943

I have gone sixteen days without writing you and apart from feeling guilty that always makes me feel so far away from you . . . But these last sixteen days, except perhaps for the first two of them, it has been impossible for me to write. Two days after I last wrote, I was rung up by the Air Ministry and informed that my long-standing request for a Coastal Command trip had been approved and that I should report in Belfast two days later. (That isn't revealing any secrets since my dispatch is permitted a "North Ireland" date line). There I was met by an RAF flight lieutenant who drove me on to the base where I stayed for five days in the miserable huts that the RAF furnishes their men. It was cold and muddy and horrible. I made my trip—[blacked out by censor] one below zero over the North Atlantic in a Sunderland Flying Boat. We didn't see a thing and my story is so dull that I'm going to send it back by mail instead of by cable. But it added that much more to my store of air knowledge, anyway. Then I stayed in Ireland, as per instructions from [Virgil] Pinkley, and toured the American Army, Air Force, and Navy installations, enjoying myself immensely during the weekend I spent at the Navy base. My old ship, the one on which I was with Ribby and Sam Read, was in and I spent a night aboard her chewing the fat until three in the morning with the few of the old hands who are still there. The next day the exec and gunnery officer from her—both of them old-timers who I knew—and I started to fly from Ireland back to London but were grounded by bad weather in Scotland. We were drenched to the skin by the time we finally got a bus to get us into Glasgow. We were too late there to get a first-class sleeper berth so we got third-class accommodations (and those by the skin of our teeth) for the all-night ride to London. Third-class is really that. Four berths in two pairs of uppers and lowers in the same compartment with no linens and, actually no bed. The berths are just mohair seats like a normal compartment seat. They give you a blanket and a pillow and you are supposed to sleep in your clothes. But not Cronkite. I undressed when everybody else was sleeping in their clothes expecting momentary torpedoing in the middle of the Atlantic, and I'll be damned if I was going to sleep in my clothes for the London, Midland and Scottish Railway. Well, anyway, the net result is that I got back here Friday morning . . . I'm up tonight, sitting in front of my little electric heater, pounding this out . . .

The thing that saved the day has been your picture which was waiting for me when I got back. It is wonderful, Darling. It looks just like the Betsy that I had to leave on the Hoboken pier . . . Also I loved the

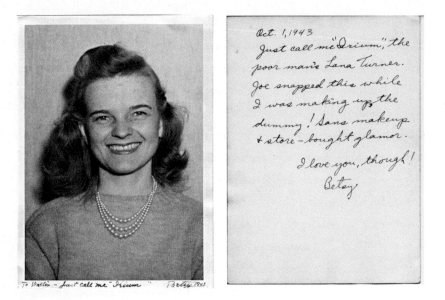

Oct. 1, 1943
Just call me "Irium," the
poor man's Lana Turner.
Joe snapped this while
I was making up the
dummy! Sans makeup
+ store-bought glamor.
I love you, though!
Betsy

To Walter — Just call me "Irium"   Betsy 1943

Betsy Cronkite inscribed the front and back of this photograph
and sent it to her husband in the fall of 1943.

Kodak pictures of you and Judy and Petty and Molo. Honey, I know
it is hard to get films but do send me as many pictures as you can like
that. They are worth so much . . . And I had half a dozen more pack-
ages. I've been opening all of them—that is, the outer wrapping—to
determine whether or not there are edibles therein which require
immediate eating, or whether they are intended as birthday gifts. My
first intention was to save even the birthday gifts for Christmas, but
you all have been so lavish that I opened a couple of them . . . More
tomorrow . . . Walter

CRONKITE'S FAVORITE OF his wartime dispatches went out on the wire
under the title "Nine Weeping Boys" and appeared in some American
newspapers on Armistice Day. It appeared on page 12 of the *Lowell*
(Massachusetts) *Sun* on November 11, 1943, under a different headline:

YANK FLIERS DON'T CRY

Epic Story of Americans Back from an Air Raid

(Editors' Note: Correspondents who cover the air war say they write only of heroes. There are dead heroes and those who come back to fight again. Walter Cronkite of the United Press has lived with the airmen, trained with the Eighth Air Force and been out over Wilhelmshaven. He has told many times the story of those who went down in flak and flames; he tells here the story of those who come back.)

By Walter Cronkite

United Press Staff Correspondent

A BOMBER BASE IN ENGLAND, Nov. 11 (UP)—On an RAF airdrome somewhere on the south coast the sun was shining. There was the smell of falling leaves in the air that wafted through the open windows of the buildings. Back home weather.

Out on the edge of the field a Fortress squatted, a little apart from the perky Spitfires and Typhoons. She was sitting at a cockeyed angle.

Her right tire was wrapped in strips around the hub. Where her nose had been was shattered Plexiglas. The underslung radio antenna hung in frayed ends.

The ball turret hung limply on one side: the other side was accordion-pleated up into the fuselage. Sunlight penciled through cannon holes in the wings and tail.

Inside the ship, the wreckage followed the pattern cut outside by Nazi gunners. But inside there was blood. There was the blood of the ball turret man there in the waist where they'd hoisted him up and given him first aid. There was the blood of the tail gunner outside his cramped compartment where they'd dragged him out.

And in the nose was the blood of the pilot. Down to the nose he had crawled because he couldn't fly with one good arm—and the other had been shattered when German "ack-ack" burst alongside his window.

He'd crawled there because he must have known he was dying and he wanted to be with his navigator, his school days pal.

Lieut. Harold Christensen was that pilot, a nice lad from Eagle Grove, Ia. He had a nice crew too, but I'm not giving their names because fighting men don't want to have it reported that they have emotions. But I have to tell you that every one of those three officers and six enlisted men was blubbering like a baby when they lifted Chris down from the nose and took him to the hospital, where he died a few hours later.

The crew lugged away its personal equipment and left the big ship standing forlornly with the wounds she'd earned over Schweinfurt. None of them had gone back since. Some day they have to go back to the plane, but not yet.

Now they were up at the Officer's club in their dirty, stained OD's, slumped in chairs and trying to read with eyes that stung. One or two tried to play pool but gave it up. They'd offered their blood for Chris but now that was over.

The RAF boys knew what they were going through. They'd been all through it and they knew it wasn't any use saying anything.

Maybe that's it. Maybe there isn't any use my saying anything about it now—but I can't help remembering it over all the recollections of blood, noise and battle—that forlorn old Fortress and those nine weeping boys.

Irving Berlin's musical *This Is the Army* opened on Broadway in the fall of 1942 with a military cast, and was later released as a Hollywood feature film starring Ronald Reagan. Berlin took a touring company of the show on the road, which opened in London at the Palladium Theatre, the production that Cronkite was sorry to miss, as he reported in his November 20, 1943, letter to Betsy.

As in the previous letter, the reference to "my old ship" was to the battleship U.S.S. *Arkansas*.

November 20, 1943

. . . This week I've covered two press conferences, done a little "master minding" of the air coverage, written about two stories—and that has been my week's effort . . . "This is the Army"—the stage version with Berlin and cast—is playing here and I'm dying to see it, but I guess I'll miss it after all since there are no seats for this weekend and I must get out of town early next week. Besides this is a slightly lean week financially inasmuch as Commander Sergeant and a couple of the boys from "my" old ship popped into town yesterday morning and I took them to lunch to the tune of a neat eight bucks—which, as up to now, I haven't thought of a way to get onto the expense account . . . Walter

DIXIE TIGHE, WHOM Cronkite reports having dinner with in his letter of November 21, 1943, was an International News correspondent "famed for her blunt language and flamboyant life style," according to Nancy Caldwell Sorel's history of women correspondents in World War II, *The Women Who Wrote the War*. Phil Ault, Bill Disher, and Johnny Parris were United Press correspondents in London. Drew Middleton was the *New York Times* military correspondent in London.

1:30 pm Sunday, Nov. 21, 1943

My precious wife:
  This is the England I'd read about. The fog has been so thick the last two days that most transportation is paralyzed. Cabs and busses run during the brightest hours of the day, but by four in the afternoon they have stopped—"grounded." Last night the fog was so thick that my powerful

Army flashlight barely penetrated to the sidewalk, and certainly not far enough for me to determine where I was, or what block I was crossing. I went up to Dixie Tighe's flat for a real Bourbon cocktail about six and opened my big trap to invite her to dinner, knowing damned well there weren't any taxis on the streets and suspecting strongly that none of the places around Mayfair, which are very snooty, would have any tables left on Saturday night. So I confidently called one of the most expensive, le Coq d'Or, only to have the damned fools tell me that they could arrange a table for eight o'clock. Well, we groped our way the three blocks around to there and had a very good, not too expensive (at that) meal. I had hors d'oeuvres, raviolis, and apple pie which, of course, they didn't call apple pie but which fancy name I couldn't possibly remember. Le Coq d'Or, which I thought for months was "The Cocked Door," is very nice with tapestry and old wooden walls and great iron chandeliers. It has a huge spit filling one wall which in my previous two trips there I'd never seen in operation and which I assumed had been inactive since the war. So I showed off last night by telling the head waiter: "I can't wait until that spit is working again." To which he answers, "Oh, sir, it operates four or five nights a week." Steady-customer Cronkite, they call me. I managed to get Dixie home through the fog and then proceeded to get myself lost a couple of times trying to get home from there, a distance of some eight blocks through Berkley Square . . .

I worked yesterday afternoon at the office without accomplishing very much . . . I seem to fool the management, however. Jim [McGlincy] tells me today that he was talking to [Virgil] Pinkley last night and Pinkley remarked on what a hard worker I was. Ah, well.

I have told you, haven't I, the amazing fact that I am one of the highest paid workers in the office? It is a slightly frightening fact since I don't consider $82.50 a week a particularly high wage, although we could certainly live well in Kansas City on it—not counting income tax deductions. With the living allowance here boosting the figure to around $105 a week, we could live fairly well even in London if you could only come *here and join me. We'd have to pay a good $100 a month for something decent in which to live, and entertaining would be rather expensive, but we'd manage and it would be fun. Several of the boys here have married girls on this side, and they are all swell people although I've never been invited into any of their homes. Ned Russell recently married a lovely White Russian girl who has lived here ever since her family fled the Bolsheviks twenty-five years ago. Phil Ault is married to a Norwegian refugee who I haven't met but who is described as very nice. Bill Disher is married to a daughter of a refugee Czechoslovakian Minister of Treasury. Johnny Parris is almost married to a girl whose husband is with the British Eighth Army somewhere in Italy and who she plans to divorce, as I get it, when the time is ripe. She is not on my list of the better types like Madames Russell, Ault and Disher, however. I think the line-up is for Russell and Parris to be in the Paris bureau after the war. Disher, I suppose, will go to Prague if we reopen a bureau there since he will be right in with the Czech government. I don't know what the plan is for Ault. Drew Middleton of The New York Times also has married an English girl and I suppose they would be part of any set in which we circulated, although Drew is the most conceited ass I know at present, not counting the millions of such in the officers' ranks of the Army.*

Jim and I are having apartment trouble. First of all, the electric heaters we have in each room and our reading lamps are all on the same power circuit. Wednesday it started playing tricks, blowing fuses and burning wires every couple of hours . . . For two days we huddled around the grate in which we kept a coal fire going. We managed to toast our faces and freeze our fannies. Now an electrician is coming in Monday to rewire the basement, or some such rot, so that we can have the electric fires again. The other problem is that of continuing thefts. Most recent disappearance has been my officers' cap which is irreplaceable since British caps are of much inferior workmanship. Also my Schick razor, for which I've amassed a nice collection of blades, has disappeared. That cannot be replaced either, but I thought perhaps you could rush me one from there . . . I'd appreciate it, honey, if you could airmail one to me as soon as possible, inasmuch as I'm now shaving with an old-fashioned Star-type razor that isn't any too kind to the old puss, plus the fact that I can only get two inferior blades a week for it, whereas I have all these Schick blades piled up . . .

I'm reading a pretty good book by Sholem Asch. It is called "The Calf of Paper" and is about the Jews between wars in Germany. Incidentally, Asch's son, a writer in his own right, is a sergeant with the Air Force public relations office here. He talks with a terrible lithp.

I ran into Josephine Sippy, a former airline hostess from St. Louis now in the Red Cross, in the PX last week and she had with her Adele Astaire, who also is working with the Red Cross here. What a screwball she is. Strictly Billie Burke, chattering on and on and making very little sense, switching conversational topics so rapidly she sounds like Alec Templeton doing his radio tuning stunt . . .

Which reminds me that Ronnie, the queer bartender downstairs, looked particularly glamorous the other afternoon and I heard some girl ask him what he had done to himself. "Well, please don't utter a word of this," he said, very confidentially, "but I've got on false eyelashes." He batted his eyes in a dainty flutter, and sure enough he did. Decadent civilization department.

The office just called and I've got to run down there . . .

Honey, it is now Monday morning. I didn't get a chance to finish this at the office yesterday and intended to do it when I got home but Collie Small and I were too weak-willed to pass up the Bob Hope version of "Let's Face It." It was very funny, but it kept bringing back memories of Danny Kaye singing to you to the exclusion of all the rest of the audience. That cad—but I can't blame him. I worship you, darling. I'll write more tonight. I worship you, Walter

JIM MCGLINCY'S PENCHANT for heavy drinking, previously treated as a kind of running gag in Cronkite's letters, now presented a practical problem, as Cronkite reported to Betsy.

———————

[Tuesday], Nov. 23, 1943

My darlingest wife:

I've just gotten home to find that all hell (namely, McGlincy) has broken loose and we are evicted from our lovely flat as of Saturday. Well, that isn't quite right, in that I was given the choice of staying on, but I couldn't think of anyone else I'd like to have share the place with me, and, secondly, I've been wanting to move, perhaps into a place by myself, for some time. It seems that last week when McGlincy was sober and in the bar downstairs some drunken Navy commander kept trying to pick a fight with him and Jim kept backing away. Well, tonight was Jim's night off and he managed to get himself pickled downstairs. Yep, you're right. The Navy guy comes wandering in. This time he's sober, but Jim doesn't give him a chance. He just walks the length of the bar, spins the guy off his stool, says, "So you want to fight, eh?" and pokes him a terrific wallop that handily removes two front teeth. The management took an exceedingly dim view of the proceeding, and since Jim has created other such scenes down there in the past, asked him to kindly move by noon tomorrow. I missed all the fun, being across the street at the Dorchester for the cocktail party about which I wrote you. I then went to Sandy's for dinner with Bill Dickinson, and thus came in long after the excitement. I argued the management out of kicking Jim out until Saturday, and said that I might as well go along—something I don't think they had figured on, since this flat is comparatively inexpensive and handy. Where in the devil I'll be moving I don't know, I've got Bill Dickinson and Sam Hales alerted already since they live in large blocks

*of flats and might be able to wangle something through their agents. If
I'd known this blowoff was coming I could have had Dickinson's flat.
He'll be leaving for home in a few days, but Collie Small already has
spoken for it . . . I'd like to find something out in Chelsea, London's
Greenwich Village, but that takes more time than I have. I just have
to get out of town a couple of days this week, and that is going to cut
down the search time considerably. Things are in a mite of a mess, I'd
say . . . I love you, Betsy. Walter*

———

IN HIS NOVEMBER 25, 1943, letter Cronkite again confessed to boredom
with the air-war story and expressed his wish to begin a new assignment. He also reported that he and McGlincy had moved into what he
thought would be temporary lodgings at 78 Buckingham Gate. In fact,
he would remain in that building (although changing flats in January)
until July 1944.

———

Thursday, Nov. 25, 1943

My darling wife:
    *This, according to the calendar, is Thanksgiving. You'd never know
it here . . . I'm up country again on what was to have been the first leg
of that extended trip I planned, although the situation has changed so
that I'm going to have to return to London today, and probably won't
get out of there again until next Monday. It is now eight-thirty and
I'm a little shocked to find myself up so early. I have done this uncivi-
lized thing because the train I plan to catch back to town takes more
than three hours and leaves here just before lunchtime. It has no diner
and, without breakfast inside, I'm afraid the trip would be a little too
Robinson Crusoe for me. I have to get back for three reasons (1) an*

afternoon conference with Mr. [N. D.] Blow at the Air Ministry (he's the public relations officer, honest!), (2) get out the weekly column with [Jim] McGlincy, which has to be radioed today, and (3) get packed for the moving, about which I told you in the airmailer sent Monday. Jim and I haven't found a place to live yet and temporarily are going to have to go into St. James' Court, a hotel development in Buckingham Gate right behind the palace . . . I'm still going to look for a place by myself but I don't have much hope . . . I'm up with [Collie] Small now, at the division headquarters where he hangs out. He's quite a lad and I'm glad to have him working with me on this air stuff, which, incidentally, I wish to hell I could get off of for just a little while. I'm afraid I'm just a bit "browned off," as the RAF says, with the assignment. Things bore me instead of interesting me. Maybe that would be remedied if I could get you over here. I've been getting more and more lonely for you as the days go by. I didn't think that was possible, my loneliness was so great at the very first. Thanksgiving is going to be like any other day, apparently. They are planning a turkey dinner and a dance here tonight, but, of course, I'll be back in London. I'll miss lunch altogether, work through to dinner, and probably eat at Sandy's. Golly, how I'd like to be looking forward to a dinner with Molo and the family . . . I love you. Walter

---

IN HIS LETTER to Betsy of December 6, 1943, Cronkite mentioned the "loss" of a fellow correspondent. Lowell Bennett, who worked for the International News Service, was shot down on an RAF bombing mission on Berlin on December 2, but as it turned out was not dead. He survived the next 18 months as a prisoner of war. He was not the first, and would not be the last, American war correspondent to fall into Nazi hands. Cronkite's UP colleague Ed Beattie was taken prisoner by the Germans in September 1944 in France; after the war he published a book, *Diary of a Kriegie* (1946), about the experience. As for Lowell Bennett, he managed to practice journalism even while a prisoner in Stalag Luft I, editing the camp's underground newspaper, *Pow Wow*.

The "Lt. Dabney" referred to in Cronkite's letter may have been 379th Bomb Group pilot William Dabney.

Hollywood star and Army Air Force captain Jimmy Stewart arrived in England in December 1943 with the 445th Bombardment Group. He flew more than a score of combat missions over Europe as a B-24 pilot, was twice awarded the Distinguished Flying Cross, and ended the war with the rank of colonel.

Monday, December 6, 1943

My dearest darling:

This should be dated December 7, for it is now 12:30 a.m. and I have just finished work. I'm staying at the office until I finish this, though, because the present unsettled conditions at the flat make it difficult to write there. When we left the Deanery, Jim [McGlincy] and I went into the St. James Court for a few days but it obviously was a stop-gap measure because of the expense—about ten bucks a day. Wednesday, in the nick of time, we found a small flat just across the street from the St. James on Buckingham Gate (that is the name of the street). The flat has bedroom, living room, hall, and bath, with room service. It is not so convenient as the Deanery but not too out of the way . . . The place we have now is the flat of a colonel in the Grenadier Guards who currently is on foreign duty. It is strictly Victorian but a slightly tight squeeze for two of us. Buckingham Gate is one of the streets leading into Bucking-ham Palace, which is only a block and a half from us. Incidentally, we find we are being awakened at 6:15 a.m. each morning by the blowing of thousands of bugles, followed by the skurling (or whatever that word is) of millions of bagpipes. Seems the Guards barracks are right behind us—between us and the Palace, which probably is a good idea . . .

Thursday I left for an RAF base and covered from the ground the Berlin raid on which INS' Lowell Bennett was lost. (UP has refused to let me go on any more raids, at least until invasion time, whenever that might be.) I returned here, after a six-hour train ride, two hours of which was spent standing up, just in time to dash dirty and filthy to a six-man party with Jock Whitney, General Tupper, head of the theater FRO, and the four of us still left of the "Writing Sixty-Ninth." Tupper gave us each a swell-looking shoulder patch, gold-embroidered, with a winged design and the words "Writing Sixty-Ninth." I never, never play poker but I did Saturday night—and won two pounds . . .

Sunday, with a notebook full of stories (at RAF bases, besides being difficult to write letters it is also almost impossible to write stories because of lacking facilities and difficult communication), I got up early, wrote furiously for three hours, took time out to run out to White City Stadium and watch the Eighth Air Force football team beat the Ground Forces team, six to nothing, and then came back to the office where I worked until about midnight. I've been at that same sort of grind again today, just having finished when I set down to write this. The flu epidemic here is frightful and has decimated our staff as it has everyone else's. Doug Werner, who with Collie Small helps me on the air run, has had to be recalled to the office to fill in on the desk. That leaves half the Eighth Air Force for me to cover again, as well as the RAF, and the past two weeks have been the busiest air war weeks we've had yet, what with the Berlin raids and all. I have so much back-work piled up now that I'm frightened, always scared to death that some of the story hunches I have will be snatched off by the AP before I can ever get around to them. Late tomorrow I'm going out again, to be gone for four or five days. Meanwhile, I've got to write at least three stories for which I have the notes already, I've got to make arrangements for a couple of stories I want Collie to get, I've got to write thank you and appreciation notes to RAF people who have been helpful in the past, and I've got to make up an expense account for the last four weeks— that's how busy I've been. Additionally, we no sooner get rid of Gable than Jimmy Stewart hit the air force in this theater, but thank goodness he is in the territory for which Collie is responsible. Although I still worry about it. But enough of this prattle. I got two sweet letters from you today, one air mail and one V-mail. They confirmed that you had gotten my package. Despite its meager character, I am glad it arrived. I was worried about it. I'm curious to know if it was mailed from England though. I gave it to Lieut. Dabney to mail when he reached the States, and I'm wondering if perhaps export rules or something of the kind forced him to mail it from here. All this speculation is inspired by your mention of the stamps that your mother wanted saved. By the way, honey, there still aren't any gifts for the rest of the family—only you—so don't feel hesitant about getting them nice things from both of us there. When I was in the bosom of the family I'm afraid maybe I was a little petty and small about things, but now that absence has impressed on me how wonderful everyone really is, I want to show them how I feel—and now I can't. Strange, isn't it? . . .

As THE ONE-YEAR anniversary of their separation approached, Cronkite was moved to write Betsy his most ardent love letter yet.

Tuesday night, December 7, 1943   To be read Christmas Day

My precious wife:

   It is nine-thirty. The huge grandfather clock in the hall has just struck its blow, and a moment later the tardy, smaller clock chimed out its tiny echo. I'm sitting in front of the Georgian fireplace whose small grate now holds a sometimes roaring, more often flickering coal fire. An electric grate also is on in another corner of the room, strangely out of place amid this Victorian furniture. The blackout curtains of course are drawn and they do their share of keeping out the cold, which wouldn't be severe if it were not for the dampness of the fog rolling up from the Thames a few blocks away.

It is in these surroundings I'm going to make another try at a Christmas letter for Betsy. I've tried twice before with much the same results I had just three hundred and sixty horribly long days ago when I wanted to leave a note for you but couldn't. Do you remember, darling? Perkins sitting out there in the living room, and my typing to hide my emotions. And I never got the note written, and you didn't have anything from me on Christmas but a silly little horse with a tender whatsis. In return I had a wonderful letter from you and packages with individual notes on them that I opened in the two-by-four cabin on the horrible S.S. Westernland while a North Atlantic gale raged outside.

I'm already becoming frightened that I won't be able to finish this. But I must, because I want you to know, and be reminded on Christmas Day, that no amount of water, land or air can ever really separate us—that I am yours forever, and you are mine, and that we really are inseparable.

I know I'm going to feel guilty again when I open those dozens of packages from you, because you have only that tiny one from me. You know how I like to shower you with presents on Christmas, even when you throw them across the room and drop them down the toilet, and that mean little Miss Judy aids and abets by chewing hers to ribbons.

Because they don't look like much in the horrible makeshift wrappings of mine (from your wrappings on my last year's presents saved for the occasion), maybe I should say just a word about those presents. I'm sort of proud of the little signets, although not very proud of the fact that I didn't get a bracelet to put them on . . .

The purse is a real Scotch importation. It is, as you undoubtedly know, a man's purse, to be suspended on the hip when he's wearing *his kilts. I bought it in a Scotch shop where my mouth watered for the wonderful tweeds, and I almost bought myself a knarled walking stick. Although I know the purse, without mirrors and compartments and stuff, isn't very practical, I thought perhaps you could use it some way, and it would be different.*

The engraved cartridge case, I'm afraid, is just a souvenir, but I sent it along for your stocking. It was from one of the bullets I fired, and managed to miss with, at German fighters on that certain day.

Not much as gifts, I guess. Perhaps they won't compare with the Irish linens, the silk scarfs, the trinkets and bobbles that must have filled the mail from here. But, darling, of all the things for which I shopped, I thought you'd like them best. I'd love to have gotten you some more tweed, but with so many Americans here now another couponless deal like mine of last year with Lieutenant Fergusson is impossible and once I got enough tweed for a suit I'd have a devil of a time mailing it home. I thought of some fine English China, but that isn't very practical either, and we'd better save that until we are together over here.

I don't know how I can possibly miss you Christmas Day any more than I miss you on all these other days, but I'm certain that somehow I shall . . . Oh, sweetest, how I'd like to dig under the tree with you Christmas morning, and have Miss Judy poking her nose into all the presents and tramping through cotton and snow and making a lovable nuisance out of herself, perhaps even having a little fir tree asthma just for the nostalgic touch. And Christmas dinner with the Maxwells and Craigs and Manrings and Carrs, to be considerably sharpened with Aines eggnog.

This past year without you has been a horrible one. There have been so many terribly lonely days, so many more impossible nights. There have been so many experiences that were wasted because you weren't there. Only for the fact that we have built something professionally that will make our future so much brighter has the situation been saved. But that doesn't alleviate the pain of being without you.

It seems so long—much longer than just a year—since I ran my fingers through your hair, and felt you close to me. It has been a hundred years since we danced together, and now I'm sure I've forgotten how to dance. It has been a century since I heard that giggle that everyone loves and I adore.

I've got a store of memories, my darling, that could last fifty years if need be. I could relive every moment with you ten thousand times and never grow tired of them. I could start with a July day when a saucy "blonde" in a big hat interrupted an imaginative jam session and carry on until a bleak December morning when a beautiful red-head drove away from a Hoboken pier. There is nothing that happens to me that, in some way, doesn't remind me of wonderful moments with you. The simple (or is it so simple, anymore?) process of eating brings back memories of restaurants with you, and those lovely evenings at home with the best meals I ever ate. I think so often of the Crossroads, that steak place on Thirty-First street, the Savoy, and later, Barbetta's and Keen's. And it isn't the food they served, but the fact that you were with me, that brings them to memories. And remember the little Jungle Bar down on Seventy-Third street where we stopped for a reviving beer the day we rented that lovely apartment?

But we won't have to live on memories long, honey. [Virgil] Pinkley knows that I'm interested in getting you over here at the earliest possible moment, and he is sympathetic. I'm sure there won't be another Christmas apart, and, with luck, not another summer. To date I haven't had an answer from you on the [Kansas City] Star foreign assignment idea, which I still think sound, but I suppose it is in the mails. The more I think about the matter—and the more I miss you—my confidence grows that it would be right to get you over here even before the finish because even though I go across the Channel when and if there is an invasion there will be frequent opportunities to return here. On the other hand, I don't see any possibility of a home leave for another year at least.

That is business, though, and doesn't belong in a Christmas letter, which is to tell you only that I love you more than anything in the world. I shall always love you as it seems that I always have. There has never been anyone but you. There never could be. I love you passionately, in every sense of the word. And at the same time I'm proud of you—proud of your beauty, your personality, your wit, and, right now, your bravery. I know it must be terrible for you, darling. I'm so sorry it must be this way. Please be sure, despite the sometimes dearth of letters, that I'm thinking of you every moment, and, if possible, loving you more with each tick of the clock.

It doesn't exactly seem appropriate to say "Merry Christmas." But it certainly is right to ask for a "Happy New Year." And to pray for one.

I do hope though, honey, that your Christmas is as merry as possible. I hope you all have the best possible holiday season. And on Christmas morning please remind that little red-headed ragamuffin of ours that I love her and miss her too. And tell the family that I miss them very much. But the bulk of my love and the bulk of my missing is yours—forever and ever.

If I could only feel your nice warm lips against mine again. I want to hold you tight, cuddle you in my arms, ruffle that wonderful hair and say—I love you, darling wife, Walter

------

DECEMBER 12, 1943, marked the first anniversary of Cronkite's separation from Betsy.

Sunday, December 12, 1943

My darling wife:

Another gloomy Sunday, this time made even lonelier by the fact that it is just a year ago today that I left you on this last, longest trip of all. I knew then, when they said I was going to London, that the easy days of the Navy assignment with frequent returns to the United States were over, *but I held a secret hope—almost a belief—that nothing could really keep us apart for long and that somehow we would be together before many more months had passed. Well, now it has been a year and, although some say the end is in sight, it still seems to be a far stretch down the road. Every day of this last year, and every day until we are together again, I miss you more, love you more, and more lonely for you. There have been a few exciting moments in this year, but even they could not replace the ever-burdening loneliness for Betsy and Judy. Most of the year has been just hard work—cold, long hours of hard work—with nothing to come home to, no one to praise the good stories, or for sympathy for the bad. It hasn't been much fun. It won't be fun until we can be together again.*

I wrote you a Christmas letter last week, and sent it airmail-special. I've got it plainly marked, inside the envelope, "Not to be Read Until Christmas" but, just to play safe, if such an airmail-special should arrive after this v-mailer, that is it and you can just leave it unopened until Christmas. Also, it should be read AFTER you have opened the meager little box.

There is virtually no hope of this reaching you before the event, but if it should: Virgil Pinkley is coming to the States on a short jaunt. His schedule calls for him to catch the Santa Fe Chief out of Chicago on December 22. That, I believe, puts him in Kansas City for about fifteen or twenty minutes around nine o'clock the same night. He has heard so much about you, and plans so on your being a member of the Unipress post-war family in Europe, that he is anxious to see you if possible. He suggested that, if not too inconvenient, you might be able to meet him for a drink or, at least, a short chat, at the Union Station. He said he would try to telephone you from Chicago to confirm the arrangements, though, as his schedule might be altered in New York. I'm going to see if I can't crowd some of the above paragraph into a cable to warn you ahead of time. Give Pinkley the old build-up on your journalistic experience—women's editor of Kansas City Journal (not mentioning length of tenure), radio continuity including news at KCMO, some work on

Star. There might come the day when we can even get UP to sponsor
your trip over before the armistice. When Pinkley once sees you that
should be three-quarters in the bag.

This week I've had another wonderful picture of you, and boxes from
the Grandfolks and Mother. Thanks to all, I love you . . .

WESTERN UNION   Commercial DEC 11 1943

NLT BETSY CRONKITE=

3920 AGNES KANSASCITY MO=

DARLINGEST UNHAPPY ANNIVERSARY STOP SAILED JUST
YEAR AGO. MAY NEVER ANOTHER YEAR BE SO LONELY
STOP LOVE, YOUR=

WALTER CRONKITE

Eleanor and Reynolds Packard, mentioned in Cronkite's letter of
December 19, 1943, were both United Press foreign correspondents and
often covered stories together. Cronkite saw them as a model he hoped
to emulate with Betsy.

V-MAIL   *Sunday, December 19, 1943*

My darlingest wife:

. . . I have been hoping to get out to send you a cable which should
have gotten off several days ago. It is one I can't send from the office
and should go by a cable office to file but now will have to telephone in
tonight so you will get it tomorrow. By now you know its contents, of
course. It is the one about Pinkley's suggestion that you might be added
to the London staff. Further details regarding it are this: I have men-
tioned to Virgil on several occasions, sometimes in a kidding vein but

more often serious, that a cheap way to add to the London staff and at the same time give experience to what might post-war become a valuable European writing team, would be for the United Press to bring you over. He had shown a little interest, but I'd thought it was dictated by politeness. Well, Tuesday, just before he left for his quick six weeks Christmas trip to the States, he called me in and said: "Do you think Betsy would be interested in coming over here before the end of the war?" To that I answered, "Certainly." "Do you think she could help out on the desk here, and maybe cover some outside stuff?" And to that I also answered, "Certainly." Then he asked me to review your experience again, and I told him you had been for some time on the women's section of the Journal, editing the same shortly before the paper folded. Also that you had done some feature work for the [Kansas City] Star.

Also I told him you had done news and women's continuity for KCMO for a year. I told him flatly that your experience on a news desk or in writing straight news had been meager, but he seemed personally sold on the idea of meeting you when he passed through Kansas City and then suggesting you to New York as an addition to the London staff. Although we didn't have time to go into the matter at length before he shoved off, I imagine that his idea would be to accredit you to the Army as a correspondent so that the United Press could bring you over here, then use you as a sort of part-time, piece-work helper on the desk here. This foreign newspapering always seems to have been a sort of happy-go-lucky sort of thing, with wives pitching in to help husbands when the work got heavy, and I suppose it is somewhat in that sort of role that Virgil pictures you.

I know you could do the job, and do it better than some are doing it now. The desk work here is mostly routine which takes anybody and everybody only a few weeks to absorb. As far as outside assignments go, you could whip most of these pretending to be writers here now.

I don't know how sincere Virgil was, or how likely is his selling the idea to New York. One difficulty may be that Virgil's brainstorm comes on the day after a ticklish situation with Reynolds and Eleanor Packard. Reynolds is in Italy, Eleanor in Ankara, and they are trying by frantic cables all the way up to Hugh Baillie to get together on the same assignment.

As I wrote regarding the Star idea I had, it seems there is not the slightest chance now of my going to any other theater but this, although I'll probably cross the Channel whenever the invasion comes. But even so, that will mean frequent—perhaps as much as twice-monthly—returns to London. It also probably will presage a rapid reopening of Continental bureaus, which would mean our being permanently together again.

I'm trying not to get excited about the plan, because I'm afraid it is too good to be true. But by now you have met Virgil, I hope—or at least will be meeting him within a couple of days or so. I'm waiting anxiously to hear from you, and for Virgil's return here to get his side of the story.

There isn't much else that is news. No parties or anything lined up for Christmas and with that dread day only six days away I'm beginning to feel more lonesome every minute—if such is possible. I miss my two red-heads so much. I told you, didn't I, that I got the other one of the pictures taken at the office? They are both wonderful. Everyone likes them and I'm now looking for twin folders for them. I worship you, honey. I love you, Walter

———

CRONKITE MARKED HIS second lonely Christmas without his wife in his December 25, 1943, letter.

———

V-MAIL   Saturday, Christmas   December 25, 1943

My darlingest wife:

This is a lonely day, brightened only by the stack of wonderful gifts you all sent me and, perhaps later, by a drink or two at Sam's. The flat looks a little more Christmas-like this morning with the wrappings from my presents scattered over the floor. The only decoration Jim and I have are our Christmas cards displayed on the mantle. I got one from the Moorheads and one each from two bomber groups besides all those you sent me. I know you were just trying to make up for all those years when Betty kidded me about the few cards I got compared to the more popular members of the family.

I had to go up to a bomber base yesterday and I got back about eight o'clock completely worn out. But since Jim had opened the one or two packages he received upon their arrival weeks ago and had none to open Christmas day, I thought it would be better if I opened mine in solitude while he worked last night. So after I got home I changed into comfortable clothes, got a fire going in the fireplace, piled all my packages (and there were dozens, honey) alongside the easy chair, and dug in. Everything was perfect—exactly what I needed, things impossible to get here, luxury items I'd never have bought for myself, and wonderful surprises. I think I got the biggest single kick out of the Mixture 79. It was so unexpected and so wanted. You were a darling to remember it as my favorite. Mixing it with the big box of Bond Street Judy sent me, I'll have my favorite pipe smoke again . . . That Wolferman fruit cake was a godsend too. I opened it early this week to make the week a little more of a holiday one. It is delicious, darling, and I bet you didn't have anything like it yourself. I wish you could be here to share it with me. Or even without a fruit cake, I wish you could be here. I miss you so much, my darling, and need you so . . .

Walter

CHAPTER FOUR

INVASION JITTERS

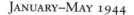

JANUARY–MAY 1944

In a mid-May 1944 letter, Cronkite mocked himself for the state of nerves he had displayed a few nights before in a crowded London restaurant. Following his meal, he had "sauntered" up to the bar, where he found himself in casual conversation with an acquaintance. "I was standing there chatting . . . when Mrs. Gaston, wife of the owner, lit the gas heater in the fireplace. It went PUFF as gas heaters have a way of doing. I jumped a foot and threw my beer half way across the room. That amused everybody—U.S. war correspondent with invasion jitters."

Invasion jitters were common that spring. Millions of Americans, Britons, and captive peoples in Nazi-occupied Europe anxiously awaited the cross-channel invasion of France. "The whole world knew that the invasion was imminent," Cronkite recalled in *A Reporter's Life*. "The secret being guarded to the very death was exactly where and when." Everyone also knew that D-Day would start the western Allies' decisive phase of the struggle against the Nazi foe—a series of battles whose outcome would, without exaggeration, determine the fate of the world.

In those last months before the invasion, Cronkite's professional star continued to rise. His expertise in covering the air war in Europe was unrivaled, within the United Press and the broader community of war correspondents in London. He wrote the leads for most of the air-war stories, making his byline a regular feature on the front page of American newspapers. He had excelled as an administrator as well as a reporter, overseeing a stable of other UP reporters, including, at various times, Collie Small, Bill Disher, Phil Ault, Jim McGlincy, Sam Hales, Ned Roberts, and Bill Higginbotham. UP management had marked him for great things in the future, promising that after the invasion he would be given a position as bureau chief for the Low Countries (Belgium, the Netherlands, and Luxembourg), as a stepping-stone to a top bureau chief assignment like London, Paris, or Berlin in a few years' time.

The new assignment would come none too soon, for Cronkite was heartily sick of the bombing beat. He was taking German lessons, anticipating scoops and exclusives once the ground fighting began in western Europe. No wonder he was jittery as the prime invasion season arrived in May 1944.

The one constant in his life was the ache he felt for his wife. He wrote in a letter at the end of March 1944, on the eve of their fourth wedding anniversary: "Two whole years out of our lives. It makes this war with Hitler a pretty personal matter. I want to take out on him and all those responsible the months that we have missed and the hundreds of days that we never shall be able to regain."

In his January 1, 1944, letter to Betsy, Cronkite marked his second New Year without her.

Wilmott Ragsdale, part of the crowd of correspondents with whom Cronkite saw in the New Year, reported for Time Life. Cronkite's description of him as "a real life Hiram Holliday" is a reference to Paul

Walter Cronkite, right, stands with the crew of the B-26 Martin Marauder
U.S.O. On February 9, 1944, Cronkite flew with the crew to bomb a V-1
rocket site in France.

Gallico's 1939 novel, *Adventures of Hiram Holliday,* whose title character is a mild-mannered newspaper proofreader who travels around the world fighting criminals and Nazi spies. Ragsdale doesn't seem to have battled any spies, but he had spent much of the 1930s seeing the world as a merchant seaman.

Geoffrey Parson, mentioned in the second half of the letter, was chief editorialist of the *New York Herald Tribune* and had won the 1942 Pulitzer Prize for distinguished editorial writing. Cronkite also mentioned Joe Evans, *Newsweek's* London bureau manager, and Ed Murray, Bob Richards, and Ned Russell of the ever expanding United Press London bureau, along with names by now familiar to Betsy, including Sam Hales, Ed Beattie, and Jim McGlincy.

Dudley Ann Harmon and Joan Twelftrees are worth noting because they numbered among the rare female UP correspondents of the era. Harmon's case is particularly interesting. Both of her parents were journalists, and after graduating from Smith College in 1934, she went to work for the *Washington Post* as a society columnist, one of the few regular newspaper positions open to women. In 1941 she traveled to North Africa as a correspondent for the *Christian Science Monitor* and then to London, where she was hired by United Press. The United Press made her add her middle name, Ann, to her byline so that readers would know the author was a woman. As she wrote to her father in late July 1943, three days after starting to work for the UP, "I am not getting a corroded idea about treatment of women, but I think you'll agree with me it is a well-known fact that newspapermen are prejudiced against them." That generalization did not apply to Cronkite, whose own wife was a journalist.

Apparently, Cronkite's description the previous summer of his letters as a form of war "diary" had not pleased Betsy; he began his first letter of the New Year with an apology.

———

January 1, 1944

My darlingest wife:

A new year, started in the typical fashion. I just wrote "1943" instead of the correct year on the line provided for same above this letter. I'm starting the daily letters to you again, honey, effective with this letter. They are letters to YOU and not diary pages as I crudely suggested last fall.

I'm at home today and not in the least hung-over. I worked at the office yesterday until about eight-thirty getting out the lead on the day's USAAF activities—a lead which had to be held for the communiqué and as a consequence didn't move until this noon. I suppose the Eighth Air Force communiqué writers took the evening off. There could be no other excuse for the long delay, which just serves to botch every thing up on our desk and also cut the Eighth out of getting any play in the afternoon papers at home. From the office I went to Sandy's, which was pretty dead. By the time I got there Ed Beattie and date and Drew Middleton (of NY Times) and wife were almost through eating, so I joined Wilmott Ragsdale (of Time, Inc.—the guy I told you was a real-life Hiram Holliday) and wife. We had some wonderful soup, shoulder of lamb, huge baked potato and cauliflower, topped off by celery and cheese.

New Year's Eve among the newspaper colony here is an excuse for playing at diplomatic intrigue. Each clique has its own party, and it is strictly <u>declasse</u> (for God's sake, don't look that up) for members of one group to let on to members of another that a party is being held. So when it came time for the Ragsdales to leave, there began quite a session at conversational parrying while we tried to determine where each other was going. Slowly I got the Ragsdales pinned down to the Marble Arch area. Then I closed in rapidly and, catching them off guard, determined that they were going to the Park West, a block of flats. Then came the showdown. I bowled them over with: "Not by any chance Sam Hales?" They were trapped. So we went out to seek a cab together, since that was where I was going. We failed in our quest, naturally, so wandered three blocks through drunken American soldiers to the Piccadilly Underground station.

Sam's was mostly a UP party—or, I should say, the Middlewest clique of the UP. Besides the Ragsdales and me and co-host Tom Wolf (at his most boring) were Bob Richards who before coming with the UP was with the Memphis Press-Scimitar, Dudley Ann Harmon who before joining the UP over here was with the Maritime Commission and originally stems from Milwaukee or some such hole, a Canadian army captain whose name I never caught, a girl named Joan from Exchange Telegraph

(British news agency), Joan Twelftrees who works for UP and BUP [British United Press] filing to Sweden, Switzerland, Spain, Portugal and other neutrals. (More)

Later Ed Murray, who is from Minnesota somewhere and used to be in the Chicago bureau, joined the party. I was supposed to go also to a party at Geoffrey Parsons' (NY Her-Trib) where Ed Beattie and Ned Russell of the UP, Joe Evans of Newsweek, and others were gathered. So I called Jim [McGlincy], who was working—and getting a bit tightish— to hold on to the hire car driver who nightly picks up our late workers. (Transportation on the calmest evening is impossible here. New Year's Eve, although I only had that one run-in with the situation, I'm sure was worse than impossible.) First of all the driver was late getting to the office, and, second, when he and Jim got to Sam's they were bosom bud- dies and the driver came right along to the flat to have a drink. An hour later the driver was the middle of the little conversational group. Only by promising the driver that Parsons' party would be better than Sam's could we get him to leave at all. By that time it was 3:30 a.m. and I was terribly sober with not the slightest desire to become a belated entry in the Parsons' brawl. By this time everyone had left Sam's and he invited me to use his normally empty twin bed, which I did.

Summary: It was a dull but nice New Year's Eve. Nothing hilarious, but that was the way I preferred it. It could have been gay if you had been here—or if we have been together anywhere. I was thinking of you at midnight and giving off with a silent little prayer that not too many months would go by before we were in each other's arms again. I love you and hope you know . . .

Incidentally, darling, Give my love to Judy, Walter

THE JANUARY 3, 1944, letter contained Cronkite's first reference to the "big push," wartime slang for the forthcoming cross-channel invasion of Europe—the anticipation of which became a continuing theme in his letters that winter and spring.

Over Christmas, Cronkite's United Press colleague Bill Dickinson, on leave in the United States, met Betsy in Kansas City. He was scheduled to return to London when news arrived that UP correspondent Brydon Taves had been killed in a plane crash in New Guinea on December 27, 1943. Dickinson was reassigned to take Taves's place as UP's point man in the southwestern Pacific, where he wound up covering Gen. Douglas MacArthur's liberation of the Philippines.

Plans for Betsy to meet Virgil Pinkley, London bureau chief, when he briefly stopped by Kansas City fell through when neither recognized the other in the city's train station. Cronkite rued the missed opportunity, because he was hoping that Pinkley would find a way to bring Betsy to London to work for the United Press.

———

Monday, January 3, 1944

My darlingest wife:

I got your air mailer of December 23rd today—in the remarkable time of ten days. That is getting down to an almost bearable time span. I had been waiting anxiously to hear about your visit with Bill [Dickinson]. I'm so glad you had a good time and liked him. He is really a great guy . . . As far as we in the London bureau are concerned, we got some bad news last Friday. Bill is not coming back here but is going to Australia to take Brydon Taves' job. Taves was our Southwestern Pacific manager. He was killed last week in a combat plane crash somewhere in New Guinea. We haven't figured out yet whether the change means a promotion or something not so good for Bill. We know darned well it is tough in one way: He sat it out over here two years waiting for the big push, and now that it is about to come, he gets transferred to another "waiting" job. I'm particularly grieved because, first of all, Bill was a close friend of mine, and, second, I had been looking forward to getting a first-hand report about you—how you look and what you're doing and if you still say marvelously witty things and still giggle hysterically. And I had planned on Bill's corroborating for me the stories I've been telling of my beautiful wife.

As happy as I am about your seeing Bill, I'm equally sorry you missed [Virgil] Pinkley. It was stupid of all of us—me, Pinkley and you—not to take into account the fact you two wouldn't know each other. I should have been the one to think of that and to have done something about it over here, and right now I'm kicking myself in the pants. It must have been horrible for you, honey, standing around that dreary station and worrying your head off. (Maybe that is why he didn't recognize you? Are you sure you hadn't lost your head?) . . .

I'm glad you liked the little bracelet. I hope you have gotten by now a Christmas letter I sent airmail-special to be read Christmas day which explains partially the gifts.

This is moving day, again, for Mac [Jim McGlincy] and me. We are moving upstairs into a larger flat in the same building. I haven't even seen it yet. I have just gotten here from a busy but routine day and the porter is coming in a minute to help move. Love, always,

———

IN RETROSPECT, CRONKITE and McGlincy seem to be an odd couple. The former tried to assemble around himself some measure of domestic normalcy while pining away for absent Betsy, while his wayward colleague made the most of the bachelor's life in London. But somehow the relationship worked for both of them, as they shared close quarters in a succession of apartments for more than a year.

Wednesday, January 5, 1944

Darlingest:

Well, Monday we started moving, and things have been in such a
godawful mess that when I finally finish a full day's stint of work I just
haven't had the energy to clear them up enough to get this portable out
from under the debris. (I told you, didn't I, that I held up the office for a
Hermes, one of the tiny Swiss typewriters that operate with some degree
of efficiency and weigh just half what my Royal and other portables
do?) We have moved up to the sixth floor of this somewhat ramshackle
late nineteenth century building. We now have two bedrooms and two
sitting rooms and, of course, a bath. One of the sitting rooms should
be a dining room but Jim [McGlincy] and I talked them into making a
study of it, and it is not bad now. It has a fireplace (with electric heater),
dormer windows (leaded) and paneled walls. They have put a huge,
oaken, carved desk in it with small library table (suitable for our lonesome meals) to match and leather chairs and sofa with velvet cushions. It
doesn't make such a bad room. The other living room is typical rococo
turn-of-the-century. Enough said. By this time next week I should start
missing things, inasmuch as the staff moved my stuff up here and I have
never yet had a hundred percent operation on that basis. Just one bit of
luck have I had: One of the bedrooms is larger and a little nicer than
the other and, in the flip with Jim, I won. That really is only fair since he
had the larger bedroom on Deanery street. (By the way, did you see in
one of the late November or early December issues of Time a mention of
the Deanery? It said something like: "From the politely raffish Deanery
to the Grosvenor Hotel, there was moaning at the bars last week as the
United States Army cut officers' per diems.")

Christmas still continues. I got your father's razor today. Honey, you
shouldn't have done that. What is he shaving with? It was a real blessing,

though, to get back on the Schick standard. Thanks so much, both to you and Petty. Incidentally, I have a gift to bring back to him when that day comes. It is a real Commando knife, lovely for slitting throats, with massive grip, dagger point, both sides sharpened to razor thickness, and perfectly balanced for throwing or jabbing. It has its own scabbard, too, with slots through which a belt will fasten. It was given me by old Tom Beasley, the octogenarian sword maker, who forged the Stalingrad sword.

Thank everyone for the lovely gifts again. I'm carrying that knitwear around in my pocket to amuse my haughty friends, but if it turns any colder I expect to start wearing it. I have put the picture of you with the bow in your hair holding Judy into the frame Betty and Allan sent because I like it better that the one in cap and gown. I worship you. Forever, Walter

---

THE INVASION WAS a preoccupation difficult to escape. Even the gift of a Boy Scout knife became an occasion for Cronkite to look forward to his time "in the field," i.e., covering the ground war in Europe, "where if all goes well, we will all be before long."

Hollywood director Preston Sturges's screwball comedy *The Miracle of Morgan's Creek* was both popular and controversial. Its plot centers on a small-town girl who, having had too much to drink at a farewell party for departing soldiers, marries and becomes impregnated by one of them—and can't quite recall his name. Racy stuff for 1944, as Cronkite's comment in his January 10, 1944, letter suggested.

Monday, January 10, 1944

Mein Leibling,

It now looks as if my chances of getting your birthday gift to you by the twenty-fifth are practically shot. I figured that if I was able to get it

today, what with the improved mail service, I might still have a chance
of presenting it to you (with the help of the Army postal service) on
time. But I have been stalled off again, and now it seems that I might
have to suffer another week's delay . . .

Christmas might come to some folks but once a year, but to
Cronkite it is beginning to look like a year-round proposition. Today
the civilian box with Molo, Betty and Allan, and the Manrings' pres-
ents arrived. The chess set from Molo is a little darb and I'm looking
forward to inveigling [Jim] McGlincy into a game . . . And tell Molo
thanks also for the Nestles chocolate which is the most appreciated
and handiest single food item. I'm munching one of Betty and Allan's
jumbo Hershey bars right now. No testimonial is needed there. Thanks
to you, honey, for the Scout knife which, as you know, I did need and
want very badly. I could never face the other boys on the hikes unless
I had one. Kidding aside, such a knife is a <u>must</u> in the field, where, if
all goes well, we will all be before long. I appreciate the typewriter
ribbon from Betty, although, as you see, I haven't taken the hint yet
and replaced this worn one. I don't know who to thank for the socks,
which were unwrapped, but whoever is responsible is a guardian angel.
I'm sorry the box arrived too late for me to get the "thank you's" in
my earlier letters, and I hope the fact that I didn't, did not cause too
much anxiety around. The box was mailed November 19, so you can
see how much slower is the civilian mail.

After I wrote you yesterday I discovered that "Morgan's Creek"
was playing right up the street at the Metropole Theater in Victoria on
a double bill with "Best Foot Forward." It was the first non West End
cinema I had been to, and I was amazed to find that the highest-priced
seat was 4/6—ninety cents—as opposed to the 12/6—$2.30—top in
Leicester Square. I only had to queue for five or ten minutes and got a
pretty good balcony seat for 3/6—seventy cents. That's for me. I thought
"Morgan's Creek" was a screamingly funny movie, with all the Sturgess

touches, but in something of bad taste. It hardly seemed that the subject
was the laughing matter they made of it . . . More, I love you, Walter

---

BEST FOOT FORWARD, a movie musical featuring Lucille Ball, was based
on a 1941 Broadway production of the same name. Its finale is a number called "Buckle Down, Winsocki."

The German battle cruiser *Scharnhorst* had preyed on Murmansk-
bound Allied convoys from its base in Norway. It was sunk in an ambush
by the Royal Navy in Norwegian waters on December 26, 1943.

Cronkite's unexpected discovery of a decent restaurant with lobster
and steak on the menu saved an otherwise forgettable night out, as he
reported in his second letter of January 10.

January 10, 1943 [1944]

Betsy, darling:

Continuing where I left off: "Best Foot Forward," which was sup-
posed to be a pretty good film, wasn't even a good "B" picture and I
almost left in the middle but wanted to hear the "March On, Winooski"
finale—which also wasn't so hot. The Gaumont-British newsreel—
"Presenting the truth to the free peoples of the world"—was taken up
almost completely with shots of seamen telling their parts in the sinking
of the Scharnhorst. You can have no doubt that this is a seafaring nation
and that the people's first love is the sea when you watch them react to
naval news. It is now almost two weeks (or is it more?) since the Ger-
man battleship was defeated but rehashes of the news with more and
more personal experience stories each just like the last are still front
page despite the tightness of the papers, the sensational developments
on the Russian front, and the jet-plane.

It was raining when I left the theater . . . I stumbled onto "Chez Gaston's." It seemed to be a very plain, ordinary French restaurant and practically everything was, as they say here, "off"—meaning "off." The only thing on the menu that they still had in the kitchen was roast beef. I had that, and "grande hors d'oeuvres" which I assumed to be something special in the way of hors d'oeuvres, but which turned out to be the same tiny hunk of sardine, beets (quaintly referred to in this beknighted land as "beet roots") and a dab of potato salad. Needless to say, the meal wasn't so hot, but just as I was finishing who should walk in but John Parris, who covers refugee governments for us. Well, it turns out that in the basement of this restaurant is the refugee Belgian club of which I'd often heard John speak. So he took me down to this lovely, intimate little club over which Gaston presides with its tiny bar at one end, its few tables with checked cloths at the other, and its walls lined with pictures of Belgian pilots in the RAF, many of whom aren't around any more. I sat there and drooled while John had beautiful lobster neuburg—so much that he had to turn down the steak Gaston offered. Gaston made me a member, and home to bed. I love you, Walter

---

FROM THE FRONT-PAGE lead story of the *New York World-Telegram*, January 12, 1944:

AMERICANS BLAST PLANTS WEST OF BERLIN DESPITE FURY OF ENEMY RESISTANCE

By Walter Cronkite

United Press Staff Correspondent

LONDON, Jan. 12—Sixty-four American planes—59 heavy bombers and five fighters—were lost yesterday in one of the biggest sky battles of the war over Germany, in which the U.S. bomber gunners and fighter pilots shot down more than 100 Nazi interceptor planes, it was announced officially tonight . . .

More than 700 Flying Fortresses and Liberators, escorted by hundreds of Thunderbolts, Lightnings and new-type long-range fighters smashed through an all-out Nazi fighter and flak defense to attack German fighter assembly plants at Oschersleben, Halberstadt and Brunswick, west of Berlin, "with excellent results," a communiqué said . . .

This raid proved a significant harbinger of things to come. For the first time the new P-51 Mustang fighters (the "new-type long-range fighters" mentioned but unnamed in Cronkite's January 12, 1944, dispatch) rendezvoused with bombers to escort them home after a mission over Germany. Eighth Air Force bombers soon intensified their attacks on the German aviation industry, especially during "Big Week," February 20–25, 1944. These attacks were intended both to disrupt the delivery of new planes to the Luftwaffe and to lure German fighters into dogfights with the new American escort fighters. Despite the attacks, German aircraft production continued to increase until September 1944; on the other hand, the Germans were losing 2,000 planes a month in aerial combat in the spring of 1944, and those planes (and more important, their pilots) could not be replaced. Because of Luftwaffe losses that spring, the coming invasion of western Europe would not face serious challenge from the air. On D-Day, the Allies sent more than 12,000 aircraft, including over 5,000 fighters, in the skies over Normandy; the Germans mustered barely 300 planes, most of them quickly shot down. Strategic bombing of German transportation systems and oil supplies also aided the Allies' ground forces by hampering German counterattacks.

The "big air battle" that Cronkite referred to in his January 14, 1944, letter had taken place three days before, when 529 B-17s and 138 B-24s were dispatched to attack three aviation industry targets in Germany: Oschersleben, Halberstadt, and Brunswick. More than 500

German fighters rose to meet them, and more than 60 U.S. bombers were lost. "DNB" was the official Nazi German news agency, Deutsches Nachrichtenbüro.

Cronkite's use of "shhh" was meant to avoid censorship; in the context it was used, he seems to be referring to plans being laid for reporters to cover the story of the invasion.

His trouble with "kindergarten color stuff" in his German language lesson is a reference to the color blindness that led to his draft deferment back in 1941.

———

Friday, Jan. 14, 1944

My darlingest:

This is the first letter since Monday, but believe me, it has been a vicious week. The big air battle broke Tuesday and ever since then, until today, I have been constantly on the go. I handled the story here in London on the desk, directing [Collie] Small and [Doug] Werner in the field, writing their telephoned stories, and typing the whole thing together into our air lead. We hopped all over the yarn, which the Air Force public relations staff stretched into a three-day story for me by not getting out a communiqué until late Wednesday night. I was having dinner Tuesday night at Sandy's with [Ed] Beattie, Drew Middleton of New York Times, Mrs. Middleton, and Gladwin Hill, my direct competitor on AP, when the office phoned to say that German radio was claiming [censored] American planes, [censored] of them four-motored bombers, shot down. DNB normally exaggerates, but not that much, so suspecting that something was in the wind, I beat it back to the office. I called Collie and Doug, who now spend all their time on the fields, and we began wrapping the thing up. We did all right. The Ministry of Information's "impact sheet" which is radioed over here daily and shows the play various stories are getting in the New York, Washington and Chicago papers, showed our UP stories in most competitive papers. We collected five congratulatory cables from the New York officials including one from [Hugh] Baillie which said: "Congratulations all participating our terrific airwar eyewitnesser which most interesting, graphic, vivid description monthalong." Harry Ferguson, [UP] assistant general news manager, cabled: "Congratulations to Cronkite, Small, Werner on airwar eyewitness stuff. It's very fancy reporting and exclusive so far." What pleases me most is that we did our job with just half the number of staffers AP turned out on the job. As I started out to say, it took a lot of work. I was at the office Tuesday night until one a.m. Wednesday I was on the job at eight-thirty (two hours earlier than usual and didn't finish until six-thirty when I had to dash to the Savoy to meet and eat with four other air correspondents (Hill, Fred Graham of NY Times, John Dursten of NY Her-Trib, and Joe Willicombe, INS) and Colonel Bob Parham and Major George Kirksey of the shhh planning our parts of the shhh. We had violent arguments, got a little business done during which we sold Parham, a former Unipresser I once knew in Texas, a bill of goods on the communication set-up we want, and broke up about midnight after which I had a series of telephone talks with the office. I was worn out by yesterday and intended to come home and write you and get to bed early. But other things were in the wind, it turned out. I was invited to go with Beattie to a cocktail party at the MOI (Ministry of Information) to introduce a couple of new censors but I never made that either because the long-awaited announcement that the new Mustang fighter is here was released . . .

That kept me tied up in the office until seven-thirty when I went down to the Wellington in Fleet street for dinner. I went back to the office later and battled with censorship on the Mustang story, finally getting away about ten o'clock . . . I collapsed into bed and slept until nine-thirty this morning. I had breakfast (sausage and bacon, cold toast, jam and tea) and dressed leisurely, finally reaching the office about eleven. I was to take N.D. Blow, public relations officer for the Air Ministry, to lunch so I invited him to come along to Gaston's. We were having a sherry brandy at the bar there when Beattie, Middleton and Henry J. Taylor of Scripps-Howard, a visiting fireman, came down. We all teamed up and were bored by Taylor's personal experiences for a couple of hours. (By the way, the Times had an editorial page feature about him in one of the editions Betty has recently sent.) Taking him back by the Dorchester later, he said that he had broken one of the keys on his typewriter that morning, and I said, "Not the letter 'I', I hope?" Beattie almost exploded and Middleton in his dour, I-can't-be-too-tolerant way, said: "You can always spell it "Eeye" in the cable copy." The result was that Blow and I didn't get to talk business and I'll have to repeat the luncheon performance again next week.

This afternoon I crowded in my second Berlitz lesson, this time from a different teacher. They change teachers on you as often as possible so you won't learn to understand just one person's foreign language. This teacher, Frau Schultz (honest!), wasn't half the teacher Fraulein Green was, and the lesson was sort of disappointing. Also I am disturbed by the fact that I called for a lesson Monday afternoon but was told it would be impossible that day, and after Berlitz' solemn promise that I could call any morning and get a lesson that afternoon. Whereas after the first lesson I could say only "the door is green," I can now say, "the door is not green, it is blue." Now if I could just tell whether it is green or blue I would be okay. I have, of course, thrown the Berlitz system in to a spin inasmuch as they depend on this kindergarten color stuff—and I never know whether the pencil is brown or green or red. The same goes for das buch, dar schuh, dis feder, die karte, das papier.

There was air action today and I got back to the office in time to do that story. I had dinner at the Wellington again with [Jim] McGlincy and Sam [Hales]. McGlincy is working on the desk tonight, so I came home

alone where, for the first time I remembered that I had ordered dinner
for tonight. Ah, well, just five shillings down the drain.

I love you, my darling, and think of you constantly. Tell little Miss
Judy and all the family hello for me. Forever, Walter

"BETSYMAS EVE" WAS the day before Betsy Cronkite's birthday. She
turned 28 years old in 1944.

Col. Leslie Arnold was part of a team of pilots from the U.S. Army
Air Service who in 1924 flew three planes around the world in the first
aerial circumnavigation of the globe. It took them nearly six months to
complete the journey.

Monday, January 24, 1944

My precious Betsy,

Here it is Betsymas Eve and we are still apart and I am very lonely and
unhappy. How much I would like to be with you on your birthday—as
well as the other 364 days of every year. Maybe we could go to Keen's for
a chop, and then see a show, and because it is your birthday, we would
make it a play instead of a musical (although I might put up a momentary
argument for "Oklahoma.") And if we weren't in too much of a hurry to
get home to let Little Dog in on the celebration, we could stop in Louis
and Armand's for a drink. On second thought, let's make it "Allen's" just
for old time's sake? I'd rather do that than have the party the Moorheads
suggested. I'd like to be alone, just with you. Would that be all right?

Honey, I was terribly delayed in getting your birthday present, but,
as will be apparent when I can explain it to you more fully, it wasn't
my fault. I mailed it today, air mail, and it should be along a week or so
after this letter.

Today I spent most of the hours out on an airdrome to which I went shortly after dawn intending to make a quick, one-day trip to Northern Ireland for a story. But the pilot said that, even if we succeeded getting into the Irish 'drome, there wouldn't be a chance of getting off again to return here tonight, and I had to be back for an RAF sortie tomorrow. So I didn't go. Instead I picked up a couple of small stories at the airfield chatting with a Colonel [Leslie] Arnold, one of the 1924 round-the-world fliers and, more recently, assistant to Captain Eddie Rickenbacker in Eastern Airlines. There was a fellow named Oster there too, who used to be with Delta Airlines in Dallas and knows a lot of airplane people I know, including Beattie. He informed me that Jim Shelby, who I knew when he was Fort Worth passenger agent for Braniff, is now in this theater in charge of Atlantic ferry service priorities. He might come in very handy if I should get a chance for a quick-trip home (something for which I pray without much hope) and I intend to look him up later this week. Also out there is Randolph Dyer, Charles' youngest brother, who has risen from an enlisted aerial gunner in the Pacific to a first lieutenancy over here, where he is a technical inspector. He said today that he had been accepted for pilot training and hoped to be returning to the States for it within a couple of months. Ah, youth! . . . I adore you, you know. Walter

———

SOME OF CRONKITE'S letters to Betsy in the spring of 1944 had an apologetic tone, as if he felt guilty for their long separation. Without Betsy's letters, it is impossible to tell whether he was merely imagining a possible estrangement or responding to a genuine dissatisfaction she was feeling with their situation. In any case, he reassured Betsy in his letter of January 23, 1944, that despite 13 months' absence, she need not fear any waning of his feelings for her.

In a command shake-up at the start of the year, Gen. Carl A. Spaatz was appointed overall commander of the U.S. Army Air Force in Europe,

Gen. Ira C. Eaker (in an implicit demotion) was shifted from command of the Eighth Air Force in England to command of the Mediterranean Allied Air Forces, and Gen. Jimmy Doolittle, famed commander of the 1942 "30 Seconds Over Tokyo" raid on the Japanese capital, took over command of the Eighth Air Force.

Cronkite's letter was written the day after American and British soldiers landed at the port of Anzio, just south of Rome. But the Germans were able to block the Allied advance, leaving the Anzio beachhead stranded and under heavy artillery fire. Not until late May were the Allied armies able to break out from Anzio.

———

Monday [Sunday], Jan. 23, 1944

My darlingest wife:

My good intentions to keep up a daily diary have sort of folded under the usual impact of time. But I'm continuing to try, honey, and you must know that you are constantly in my thoughts whether or not I can remind you of it every day. We have been apart nearly fifty-eight weeks—more than a year—but mere separation cannot shake the solid foundation we built in the happier years before Hoboken. There still is no sensation, no temporary joy, no observation that I do not wish you could but share with me. The sensations, the joys, the observations just don't seem to jell without you. Betsy, I want you so, and I miss you so, and I'm disturbed because I read into your letters a fear that perhaps you still aren't the most important thing in the world to me. You are, sweetheart, and you always will be. If I can't convince you by letter, I shall when we are together again. I know my letter-writing doesn't stack up with what it should be—or with what I want it to be. It probably doesn't come near equaling the flow from some soldiers to the wives they couldn't possibly love half as much as I love you. But whereas they have dozens of idle hours, I have none. I write to you every opportunity

I get—opportunities which mostly I have to manufacture out of already
crowded hours. Because I want so to feel closer to you, and I do feel closer
when I am writing to you, I'd rather pound out these letters than do any-
thing else, but that isn't very practical, is it? And even if the most far-fetched
situation existed, even if I didn't want to write to you, I would because
I want you to be happy, as happy as you can under the circumstances. I
know how impossible it would be for me to go on without your letters,
how the occasional week that goes by between letters is almost unbearable.
I wouldn't ever purposefully or even willfully let you suffer like that, too,
honey. I adore you. I'll always adore you. Please know that, darling . . .

*   Forever and ever, Walter*

CRONKITE'S COMMENT ABOUT "'old' pals" among fliers of the Eighth
Air Force demonstrates once again the strain he felt in seeing so many
young acquaintances turn up on mission casualty lists.

Roy Roussel was city editor of the *Houston Press* in the 1930s when
Cronkite was starting out there as a reporter.

The B-26 Marauder was a twin-engine medium bomber used on
shorter-range and lower-altitude bombing missions than the more
famous B-17s and B-24s. Most of the Marauders in England were
assigned to the Ninth Air Force, the unit charged with providing tacti-
cal air support for the upcoming invasion.

"Forts and Libs" refers to B-17 Flying Fortresses and B-24 Liberators.

Thursday, February 3, 1944

Darlingest Betsy: I love you, honey.

*   You saved my life today. After a long train trip from up-country, I*
got to London tired and discouraged and stopped by the Army Public

*Relations office on my way from the station to see if I had any mail.
And there was the picture of you in the new suit. The suit certainly looks
stunning, and the hat, too. I do hope you like them. I didn't think the
picture was particularly good of you, but I liked it because you are so
cute, and it showed you haven't changed. You are still like a little kid
in the barber chair. When that nasty man points his camera at you, you
set your mouth and stick out your jaw. There's certainly no ham in you,
honey, and I say, "Thank God, we've got enough in this family."*

*Speaking of ham, I'm sending along a picture of Jim [McGlincy]
and me taken by the same kind but stupid Army photographer who
took the lousy photo I belatedly sent for your birthday.*

*I had a pretty good trip this week, getting several pretty good
stories and visiting a lot of old Air Force buddies I haven't seen in
several months. (They become "old" pals after you've known them
a few weeks in this stepped-up existence where life is so cheap and
sometimes so short.) Monday night I stayed with Roy Roussel, the
old Houston Press managing editor, who now is a major and in a very
responsible job. Tuesday night I was with Clayton Smith, a fortyish
Houston oil man who I met over here and who is PRO [public relations officer] for one of the Marauder groups. He also is a major, but a
great guy despite that. He's a typical oil field lease buyer—rough-hewn
but polished smooth by years of fast-talking. He's loved by every man
on the base because within a week after they had hit England he had
located supplies of liquor, eggs, hotel rooms, and nice girls for Saturday night officer's club dances—commodities that long-established
bases had done without and for which they were still wangling after
months over here. Wednesday Colonel Wilson Week (25) and Lieut.
Col. Bill Byers (24) flew me in a Marauder up to another area where I
had to go and which would have been devilishly hard to reach by train
without their help. We got tangled up in some nasty weather and had
to get on top of a solid overcast. When we got up there we ran smack*

into scores of Forts and Libs forming up for a mission. Of course I have flown over clouds before, but never above solid overcast that was without a single hole, and never when on that overcast like on an ocean of white floated a convoy of hundreds of great four-motored ships, as far as the eye could see. It really was a thrill . . . I love you and little Miss Judy. Walter

———

WESTERN UNION

CABLE=LONDON VIA COMMERCIAL FEB 10

BETSY CRONKITE

3920 AGNES KANSASCITYMO=

MY EYES ARE RED MY HEART IS BLUE LETS GET TOGETHER CAUSE I'M MISSING YOU STOP YOULL ALWAYS BE MY VALEN-TINE DARLING = WALTER CRONKITE

On February 8, 1944, Cronkite flew in a B-26 Martin Marauder named the *U.S.O.* from the 323rd Bomb Group's 454th Bomb Squadron, piloted by 1st Lt. Jack W. Nye. Fifty-three B-24s hit the V-1 site at Sira-court, France, that day, and 57 bombed the site at Watten, France. It's not clear which mission Cronkite accompanied. He described the attack as being unexciting, and none of the aircraft were lost. But the mission was not without risk; 41 of the attacking planes were damaged by flak, and ten airmen were wounded. Despite continued attacks that spring on "German secret rocket-gun emplacements," in mid-June the Germans unleashed the V-1 flying bomb, or buzz bomb, attacks on London. Unlike the Wilhelmshaven raid a year before, Cronkite's account of his second combat flight did not create much of a stir among American newspaper readers.

From page 2 of the *Berkshire Evening Eagle* of Pittsfield, Massachu-setts, February 10, 1944:

SECRET NAZI COAST DEFENSES SEEN BY AIR REPORTER

Cronkite, First War Correspondent to Fly Over "Invasion Coast,"
Tells of Memorable Flight

By Walter Cronkite

United Press War Correspondent

MARAUDER MEDIUM BOMBER BASE, England (UP)—I saw
the secret German military installations studding the Pas de Calais
coastal strip of France today, the defenses on which the Allies have
heaped 10,000 tons of bombs in the past two months.

An hour and a half ago I was over France with 1000 other young
Americans. While they flew, navigated, bombed and watched the sky
for enemy fighters, I stared through binoculars while another 200 tons
of explosives rocked the camouflaged acres below.

Censorship forbids describing what I saw down there during my
flight, the first by a war correspondent over the forbidding strip of coast
about which secrecy and rumor have cast a fascinating air of mystery.

Neutral sources have insisted that the installations are long range
rocket gun emplacements—an assertion which tight-lipped military
authorities have neither confirmed nor denied . . .

CRONKITE'S DISPATCH CHRONICLING the February 10, 1944, mission
against factories in Brunswick, Germany, drew more notice, as he mentioned in his letter two days later. A total of 141 B-17s flew on the mission, and 29 were lost.

Earl Johnson was the United Press New York bureau manager.

The 1943 film *Phantom of the Opera* features Nelson Eddy, Susanna
Foster, and Claude Rains (the phantom). Rains is better remembered for
his role as Captain Renault in *Casablanca* (1942), another film Cronkite
saw in London.

The reference to "hyped up dramatized shows" was to the weekly
syndicated 15-minute radio program *Soldiers of the Press,* which

featured a Cronkite dispatch in May 1943. In contrast to the actor-voiced *Soldiers of the Press* broadcasts, Cronkite occasionally spoke himself on CBS radio broadcasts.

———

Saturday, Feb. 12, '44

My darlingest Betsy:

...This has been a pretty busy week. Maybe you have heard by now, but Wednesday I made another operational flight. I went with the Marauders (twin-engined bombers) to France, to the Pas de Calais area where we announce only that we are hitting "special military targets" but neutral sources insist are German secret rocket-gun emplacements. The trip was about as exciting as a windy day in a Piper Cub. We got no fighter attacks what with our Spitfire escort, and only a couple of score bursts of flak which, except for one or two bursts, weren't even close enough to be exciting. Censorship permitted me to say only a little more than I have told you here, so they sort of played hob with my story. It got front-page play here in the Daily Herald, Daily Sketch and News-Chronicle and I see that a couple of papers at home used it. New York was not exactly happy about the story in that [Earl J.] Johnson and [Virgil] Pinkley forgot that they had authorized the flight two months ago and they thought that I had taken it without their approval. (I think that secretly they probably admired the initiative. At any rate, I hope so.) Thursday [Doug] Werner, [Collie] Small and I made a big splurge, however, by swarming all over the day's big air battle over Brunswick. Werner and Small were out at the bases, and I did the rewrite job at this end. The result was a couple of congratulation cables, one from Harry Ferguson saying our story was sweeping the country and one client had reported we "covered ourselves with glory." Pinkley said that "such reporting such writing carrying United Press banner high and higher." Well, that's corny, but it's nice to hear anyway. Yesterday I

finally took it a little easier. I wrote the air story again, although it wasn't as sensational as Thursday's, and knocked off early to see "Phantom of the Opera" which I thought stank. It just didn't jell. There was the "Figaro and Cleo" Disney short which I had read of but never seen, and it was worth the price of admission. Also helping to break the boredom of the movie was this: Right in the middle of the scene where the prima donna is being examined by the doctors in her dressing room, a slide flashes on the screen at the Odeon asking for a doctor in the house . . .

A few minutes later another slide came on the screen which said almost too calmly: "An air raid warning has been sounded. The performance will continue." Five minutes later, after only a few persons had left the crowded theater, the gun barrage got so loud it almost drowned out the picture, but it only lasted for a moment. The warning was still on but apparently there was nothing overhead when I left the show . . . Tuesday morning I had to get up early to get out to an air headquarters to make arrangements for the flight the next day, and Wednesday we were aroused at five-thirty for the briefing and then the flight.

Speaking of the flight, the biggest disappointment was the fact that Ed Murrow wanted me on CBS but New York was unable to clear the time for the broadcast. There is still just some vague hope that I might get on to the Report to the Nation broadcast Tuesday night, but since Ed said he would let me know by the end of this week, and I haven't heard anything, I suppose that is off, too. Incidentally, I've been meaning to ask you this for a long time: How about explaining to my mother that when her friends keep telling her they heard me on the radio they are just cockeyed. Every time I've been on I've been able to let you folks know in advance. That is the main reason I like to go on, is to feel a little closer to you. These other things are either commentators quoting me (which is even standard procedure on the UP radio wire) or one of those hyped up dramatized shows . . .

Judy THE COCKER SPANIEL was clearly the surrogate child in the early Cronkite marriage. Now Cronkite began to think about the real thing, as he confessed in his letter of February 15, 1944.

The Berlitz lessons did not pan out; Cronkite would have to cover the invasion with a command of no language beyond his mother tongue.

———

Tuesday, February 15, 1944

My darlingest Betsy: Give my love to the family. I love you.

You are still my Valentine, aren't you? . . . I sent your Valentine cable four days early and I do hope it arrived in time. Darling, remember the Valentine's Day when we sort of formally engaged ourselves and I gave you the little jade ring under circumstances that you didn't think were nearly romantic enough? And how we quarreled about it, and how old dumb, juvenile me didn't get the pitch at all? We did have fun, didn't we? We have so many wonderful memories—and what is more important, so much more fun to look forward to. This separation is awful hard to take, but there is still the Pollyana outlook; tiz: the future we're building. I have officers tell me: "What are you bitching about? You don't have any children. You'll have years and years yet with your wife but I've been away from home two and a half years and I'm missing most of the few years I'll ever get to spend before my children are grown up and move out on me." And when they tell me that I get mad, because I think of little Judy and how she is getting older and how it is impossible for me to tell them that I feel pretty strongly about that, too. And children is another thing I think a lot about. Sometimes I'm crushed when I think about our not having made any start on a family. And other times I think it is probably for the best and how perhaps it would delay indefinitely your coming to me . . .

My great start at even further solidifying our future with a good firm knowledge of a foreign language (this time it was German) seems to have petered out. I haven't cracked my German book in a week, and haven't had another lesson from Berlitz in that long. I just can't find the time, darling. Every waking minute of every day is taken up with business. I know that sounds fantastic but it is gospel. I admit a lot of the time is spent over bars and in restaurants—but nine-tenths of the business in this town is transacted there. Remember how Gene Gillette and the others used to talk about Washington and the impossibility of even spending an evening at home if you were to keep up with your sources? Well, it is the same here. Half the evenings I work at the office until nearly midnight writing the air stories, so on the other half when I'm "free" I've got to take colonels and captains and civil servants from the Air Ministry and other sources to dinner, or I'm actually on an air base where if I'm to spend the time profitably I've got to use up the evening jawing with the fliers and intelligence officers and commanders. It is vicious, and you have no idea how wearing. I love you, my darling. Be mine forever, Walter

---

CRONKITE'S LETTER OF February 17, 1944, addressed the issue of their postwar future; he had no doubt by now that they would be in Europe, at least for several years.

Thursday, February 17, 1944

My precious wife:

In the last two days I've gotten a wad of mail from you. A couple of Valentines, a couple of regular letters and a couple of V-mailers. Before I forget it, let's discuss the furniture. I think the swell letter from Virgil

[Pinkley] which you quoted pretty well answers the question about our post-war future, at least for a few years to come. However, it might be smart to hold on to the stuff a few weeks longer until Virgil gets back here and I have another chance to chat with him in regard to what he might have learned in New York. I am almost certain that the status is going to be quo—that is, that we are going to be destined for an European job, and that it will be good enough that we will want to accept it. Under those circumstances we certainly won't want to hold on to the furniture. To let it mold in storage while we pay keep on it would be ridiculous. I also admit, though, that I, too, am a sissy about letting it go. I talk a good fight about getting rid of all encumbrances—but when it comes down to actually disposing of our first household belongings and the things we so tenderly picked out and paid so diligently on at David-sons and Duff and Repp's—well, then it begins to hurt, even if it is the smart economic move . . . All of this, though, I say is subject to further discussion after Virgil returns, which will be shortly . . .

About that letter from Virgil: Them are awfully kind words, but take them with a grain of salt. Virgil is slightly on the effusive side. I'm sure I'm in solid with him, and I think my work probably is satisfactory, but as far as any editors crying for my copy or considering me the greatest living authority on the American air force in England—nuts! And, beside if I were so darned brilliant I'd be efficient enough to be able to do the UP job and still find time to write the hundred articles and the two or three books which are whirling through my head but are slowly becoming lost forever in the impenetrable forest of time. The book that Jim [McGlincy] and I half finished is molding in the drawer for lack of time to finish it. There is one incontrovertible fact: Not a single correspondent has written a book while actively engaged in covering his beat. Everyone has take time out—and I haven't managed that yet.

Give my love to the family. Yours always, Walter

ON THE NIGHT of February 19, 1944, the Luftwaffe launched the heaviest air raid against London since 1941. More attacks followed over the next few nights. Cronkite referred to a colleague whose house was destroyed by an "ME": the reference was probably to a German fighter-bomber, a Messerschmitt or ME 110.

Monday, February 21, 1944

My darlingest:

Some fun! We all had a little taste Friday night and again last night of what London went through in the blitz and an even smaller taste of what Berlin must be going through now. And, believe you me, a taste is enough. I have no hankering for a full size meal of that! Friday night I had dinner with Roy Roussel at the Grosvenor House and was with him in his room there when the alert sounded and the guns started going. It sounded like just another noisy barrage like the dozens we have had recently until it was all over and I got ready to leave. Then I saw the dozen glows in the sky where the German raiders had planted their incendiaries. I took a cab to one of the areas where a couple of blocks of flats were burning. I asked a girl fire guard there if anyone was hurt and she said that most of the flats were unoccupied but that three old women had been evacuated from one and at that moment were in the parlor of a flat across the street. I went over to have a look in on them. Here were these three old gals, all of whom looked to be in their nineties, with a few pitiable possessions they had saved stacked around them. There was no light in the parlor. It was lit only by the reflection of the three old ladies' burning flat across the street. But the three old ladies were huddled around a quart of Irish whiskey. And when I looked in one was just wiping her lips, laughing uproariously, and cackling: "Gol blimey, if it ain't just like the good old days." I guess that is the blitz spirit we read about. And the firemen here. I didn't hear them

shout a single order. They went about the work with more calm, and about
as fast, as a bunch of WPA workers digging a sewer. And this with magne-
sium incendiaries still burning in the streets beside them. Last night's was
another little daisy. I was busy writing about the American raid on Ger-
many so didn't get to the top of the News of the World Building during the
raid, but later I got up there and could see the fires burning in several sec-
tions of the city, illuminating the skyline like a full moon. Jim [McGlincy]
and I went to one of the fires in an industrial section but it was no fun
with the sparks, whipped by a high wind, flying down the narrow streets
like Fourth of July sparklers. We were so busy dusting them off our clothes
and snatching them with gloved hands from our hats that we didn't get
to see much of the fire. And it was bitterly cold as it has been here the last
week or so. One of our boys has been bombed out and others have had
narrow squeezes. Jim and I have had a couple of high explosives and a few
incendiaries within a few block radius of us, but Johnny Parris' building is
the only one standing in his block after last night's affair and there aren't
any windows in his flat. Herb Radzick, a Polish fellow who files one of our
European wires, had an ME in his back yard that left him only one room
of his house. So, all in all, it is getting more interesting . . .

CRONKITE'S LETTER OF February 25, 1944, came at the end of "Big Week," during which the Eighth Air Force flew more than 3,000 sorties against German aviation industry targets. American bomber losses were high but sustainable. German fighter losses were high and unsustainable.

Between January and April 1944 the Germans ratcheted up their bombing raids on London and southeast England in what was sometimes described as the "Little Blitz" or "Baby Blitz." In the third week in February, the days leading up to Cronkite's letter, bombs damaged the Treasury, Admiralty, War Office, Scottish Office, and the prime minister's residence at 10 Downing Street.

A "Bofors" is an antiaircraft gun.

———

Friday, Feb. 25, 1944

My darlingest wife:

I finally collapsed today after the worst week I have ever put in. The greatest week of the air offensive has meant never less than a twelve hour day for me and most of the time a fourteen to sixteen hour pull. I've been getting into the office between ten a.m. and noon and not leaving until two or three the next morning. That way I miss breakfast here at the house and the busiest part of the evening is right at dinner time, so I miss dinner too. I get a good lunch (as good as you can get around here these days) but only have a couple of hot meat pies and bottle of beer for dinner and eating it off the desk while I'm hopping up to the phone booth to take some more information and slipping back to the typewriter to write it. The last good meal I had was noon yesterday when [Ed] Beattie and I took a guy named Satterwhite from the Embassy to lunch. Last night was another fierce one on the desk from which I got away about two-thirty. I didn't get up until noon today and by the time I bathed, shaved and dressed it was almost two o'clock. So I missed lunch, too. And when you miss a meal right at feeding time in this country you are out of luck. No drug stores exist where you can slip in for a roasted cheese sandwich and malted milk. You just starve until the next meal hour. A pub (El Vino's) was open in Fleet street though and I thought perhaps a couple of glasses of wine might give me a little strength until dinner time. But they bounced back in a hurry and I got so damned sick at the office I had to come home. Now it is three hours later, I've had dinner here at the flat, and I feel fine. I'm just debating going back to the office, since the air war still continues tonight, but probably will decide to stay home and direct it as best I can from here by telephone.

For the first time I really feel the limitations of censorship. I would like to tell you so much about the air raids that I'm told is censorable—stuff like where the bombs fell and the damage that was done. Some of the nights this week I have been too busy writing about our raids on them to even worry about the raids here, but other nights at the office I have been able to take a few minutes to don my helmet and go up to our rooftop observation post from which you can see all over London. Fourth of July celebrations will really be picnics after this. Hundreds of searchlights, cones of light occasionally catching a twisting, diving plane, great chandelier flares that light up whole sections of the city, sticks of incendiaries burning their way down through the sky, small balls of red fire where Bofors gunners are trying to shoot out the flares, tiny twinkling stars that actually are huge bursts of flak five miles high, and the rocket guns that burst in a barrage you expect to cover the whole sky before it is through. And the terrific noise. Then George Washington Crossing the Delaware in Six Beautiful Colors and you get to go home for another year. I adore you, my darling. Don't forget to love me too, and remind me to Judy. Forever, Walter

---

WITH "BIG WEEK" OVER, Cronkite enjoyed a day of rest. "Manning Coles" was the pseudonym for the writing team Adelaide Manning and Cyril Coles, who, beginning in 1940, turned out a series of novels about the adventures of a fictional British spy named Thomas Elphinstone Hambledon.

Sunday, Feb. 27, 1944

My darlingest wife:

This is a truly lovely Sunday. It is nice and cold and wet and gloomy outside, there is no air war for me to worry about, I have no where to go and nothing to do, there are no air force sources in town I have to have a drink with, and I'm sitting here at home reading the Sunday papers and a good book. It is now four o'clock in the afternoon and I haven't even splashed any water on my face. Now if I just had a red-haired wife and a red-headed dog to sit here with me, I'd be perfectly content. This is the first Sunday—the first day, for that matter—I have had off in more than three weeks and, after the particularly grueling last six days of never less than fourteen hours a day, it is most welcome. It is nice, too, to be able to sit and digest the papers without having to glance through hurriedly to see if you have missed anything and then hurry on to something else. The book I am reading is a good one, too. It is by the mystery author on to which Herman Allen sicked us and whom we liked so much—Manning Coles. Remember "Drink to Yesterday" and "Toast to tomorrow" and how we tried unsuccessfully to get the third in the trilogy? Well, this is the fourth, it says here on the fly-leaf entitled "Without Lawful Authority" and in which our old friend, Tommy Hambledon, of the Secret Service appears again, although this time in a minor role. It isn't as good as the other books and really classifies as just another thriller. If you want it, though, and can't get it there let me know and I'll send it along. Incidentally, along that line, I would like any good correspondents' books you run across. Frequently they are printed over here, too, but when they are the book shops seem to sell out their limited quota in a terrible hurry. I'd like particularly Bob Casey's "You Meet Such Interesting People" and [Vincent] Sheean's "Between the Thunder and the Sun." Also if there any good books kicking around about Austria. I think you probably could send them to me through the APO.

I was awfully sorry, honey, to hear about your flu. I hope you are really over it now without your bumbling husband there to irritate you with his helplessness. I do wish, though, that you would let me know immediately when you are ill rather than holding off until you are well again . . .

I love you, Walter

From the *New York World-Telegram*, March 4, 1944:

ATTACK SUCCEEDS THROUGH CLOUD BANK 30,000 FEET HIGH
By Walter Cronkite
United Press Staff Correspondent

    LONDON. March 4—American Flying Fortresses bombed Berlin by daylight today in the first attack of the war on the German capital by United States bombers . . .

After "Big Week" the Eighth Air Force shifted its attention to Berlin, once again seeking to lure the Luftwaffe into an aerial war of attrition.

    From the front-page lead story of the *New York World-Telegram*, March 9, 1944:

YANKS RANGE OVER CAPITAL AT WILL, STOKE VAST FIRES STARTED 24 HOURS EARLIER
By Walter Cronkite
United Press War Correspondent

    LONDON, March 9.—Powerful American bomber fleets skimmed the top of a four mile-high cloud layer over Europe today, converged on Berlin from many directions, and without a challenge by the German air force stoked the great fires they had started in the Nazi capital 24 hours earlier . . .

From the front page of the *New York World-Telegram*, March 13, 1944:

U.S. STRIVES TO FORCE NAZIS TO FIGHT IN AIR
By Walter Cronkite
United Press War Correspondent

    LONDON, March 13.—Flying Fortresses bombed northern France today without challenge by the German air force and a high official source said Lt. General Carl A. Spaatz might start announcing his targets in advance as a challenge to the Nazis to come up and fight . . .

A clue to the content of Betsy's letters to Cronkite that spring can be found in his reply of March 7, 1944, as he sympathizes with her being "down in the dumps."

Charles "Bill" Higginbotham was a United Press correspondent in London.

The mistaken attribution of several of Cronkite's dispatches to UP colleague Phil Ault went on for several weeks before he was able to straighten the matter out. As Cronkite commented to Betsy, "UP pays half your salary in by-lines," which was to say, since United Press was notoriously stingy in its pay scale, UP writers expected to see their names displayed on their dispatches as compensation.

———

Tuesday, March 7, 1944

My darlingest wife:

I got your February 21 letter today. You wrote it when you were down in the dumps. I'm so sorry, honey. But I wonder if maybe we are getting into a new stage of long-distance telepathy and pathetic reactions with the help of V-mail? Because the last twenty-four hours have been among my worst over here, and as a result I was pretty low myself when I got your letter. Of course, there is always that constant gnawing of separation from you and Judy but added to that this time was office problems. I won't bore you with all the details but yesterday on the biggest single day of the air war—our first mass attack on Berlin—everything I touched seemed to simply fall apart. To complicate all my other problems, we had some new boy, even more stupid than the rest and that is reaching a new moronic low, on the switchboard. After Doug Werner and Collie Small

at the bomber bases and Bill Higginbotham at a fighter base finally man-
aged to get priority calls through to the office where we were panting to
hear from them, this lout cut me off time and again. To top even that,
our wireless circuit to New York went out midway in the evening but the
New York receiving post neglected to tell us for three hours and all of that
air copy was delayed by that much. Besides that I get what I, but no one
else, thought was a pretty snotty message from Boyd Lewis, our acting
foreign editor in New York, and I fired an equally snotty one back. I'd
gone in at eight in the morning and finally got home about eleven-thirty
feeling pretty sick about the whole thing. Well, it turns out today that AP
must really have been lousy on the story because we get at least an equal
break with them. Our story was played in the Monday afternoon World-
Telegram and in the morning Daily News in New York, which is a pretty
good barometer of play countrywide. But there arose another thorn off
that too-big bush to prick me. Phil Ault was signed by the New York desk
to the afternoon story. He had nothing to do with it. The afternoon story
was completely my work. The morning story, to which I was signed, was
the joint work of Werner, Small, Higginbotham and Cronkite. I really hit
the ceiling then. Maybe I am getting to be a prima donna but, after all,
UP pays half your salary in by-lines and I want a full paycheck when I'm
turning in twelve to as many as sixteen hours a day.

Well, now I feel better that I have cried on your shoulder. I guess that
did a lot of good in snapping you back. Crying on yours and the censor's
shoulders, that is. I hear they are really fine-tooth-combing our letters
these days. I suppose it is a good idea but the thought annoys me that the
order for such searching probably went out from some gleeful general
who has always thought newspapermen were a bunch of spies unless they
put his name in the paper. Of course, while the newsmen took his story he
shouted that he didn't want any publicity—then got up two hours early to
see the morning papers.

ROBIN DUFF OF the BBC, Cronkite's new flatmate, won fame in 1940 for his coverage of the Blitz.

———

Wednesday, March 8, 1944

Darlingest Betsy:

The other day I mailed you an air mail letter with some pictures and clippings enclosed . . . I thought of a funny thing when I was mailing those pictures. Remember that somewhat dark winter of 1936–37 when everything seemed to be all haywire—and in February, when things were darkest, I said I was going down to Cairo (Illinois) and free-lance cover the Mississippi flood—and you and Betty derided me and said I wouldn't have the nerve? Well, it is funny how "little" things, say the bloodiest war in history, for instance, bring out the fact that some guys can overcome fear to go after a story, or after Freedom. I was thinking about a rather screwball bombardier, a little older than most, whose father runs a newspaper in Indiana. He was a very nervous type and talked a blue streak trying to cover up what everybody, even on his own base, thought was cowardice. Well, that boy is now in a hospital here without ears, without a nose without a face, virtually blind, his hands gone and his toes missing. He is that way because, although he knew that to expose yourself for long to the fifty below zero temperatures at 26,000 feet is virtual suicide, he stayed over his bombsight until his bombs were away despite the twenty millimeter shell that took the Plexiglas nose away.

But how did I get into that? There are more immediate problems. Such as the reason why I'm writing this hunched over my trunk where my typewriter precariously rests. It seems that a week or so ago—it is beginning to seem like a year—Robin Duff of British Broadcasting Corporation got bombed out of his flat. Good old big-hearted McGlincy, extending the helping hand, says "come live with us until you get squared away." Robin, I

gather, likes it here although he is sleeping on the divan in the living room.
At least he has made no effort to move. Tonight he is using the desk for his
typing. Actually he is a pretty nice sort of bloke. It is just that McGlincy
and I are getting a little tired of patting each other on the back and saying:
"Boy, that's doing your part. We all have to stick together in these crises—
extend the helping hand, keep the old chin up, white tie, tails, what be."
The gag is wearing out much faster, to be honest, than Robin's welcome . . .

———

CRONKITE WAS PUTTING in long hours as the furious aerial assault on
Germany continued unabated through March. The promise of post-
war professional advancement was partial compensation, as his next
letter suggests.

———

Sunday, March 19, 1944

My darlingest wife:

We have been having some nice weather in recent days, forerunners
of Spring which is going to be another unbearable period without you
and little Judy to go picnicking and golfing and bicycling and, later,
swimming. It is now three-thirty in the afternoon and the sun has been
out from behind the morning clouds for a couple of hours. The tempera-
ture is still in the overcoat bracket but it is a help to see the sun again.
It shines rarely enough in this country and during the winter with the
industrial haze hanging over this city it seldom makes an appearance . . .
[Virgil] Pinkley returned Friday [blacked out] still rather ill with a
chest trouble resembling pleurisy that he contracted in New York "from
dashing in and out of those sweltering eighty-degree office buildings."
. . . Pinkley gave forth as follows: (1) He was very sorry that he missed
you. He described his antics while searching for a beautiful red, copper,

or auburn head at both exit gates until the crowd thinned to only a few among which he saw no one resembling what he thought you should look like. He then went to Western Union to dispatch a telegram to his wife, wandered to the newsstand to buy some postcards, and departed. (2) He showed me your letter to him. (3) He said New York was highly pleased with my work, that I was slated for one of the three, four, or five-man bureaus as bureau chief with some hope that in two or three years I would be moving into top job in one of the three main-line bureaus— Paris, Berlin or London. It all listens good—but we shall see.

I'm absolutely worn out with working so hard. I've been missing a lot of meals or forcing down some horrible brown bread and Spam sandwich in order to direct every move of the air war coverage. I'd like to be able to take a rest of a week or so but with the story getting bigger and bigger every day that is, of course, impossible. Incidentally, since I seem to be on the subject of health, I've noticed in recent letters indications that your eyes are bothering you. Honey, I do wish you would see about them and get glasses if necessary. It would be better to wear them while doing close work now than have to wear them all the time later. I love you. Walter

---

NEVER BEFORE IN his life (and certainly never again) would Cronkite spend as much time fretting about food and clothing as he did during the war.

Monday, March 20, 1944

My darlingest Betsy:

If I can get my jaws unstuck I'll chat with you a little while this evening. I got the quart of lovely pineapple juice, the nuts, and the toffee you mailed Feb. 2 today. I've just finished one of the boxes of nuts and am now wrapped up in the toffee—and I do mean wrapped up. Thanks so much, honey. I feel a little guilty, though, since just today I also got a letter from Molo in which she mentioned that pineapple juice costs more points than any other. Please don't use your points for me, darling. Things probably sound a lot worse over here than they really are and I get along okay. I do miss fruit juices, though, and if you have extra points left over juice is the most welcome of all items. Right now I'm pretty well stocked on haberdashery. I need suits rather badly but even if I could get the coupons or do a little black-market dealing, I wouldn't spend the money . . . Although wartime has helped alleviate the situation a little, this country like all the old world, is still a little finicky about dress and "lounge suits" as all my tweeds are called are not quite the proper thing for dinner. Which reminds me that John Parris scored a great beat today. Through careful development for more than a year, he wangled an invitation direct from King Peter of Yugoslavia to his wedding to Alexandra, and tonight when he came in to write his story he had on the whole morning suit from top hat to grey gloves and spats. He wrote a beautiful story, too. The way he has developed his refugee government sources in the two years since he grabbed hold of that run embarrasses me in the light of my superficial reporting of the air force . . . I love you and Judy. Always, Walter

---

Pulitzer Prize–winning playwright William Saroyan was serving in the U.S. Army Signal Corps when Cronkite met him in London.

Cronkite had one brief encounter with the king of England during the war. More common were encounters with Hollywood royalty, such as Clark Gable, Jimmy Stewart, Adele Astaire, and in March 1944, George Stevens. Stevens commanded the unit in which Saroyan served, and would go on to film the liberation of Dachau concentration camp. In addition to *The More the Merrier* in 1943, Stevens had directed such films as the Rogers-Astaire musical *Swing Time* in 1936, *Gunga Din*

with Cary Grant in 1939, and *Woman of the Year* with Spencer Tracy
and Katharine Hepburn in 1942.

Grace and Holy Trinity Cathedral, which Cronkite preferred to
Westminster Abbey, was the church in Kansas City where he and Betsy
were married in 1940.

———

Sunday, March 26, 1944

My darlingest wife:

*It is now noon and, so far, this is a perfect day on all scores except the
most important which is, of course, that you are not with me. There isn't
a cloud in the sky and the sun is bright enough to penetrate the slight
haze that always hangs over this city. Apparently there is no action up
country that is going to call me into the office. I have no other obligations
for the day. All in all, it looks as if I'm going to get a day to myself. I got
up early—about eight-thirty—and shaved and dressed in my blue Bonds
suit just like I had something to do. The elevator man who usually forgets
this morning remembered the papers. I read them until breakfast—oh,
yes, there was a hitch there. The stupid little Charlie, a midget who is one
of the characters peopling this place, said there was a real, honest egg for
breakfast. But when the meal came, there was only a fatty slab of what
they call bacon. It seems Charlie was wrong. Ah, well. Then I walked the
few blocks to Westminster Abbey in which I had never been. And now
I have just come back from the morning service there. The building, of
course, is lovely but it is so vast that the service in the nave is lost in it
and, as a result, not nearly so impressive and so honestly inspiring as that
at Grace and Holy Trinity. And the Dean's sermon today barely compared
with one of Dean Sprouse's poorer ones. Perhaps I'm judging unfairly,
because this may have been one of Westminster's lesser ones. The fact is
that all sermons fall off a little in the weeks preceding Easter. They always*

wander into the theologic and I am one who believes in a little more reli-
gion for the common man—a strictly practical application.

I'm going to finish this note, take it by the APO, have lunch at the
officers mess (it is so large now that they are calling it "Willow Run," or
alternatively, the "Spam Room"), go by the Army hospital to see Pneu-
monia [Virgil] Pinkley, then to the PX for my tobacco ration, perhaps
if I have time then to a new flat I'm considering (in an effort to live by
myself where perhaps I can get some work done), then home. I suppose
Pinkley's room will be crowded again but I hope to hell I get a chance
to talk with him alone soon because I am anxious to find out what the
chances now are of getting you over here.

Last night I had dinner at Sandy's, as I have managed to quite a bit
lately, I was alone and so was the Armenian GI who had been pointed
out to me once as William Saroyan, private, USA. So Saroyan and
Cronkite, those two famous writers, hung over the bar together discuss-
ing mostly the American educational system until Saroyan's pals headed
by George Stevens, director of "More the Merrier," showed up . . .

I love you, darlingest, and will write more tonight. Forever, Walter
Love and kisses

CRONKITE'S CAMPAIGN TO bring Betsy to London proved an emotional
roller coaster. Vague assurances of interest from higher-ups at the United
Press and the *Kansas City Star* never panned out.

Tuesday, March 28, 1944

My darlingest Betsy:
This letter is all business—the most important business we have dis-
cussed in a long time. I have started the ball rolling in a new game to get

you over here but it is going to take a lot of drive, stamina, persistence on your part, honey.

I talked to Virgil [Pinkley] Sunday afternoon. He said that, because of your newspaper and radio experience, United Press would like very much to get you here and certainly could use you. But, he added, to bring you over would raise a hue and cry from other of the London staffers whose wives also are newspaper women. He suggested, therefore, that it would be far better if you could come, say, for the Kansas City Star. Because the UP would figure on perhaps sharing you with the Star on occasion, they would see that all transportation expenses were paid—thus costing the Star nothing.

Yesterday noon I talked with Marcel Wallenstein. He is crazy about the idea. As I explained to you some time ago, Wally's principal business here is a photo agency. His Star work, although paying him well, no doubt, is strictly a sideline . . .

My suggestion to Wally was that we get the Star to send you over, expenses paid by UP or even us, if necessary, and that once here you could do work for him on a space rate basis. His answer to that was that once you got here he probably would use you full time . . .

Darling, I feel very encouraged about this whole thing. I feel that chances are fairly good that our long separation will be ended and we can start living again. In all fairness, though, I think I should warn you again that living is not too pleasant over here right now. I've gone through all the horrors of it before so there is no need to repeat them, but there is need to keep them in mind. There is chance, too, that we will have further separations even if you are here—but if you are here, the separations will not be nearly so long. What we would have, is a chance to share the same experiences and the same friends again. I feel an urgent need to close the gap that with every month widens in our interests and acquaintances.

Of course I'm going to be on the old needles and pins waiting to hear from you. Write your reactions as soon as you get this letter, honey, and cable me Roberts' reactions as soon as you see him. I'm sending along a

condensed version of this by V-mail, so make plain in your answering let-
ter that you got one or both of them, will you? ...

I worship you, Walter

———

CRONKITE DECLARED PRIVATE war on Hitler, blaming him for the long
separation from Betsy.

———

March 29, 1944

Dearest Betsy:

Doubt comes sharply on the heels of hope. I have been in rather fre-
quent discussion with Ed Beattie about the possibilities of getting you
over here and he, of course, is very sympathetic and helpful—as are all
the boys who want to get a look at this glamorous red head I describe ...

Tomorrow is our fourth anniversary. I've just sent you a cable, night
letter, saying the only thing I seem to be able to think; that the first two
years seemed to go so quickly, and the last two have dragged so horribly.
Two whole years out of our lives. It makes this war with Hitler a pretty
personal matter. I want to take out on him and all those responsible the
months that we have missed and the hundreds of days that we never
shall be able to regain. I have been terribly lonely without you, my dar-
ling. I have been busy—true. I have been on the go almost constantly.
But no amount of activity, no number of new experiences, not scores
of new acquaintances are sufficient to fill the gap left by you and Judy.
Everything I see I want you to see with me and everything I do I want
you to do with me. I don't know that in these years we would have been
able to maintain much of a home life as such, but at least we would have
been together and we could have had fun ...

The Pollyana approach still is the saving feature of the whole mess.

We at least are doing the old building act for the future—I keep telling myself. It is a better fate than that of a lot of our contemporaries . . .

I love you, my precious wife. Tell all the family and little Judy that I love them, too. Walter

———

CRONKITE'S DRAFT DEFERMENT for color blindness was suddenly thrown into question on the eve of what he called "the big story," i.e., the invasion, but he had faith that the United Press would straighten out the problem with his draft board.

———

April 9, 1944

My darlingest one:

. . . Don't worry about the draft situation. The UP here immediately got a cable off to New York, after I received yours, advising them of the situation and they answered back this morning that they are appealing. I can't tell you about it, but some behind-the-scenes machinery also is working here so that I think the possibility of my being plunged into the army, at least any time in the near future, is virtually nil and certainly no better than one to a hundred. I would hate to have to leave here right now but actually I wouldn't mind being drafted if it meant seeing you even if but briefly.

I'm getting very nervous and jittery over impending developments. Much of the way in which UP fares when the big story breaks depends on the groundwork I lay now and the way in which the boys working for me function. The responsibility is great. I love you, Walter

———

CRONKITE'S STORIES THAT spring increasingly focused on the impending Allied invasion of France.

From the front-page lead story of the *New York World-Telegram*, April 18, 1944:

2500 U.S. PLANES END LULL BY BATTERING NAZI CAPITAL AND FRENCH INVASION COAST

By Walter Cronkite

United Press War Correspondent

LONDON, April 18—United States air forces thundered back into action against Berlin for the first time in nearly a month today when some 2000 heavy bombers and fighters struck heavy blows at the Nazi capital and other targets in Germany . . .

While Lt. Gen. Carl A. Spaatz's main striking force was hammering Berlin a small formation of Liberators attacked the Pas de Calais coastal strip of France under an umbrella of Thunderbolt fighters . . .

Attacks on the Pas de Calais region served a dual function. Some hit genuine targets of interest, like the Nazi V-1 rocket launch sites. But they also served to draw the Germans' attention to the region—and away from the real invasion coast of Normandy.

The story resulting from Cronkite's ten-day trip to an unspecified location in England did not make the pages of the *New York World-Telegram*. And, "pleasant and interesting" as the trip may have been, he did not offer any clues in subsequent memoirs what he did. The stories that did run under his byline in April reported more raids on Berlin and the "invasion coast" of the Pas de Calais.

———

Monday, May 1, 1944

My darlingest Betsy:

Happy May Day, Red! Pun—just couldn't help it. Like the story about

the man who yells from the kitchen upstairs to his wife: "Honey, can I
bring you a drink?" She replies: "Oh, yes, thanks, darling. And when you
come up would you mind bringing me a couple of safety pins, too?" "Come
down and mix your own bloody drink," he answers.

I've just come back from a ten-day trip which was one of the most
pleasant and interesting on which I have been since coming to England.
I'm sure if I told about it here it would be slashed by censorship but
perhaps the World Telegram will use the principal story I got out of it
and you will get the idea. The story was moved on the wires last Tuesday
night and probably would be in the April 26 issue. At any rate, the sun
shined almost every one of the ten days. It was warm and I was out in
the open most of the time. The result is that I feel better than I have in
some months and people tell me I look better. The improved appearance
is all accounted for by a hefty sunburn which I hope to turn into a tan
by getting in some tennis should the weather remain at all good.

I got in three games of tennis week before last, before leaving on the
trip. I played twice with Ed Murray (from the office) and once with Jim
[McGlincy]. The last time I played with Ed we both seemed to be back
in top form and were really slapping the ball around. We play out at
Queen's Club, one of the once swanky, Victorian London tennis clubs
that have opened their doors to "Allied officers" for the war years. We
rent equipment out there and the full afternoon's expenses run only
a dollar and a half or so. Right now play is on the clay courts but the
grass courts will be open in mid-May. The club used to have two large
indoor tennis courts and several large squash and handball courts, but
they were burned out in one of the recent raids. The club house itself got
one incendiary through the roof but it was doused by the eighty-year-old
caretaker before much damage was done.

I got three packages and quite a batch of letters from you when I
returned today. The letters practically all were concerned with the draft
situation. Honey, I'm sorry but I can't shed much light on the situation.

After receiving your two cables I cabled New York to advise them of the situation, and telling them to keep you advised by telegraph of all steps. The only thing I have heard from them was the one cable two days after mine, which I think it would be a mistake for me to go meddling in the thing from here and I'm certain United Press is capable of doing whatever is necessary. Personally, I'm not very worried. As for your handling of the matter, I think it has been perfect. I know it must be hard on you, darling, but I trust it is all right now and you can rest assured that every step you took was exactly the right one. I'll get off another letter tomorrow. I adore you, Walter

---

THE UNRELENTING PACE of the air war continued in May 1944, as did the countdown to the invasion. Cronkite had never worked harder, but he could still get annoyed by a purloined byline, as evidenced in his letter of May 9, 1944.

Tuesday, May 9, 1944

My darlingest Betsy:

It has been more than a week since I have written and I feel very guilty. Most days I have been working my cockeyed head off from eight a.m. until nearly midnight and, on at least one occasion, beyond . . . With the air war now the biggest daily story of the world I try to get in by eight o'clock to ride it right on through from the first Air Ministry communiqué on the RAF's night bomber activity until the last American day bomber communiqué rolls in somewhere around midnight. So now, whereas I used to ride to work around ten or ten-thirty with all the decent people here, fighting my way through brief cases and umbrellas and canes to get on the Number 11 bus, I now am one of the wage slaves and hack my way through a living wall of lunch buckets and Daily Mirrors. My showing up early has finally brought to a definite showdown this matter of by-lines. Phil Ault, who has the early desk shift, has been almost habitually signed by New York to the day air story with me being signed to the nightwire story. I could not, in the past, complain too loudly about this inasmuch as Phil did handle the first story of the morning—the RAF communiqué. But now I am handling the whole thing, Phil doesn't touch it, and the last two days New York has again shown total disregard for the facts and put his name back on the yarn. I don't think I'm getting to be a prima donna or anything of the kind when I insist that I get credit for the work I am doing. As long as all the responsibility for the air coverage, and the grief when it goes wrong, rests with me, by Gad sir, but I intend to get whatever credit may accrue. Jim and I have tickets for the preview of "A Canterbury Tale" tonight but I have to go back to the office to do another air piece—a "think" piece on "what it all means"—and I don't know that I'll finish in time for the picture, which is at ten o'clock—scandalously late for this town. I love you, honey. Forever, Walter

———

"WALTER'S SHIP" WAS the U.S.S. *Arkansas,* which he had sailed on to Britain in 1942. After two years of convoy duty, the *Arkansas* was given a new mission: to provide fire support to the troops landing on Omaha Beach on D-Day.

———

Monday [Sunday], May 14, 1944

Dearest:

It is now 11:20 p.m. I put this page in just exactly a half hour ago but since then [Jim] McGlincy, first, and, then, [Robin] Duff came in and

the chatter has been so heavy I haven't been able to get started. Now I
am starting in spite of the disturbance although I must admit the dif-
ficulty is almost too great to surmount. I also am disturbed because I
found that Duff has been using my typewriter all afternoon—a thing I
object to strenuously because these Hermes are not built for any endur-
ance contests and I like to save mine for my own work. To say nothing of
changing ribbons, which on these machines requires re-spooling—a thing
I intend to do tonight after this letter.

Today the air war was stepped down to a walk—the second day in
a row that I have been able to spend in comparative ease. I got to the
office about nine this morning after a wonderful night's sleep uninter-
rupted by a jangling phone. (The office calls on the average of once
every pre-dawn morning, necessitating a sleepy search for the door of
my room, a cold passage down the corridor to the living room where
I bump into the door I thought was open, a stumbling crossing to the
phone.) I got what air war there was off to a start by 1:30, including the
making of assignments for my staff . . .

I got my hair cut at the Park Lane Hotel barber shop and the barber
made his usual remark: "Been out of town again, I see." He figures I
must have been out of town and away from civilization to ever let my
locks get down to my shoulders. Then back to work after first running
into one the boys off "Walter's ship" who told me the whole gang is
around somewhere over here—a thing which, because of all the present
hush-hush, I won't be able to do anything about. Except they will prob-
ably start calling me one-by-one and that will run into more sheckels.
More. I love you. Walter

———

ROBERT W. CATENHAUSER, whose chances for survival Cronkite
doubted, was a glider pilot and Army Air Force second lieutenant.
Kansas-born and raised, he seems to have been a prewar acquaintance

of the Cronkites. Vera Hruba was a Czech ice-skating star turned film actress.

———

Sunday May 14, 1944

My darlingest Betsy:

Honey, before I run out of space or time or something, I must tell you that Friday I drew a draft on City National for $60 (15 pounds). I hated to do it all, and certainly without telling you first, but I simply was running too close to the margin and needed that much to straighten everything up. The point is that I get by just comfortably on the salary I draw here plus our meager living allowance (the AP boys get $275 a month living allowance—more than three times what we do). But I also counted considerably—how much I never realized before—on the fact that I was out of town a great deal which meant additional expense accounts and lower living costs, two factors which together made up quite a margin. All that combined with the now almost weekly appearance of somebody from "home" who has to be at least taken to dinner (a damned expensive business in this town) with no hope of refund from the office, has put me on the short side for the first time in this much too long year and a half. I finally went into debt when Jack [Fritsche] and Freddie [Payne] showed up the same week. But now, with the draft, that is cleared up and my cable and laundry bills besides. The cable company bills us only every quarter and the laundry bill is hard to pay without a checking account. That is why they had piled up.

The other thing I must tell you right now is this: When, as and if there is an invasion of the continent, please don't worry about me. I'll be sitting right here behind a desk. They have decided I'm too valuable to risk. I am going to continue to direct the coverage and write the air story. Virgil [Pinkley] is right—it must be written from here where the communication facilities are. But I am broken-hearted. I want to go along on whatever happens. I am destined though to be attached to air headquarters. I will go along when, as and if (that phrase again) it goes, but that certainly will be sometime in the future. Meanwhile I am safe and snug and hating it . . .

For me, of course, the biggest stories are right now. The air story has been the lead story in all the New York papers for the last several weeks. I have been handling all of them, day and night right around the clock, but only this week have I finally become firm and told Virgil that something had to be done about the insidious matter of the New York desk signing Phil Ault to the day wire stories. It has finally been done and I am now being signed around the clock. Friday I had a nice spread with the bannerline in both the World-Telegram and Journal-American in the afternoon and the New York Daily News and Mirror in the morning. At least that is what the OWI impact sheet that daily shows us the play the American papers are giving London dispatches said.

Darling, thanks a thousand for the little packages. I got the two of candy a week ago and Friday I got the Mixture 79. You are the sweetest person in the world. No wonder I love you so much. Forever, Walter

Monday, May 15, 1944
(continued)

So then back to the office where I finished up about six o'clock . . .

I then went and had a lonely meal at a little Belgian club—Neuf Provinces—on Buckingham Palace Road near Victoria and not so far from the flat. I had a gin and French at the bar and a long chat with the Czech waiter who is on leave from the French army and who did not used to be a waiter before the war. He ran a wine shop in Prague. A nice gent who looks like Mischa Auer. I sat then near a party of six—a

British major, some little man who looked like Laval, three British
women, and a Belgian lieutenant who, I gathered from their conversa-
tion, was a professional linguist with command of 26 languages. That
is 26 more than I have command of. After dinner I sauntered back
to the bar. (I sauntered the whole thirty-five feet from one end of the
room back to the bar.) I was standing there chatting again about Vera
Hruba to my Czech friend when Mrs. Gaston, wife of the owner, lit the
gas heater in the fireplace. It went PUFF as gas heaters have a way of
doing. I jumped a foot and threw my beer half way across the room.
That amused everybody—U.S. war correspondent with invasion jitters.
That brought Mrs. Gaston and me together and we sat and talked about
Brussels and she didn't understand me and I didn't understand her and
then we said goodnight and I walked on home.

Incidentally, after several weeks of summer it has turned bitterly cold
again. Ah, England.

Sunday before last Jack [Fritsche] and I were at the public relations
office where I was picking up my mail. As we went into the building an
officer passed us on his way out. He stared at me and a few minutes later
was standing nearby staring again. "Where have I seen you before?" I
asked. "I remember the face but—." "You are Cronkite, then," he said.
"I'm Catenhauser." He was right. He was [Robert W.] Catenhauser. He is
piloting a glider, what the fellows call a "third lieutenant"—a flight officer.
(Frankly, if I were Lloyds I wouldn't be interested in his patronage.) More
later. Forever, darling, Walter

———

JOHN F. "JACK" FRANKISH was a United Press reporter. He would be
killed covering the Battle of the Bulge on December 23, 1944.

Cronkite was looking forward to a "slack period" in his reporting
specialty, the air war, "a month or so from now," during which he hoped
he would be able to make a trip home to visit Betsy.

—————

Thursday, May 18, 1944

My darlingest wife:

Well, my best intentions always seem to go astray. For two days now the air war has been in the doldrums and I had intended to get off some nice long, chatty letters to you as well as to catch up on other correspondence of which there hasn't been any in many, many months. But Tuesday night I ran into Jack Frankish at the officers' mess and last night Bill Vaughan was in town. Tuesday, since Jack has just arrived here from the States where he was Miami bureau manager, I invited him to come along to the flat for a drink. That was the mistake. Robin [Duff] was home and we sat and killed one of my two prized bottles of bourbon. Robin and Frankish did the talking. I never got so tired of hearing two people converse. I did put in a few words which were such pearls of wisdom I'm sure they were worth more than the usual two-bits (of "two-bits worth" fame). They were talking of differences in accents of Americans and British and Robin said: "Yes, I've been covering the American army so long now I say 'get' instead of 'got.'" (That is the way it sounded to me.) And Jack said: "With the whole world on the move, we are sort of losing our sense of values." And I said: "Sort of losing sight of got." Like it? So yesterday afternoon Vaughan called. He met me at the office at five. We had one drink at El Vino (wine shop in Fleet street) and then came on out to the flat to wash up a bit. We had a couple of drinks out of my other p.b. of b [prized bottle of bourbon], and then I took him over to the Belgian club, which is just a few blocks from the flat, for dinner . . . Then we came home about ten-thirty—and with Duff killed the you-know-what. Duff sat there quietly having hysterics, and Jim [McGlincy] got out of bed and joined him in that, while Vaughan went into his funniest gags and we rehashed old Kansas City times. It was heart-rending . . . Bill has some pictures of his baby, which frankly looks as ugly as all babies do to me . . .

*In that last letter I was telling you about [Robert W.] Catenhauser.
Well, he didn't look so good. Maybe it was because his finger-nails were
so dirty. Or maybe it is that he is worried—for which in his line of business I wouldn't blame him . . . (Funny how you remember those little
things, but I still can't forget that he was the guy who picked you up
at the Little Marvel Wind Charger Company that fall evening in 1936
(eight years ago!) while I gnawed nails at KCMO.)*

*Tell Molo for me that I haven't forgotten she asked me how the
English make tea. Well, I got the BBC's famed Robin Duff to write
out a little recipe and I'll send it along the next time I use an envelope.
The secret seems to be in something silly like heating the pot first, or
heating the tea first, or not heating the tea first. Something like that,
anyway. It is a damned serious ritual, whatever it is, and it seems that
nothing will ruin it so fast as a tongue in the cheek. It is true, though,
that their tea is a refreshing beverage—and definitely habit-forming.
I prefer it now to coffee, although, as you remember, I never was
much of a coffee drinker ever. Gosh, how I'd like a cold glass of milk,
though. Hot cinnamon rolls, dozens of soft-boiled eggs, quarts of cold
milk, and Betsy—all for breakfast. That is my present conception of
heaven . . .*

*Darling, this is such a sketchy thing right now that I even hesitate
to mention it—but I've got a bee in my bonnet that I might get home
for a leave in the not-too-distant future. My idea is this: I've been over
now longer, in one stretch, than any other married man on the staff.
Pinkley, I know, is damned interested in both of us (he keeps telling
me how sorry he is he missed you, and how much he wants to meet
you). I am going to be very busy for a while, but I expect, in my particular specialty, a slack period a month or so from now. It might be, if
transportation is available and a long string of other "ifs," that I could
make a quick trip home then. One of those big "if's is "if we manage*

to open some continental bureau soon." We shall see, and pray. I adore
you. Walter

———

BETWEEN THE BEGINNING of April and the first week in June, Allied
aircraft flew more than 200,000 sorties to prepare the way for the
invasion of France. They bombed coastal defenses, airfields, and transportation networks to weaken German resistance. The attacks on air
bases in France not only destroyed many aircraft but also forced the
Germans to pull their surviving aircraft farther from the coast, contributing to the unchallenged air supremacy the Allies enjoyed in Normandy on June 6.

Meanwhile, hundreds of thousands of men, and thousands of ships,
were being gathered in southern England to make up the invasion force.
The landings, by sea and air, were set for June 5, but bad weather forced
a postponement to the following day. Invasion jitters were drawing to
an end, as the war in western Europe entered its final decisive stage.

From the front page of the *New York World-Telegram,* May 20, 1944:

YANK PLANES BATTER AIRDROMES IN FRANCE

By Walter Cronkite

United Press War Correspondent

LONDON, May 20.—American heavy bombers smashed at three
German airdromes and one rail hub in France today to continue a
new preinvasion offensive in which nearly 5000 Allied planes dropped
more than 6000 tons of bombs on Europe in 24 hours . . .

Reports up to noon indicated that the resumed aerial onslaught
softening the Continent for land attack was being pressed at a pace
rivaling if not exceeding that of the month-long campaign broken off

last week end by bad weather. Many big formations crossed the Channel in a nonstop parade by daylight . . .

From the front page of the *Nevada State Journal,* June 3, 1944:

ALLIED AIR FORAYS BLAST EUROPE FROM FRENCH COAST TO HUNGARY AND ROMANIA

By Walter Cronkite

United Press War Correspondent

London, June 2 (UP)—The mighty Allied air offensive against Adolf Hitler's defenses assumed a new pattern of invasion bombing yesterday as some 4,500 warplanes, 3,500 of them American, hammered Europe from the French channel coast to Hungary and Romania . . .

Highlighting the great assault, the U.S. Eighth Air Force in Britain made its greatest attack of the war on the Atlantic wall in France, sending up to 1,500 heavy bombers and fighters against the invasion coast on a mission to flatten fortifications before D-Day . . .

CHAPTER FIVE

ONCE THIS WAR IS OVER...

JUNE 1944–DECEMBER 1945

The final year of the war proved the hardest for Cronkite. He had risked his life on several occasions in his first year and a half abroad, flying perilous bombing missions over enemy territory, but those missions ended in a matter of hours, and at the end of the day he could enjoy the amenities of London nightlife and the comforts of his own apartment. In contrast, in the fall and winter of 1944–45 Cronkite found himself in dangerous situations, often exposed to enemy fire for weeks at a stretch. Even when he was ensconced safely in an apartment in Brussels, he and his flatmates had to scramble to find fuel and food.

Mostly the last year was difficult because, although ultimate victory was in sight, Betsy was still thousands of miles away, and he knew that many lonely, frustrating months would pass before he would be reunited with her. In their third year apart, his longing for her was undiminished. "Once this war is over, you and I ought to have a lot of fun," he wrote from Belgium in November 1944. "That is the day I'm living for. That is what will make all this worthwhile."

At a number of points in this chapter, Cronkite's wartime letters to Betsy contradict his retelling of the events of the war years. Mentioning such discrepancies is not a judgment on the truthfulness of the reporter who later became "the most trusted man in America." Rather, the conflicting accounts of long-past events suggest why, as a general rule, historians prefer to rely on the unaltered documentary record—in this case, the letters to Betsy—rather than fallible human memory.

After midnight on the night of June 5, 1944, Cronkite heard a knock on the door of his Buckingham Gate Road apartment. Eighth Air Force public relations major Hal Leyshon had come to make him an offer he couldn't refuse. As Cronkite remembered the conversation, Leyshon informed him, "You've drawn the straw to represent the Allied press on a very important mission. It will be dangerous. No guarantee you'll get back. But if you do, you'll have a great story. You can turn it down now or you can come with me. And security is on—you can't tell your office."

Cronkite was used to the elaborate security rituals that circumscribed wartime journalism. He had often received coded phone messages alerting him to Eighth Air Force bombing missions. But this time he knew that something new and far more important was taking place: the long-awaited Allied invasion of western Europe. Dressing hurriedly, he traveled by military car to Molesworth air base, home to the 303rd Bomb Group. He may have arrived in time for the 3:30 a.m. briefing by Col. Kermit D. Stevens, who told the assembled aircrews, "This is D-Day. This is the day we have all been waiting for. Make 'em know it."

The 303rd's B-17s took off just after 6 a.m. Cronkite made the short flight over the English Channel in a bomber named *Shoo Shoo Baby,* piloted by Capt. Robert W. Sheets. Although in *A Reporter's Life* Cronkite remembered their intended target as "a heavy artillery

The crew of the B-17 Shoo Shoo Baby, *June 6, 1944. From left:*
1st Lt. F. E. Umphress, Jr. (bombardier), Capt. Robert W. Sheets (pilot),
Cronkite, Technical Sgt. Francis X. Neuner (engineer).

emplacement that commanded Omaha Beach," the official mission
report recorded that the bombers were headed for a bridge at Caen
over which the Germans could bring reinforcements to the beaches.
Only one group of the 303rd's planes was able to drop its bombs on the
bridge; Cronkite's group was foiled by technical problems. His plane
returned to England with bombs still loaded in its bomb bay, making
for a nerve-racking landing. (Cronkite later inscribed a photo of himself and some of the plane's officers with the heartfelt message, "With a
lifetime of gratitude for getting us back!") The greatest disappointment

of the flight, for Cronkite and the other crew members, was that heavy cloud cover obscured their view of the Channel and the vast invasion armada steaming that morning toward the coast of Normandy.

Back in London later on D-Day, Cronkite pounded out the story of the air effort supporting the invasion, but left out any mention of his own experience. That he saved for his letter to Betsy of June 12, 1944.

"A few days" after the invasion, according to Cronkite's memoir, he flew back to Normandy in a small plane, this time landing on a hastily laid-down landing strip on the high ground above Omaha Beach. Ostensibly he was writing about the building of the landing strip, but he really was more tourist than reporter. He caught up with several colleagues who had covered the landings on June 6 and listened to the terrifying stories they passed on about that historic day. He envied them the experience. After several days he returned reluctantly to London, carrying with him a musette bag crammed with Camembert cheese, a souvenir of Normandy. Since his June 12 letter makes no mention of the hop to Normandy, his trip must have come later in the month.

In any case, what is perfectly clear from his letters to Betsy that summer was his eagerness to return to the continent, this time to stay and cover the ground fighting.

From the front page of the *Daily News* of Huntington, Pennsylvania, June 6, 1944:

BRITISH BOMBERS BLAST ENEMY WITH HEAVIEST ATTACK

By Walter Cronkite

United Press Correspondent

LONDON, June 6.—Thousands of Allied bombing planes softened up the defenses of western Europe for the Anglo-American invasion armies last night and early today, dropping more than 11,200 tons of high explosives down on the Nazi coastal fortifications in eight and one-half hours of furious assault.

It was the greatest attack launched against a single objective in the history of aerial warfare and the battered Luftwaffe took the beating without putting a plane into the skies . . .

From the front page of the *Daily News* of Huntington, Pennsylvania, June 12, 1944:

BIG FLEET U.S. PLANES HIT NAZI FIGHTER BASES BEHIND INVASION COAST

By Walter Cronkite

United Press Correspondent

LONDON, June 12—A fleet of possibly 1,750 American heavy bombers and fighters struck the chain of German fighter bases behind the French invasion coast today, while more than 3,000 other Allied warplanes swarmed over the Norman battlefields under rapidly-clearing skies that promised the embattled ground forces their strongest aerial cover since D-Day.

Striking furiously to deprive the hard-pressed German coastal armies of their last vestiges of air support, almost 1,000 American Flying Fortresses and Liberators ranged over a vast arc of northern France to bomb and burn "many" of the enemy's vital advanced air bases . . .

June 12, 1944

My darlingest wife:

I really have neglected you terribly in the past couple of weeks—but then perhaps you will understand. There <u>have</u> been a few things happening. And I have been right where I said I would be. Maybe once there was a "Walter's ship" or a "Walter's plane." I wonder if Maggie and Jack would be so proud of "Walter's desk?" It turned out that I did *fly the morning of the invasion after all but the Eighth Air Force public relations people who thought they were doing me a favor and handing me a scoop on a silver platter managed to botch things up. The result was that I went with a high altitude bombing formation instead of a low-level group, we were above a solid cloud bank all the way over the Channel and back, and although I was over the invasion beaches shortly after zero hour and on inland over Caen and Carentan, I did not see a single thing. I was never so disgusted in my life. Why, we didn't even get shot at. A dozen bursts of flak and that was my invasion experience. It was like taking only one drink on New Year's Eve. I have been getting pretty good play with the air war general leads which I do around the clock now. They are keeping the name in the paper, anyway. [Jim] McGlincy also is a little bitter about the invasion. He was left behind. His assignment was changed somewhat at the last minute without his knowledge and he awakened "D day" morning to find that the invasion had started without him. He has gone now, however, and I admit I miss the patter of his little feet around the house. But I'm not here at home enough now to make any difference. [Ed] Beattie, [Virgil] Pinkley and I sign the main stories of the day and the three of us work fifteen hours a day doing it. We cover three "communiqué and briefing" periods each day—at 10:30 a.m., 5:00 p.m., and 11:30 p.m. That means being at the Ministry of Information, where the communiqués are issued, by 10:15 in the morning, and getting away from there after writing the last story at 1:00 the next morning. It is a grueling pace and we are all wearing out. Effective today we are doing a little overlapping of schedules so each of us will get every other night off—after we clean up the stuff from the five o'clock conference, which usually is by seven or eight o'clock. It, of course, doesn't mean we will have time to do anything on those nights except catch up on our sleep. Tonight I'm writing this letter to you and then turning in. I'll write again Wednesday, honey . . .*

CRONKITE'S FIRST POST–D-DAY letter to Betsy was dated June 12. The following day, London was struck by a new weapon, a "vengeance weapon," or *Vergeltungswaffe,* as Hitler called it, the V-1 flying bomb. Purely by chance—they were in the wrong neighborhood at the right time—Cronkite and UP colleague Ed Beattie saw the first one land. Eight civilians were killed in that attack; thousands more would die over the next four months until advancing Allied armies overran the V-1 launch sites in France and Holland. An even more terrible vengeance weapon, the powerful V-2 rocket, soon began to rain down more death and destruction on the city and its inhabitants. Cronkite not only reported on the early wave of V-1 attacks but also was nearly one of their victims, as he reported in his letter to Betsy of July 9, 1944.

The V-1 bomb described in Cronkite's letter struck the Guards Chapel of Wellington Barracks at 11:20 a.m. on Sunday, June 18, 1944. The chapel was filled with military and civilian worshippers at the morning service; 121 were killed and another 141 wounded. The dead included several high-ranking British and American officers.

———————

Sunday, June [July] 9, 1944

My darlingest Betsy:

I suppose I can tell you, now that [Prime Minister Winston] Churchill has sounded off and revealed all the secret details, that I was bombed out of my flat a couple of weeks ago. As a matter of fact, I was bombed twice, but the first one didn't take and they tried again, the second time with a little more success. It was revealed today so you have read by now that one of the buzz bombs hit the Guards Chapel of Wellington Barracks. That was on a Sunday morning and at that time I had not yet seen one of the infernal instruments. So when I

*heard it approaching I threw open the window of my flat living room
and leaned out to see what I could see. Since the thing was approaching from the other side of the building I couldn't see it but I could see
all the Guardsmen leaning out their windows only a few yards from
me watching it approach. Then I saw them duck back into the barracks and at the same instant the motor of the damned thing stopped.
By that time we had begun to learn that we had five to fifteen seconds
to get under cover between the motor shutting off and the explosion.
I turned and started running like hell for the main corridor of the
apartment building. I got through the tiny living room into the hall
of my flat when the bomb hit. There was that terrible tinkle of falling
glass like in an automobile accident only multiplied a thousand fold
with the additional crumbling of plaster and ripping of wood. I felt
like someone had slapped me but hard on the back, and then shoved
me but hard on the chest. The front door of the flat toward which I
was heading instead came over to me. It wasn't blown clear off the
hinges but the Yale lock was torn from its moorings and the door flung
open. Well, a lot of windows and some window frames and doors in
the building were knocked out by that one. Wonderful sidelight was
that just before the incident I had rung down for Charles, the house
man to come up. ("House man" indeed! Charles is a valet. Sixtyish
with winged collar, striped pants and all.) Then the bomb went. A
moment later Charles came through the open door. I was hoping he
was going to say, "Did you ring, sir?" But Charles disappointed me.
He said instead, "Are you all right, sir?" and without awaiting an
answer disappeared back into the littered hall. The next one sometime
later was a real daisy though. It came while I was still asleep in the
early morning. The darned things had been awakening me and sending me fleeing into the hall all night and I finally had fallen asleep of
exhaustion. This one must have awaked me just before it hit because
I remember in half sleep curling up in a tight ball, pulling covers over*

my head and clapping hands over my ears. Then it hit. All hell seemed
to break loose. It seemed like fifteen minutes that debris was falling all
around and I kept waiting for the ceiling and the three floors above me
to come tumbling down. I suppose it was only seconds though. (more)
I love you, Walter

———

THE ARRIVAL OF Charles the valet within moments of the V-1 bomb's
explosion is another illustration of the vagaries of memory. In the version
of the story Cronkite told in *A Reporter's Life*, the valet Charles became
"George," and the conversation ended with a better punch line: "There
was a knock on the torn door frame. There stood George, holding a
towel over a bleeding eye. And so help me, he said, 'Did you ring, sir?'"

———

Sunday, June [July] 9, 1944

Page Two

The ceiling didn't come down, nor did the other three floors, I am
happy to be able to report. The thing landed immediately across the
street, it turned out, and since my flat was on the back side of the apart-
ment I was spared full force of the blast. But the front of the building
and the shops on the ground floor were devastated. The apartment
building the bomb hit was demolished, the church on the corner was
wrecked. I won't try to detail the damage any more than that. The win-
dows and their frames were blown out of my flat, the front door was
ripped from its hinges, the bathroom window, the washbowl and the tub
were shattered. I wasn't even scratched although the glass and debris
was so thick in the flat, in the halls and in the street in front that I had
to put on my thick army boots to safely get over it and out of the build-
ing. Fortunately, except for bottled toilet articles such as hair tonic and

what-not, I didn't lose a single possession. My books and clothes were
dirtied up a little with soot and debris but nothing that washing and
cleaning won't fix. So now I'm in a nice modern hotel in a very con-
venient location and almost as comfortable as I was in the flat. I don't
think I had ever told you much about the flat since I had just moved into
it. It was in the same building where McGlincy and I lived for so long
but when he went to France I moved downstairs to this smaller one—a
fortunate move since the other flat was in the front, one of those badly
blasted. The building I'm now in is modern steel and concrete and my
room is on a very small court so I figure I'm safe from anything but a
direct hit, which is a very remote possibility.

I was interrupted in this letter. It is now Monday afternoon and I'm
at my desk at the Ministry of Information where I spend more of my
time nowadays. Another package just came for me today [—] contain-
ing fruit juices and shorts . . . Please send me more of both. I'm in very
serious straits for clothing right now, but it is a matter which I want to
take up with you when I have more time. I'm going to be doing more
and more diplomatic stuff getting ready for the Amsterdam assignment.
As such I'm going to need some clothes . . . But I'll have to go into that
later. Now I must run. I love you, darlingest. And Judy. Tell her for me,
will you, please?

I worship you, Walter

CRONKITE'S NEW ASSIGNMENT, for which he needed better clothes, was
as United Press bureau chief for the Low Countries, and he was to set up
headquarters in the old prewar UP office in Amsterdam. The only hitch
was that the Germans were supposed to depart Amsterdam—which
they did not wind up doing until after V-E Day, in May 1945.

In his letter of August 6, 1944, Cronkite described a recent trip to
France (probably his second since D-Day) as a welcome break from life

in London. He wasn't the only London-based correspondent that summer to find relief in traveling to a combat zone. Dudley Ann Harmon, one of his colleagues in UP's London bureau, had a similar reaction. As she wrote in an undated letter to her father, sometime in July–August 1944: "Dearest Daddy: This is written from Somewhere in France . . . It is a great relief from buzz bombs in London and I feel as though I were on a vacation." On the other hand, those who had left loved ones behind in London were not as pleased. Drew Middleton of the *New York Times* had been in the enviable position, in Cronkite's eyes, of having his wife living with him. But as Middleton recalled in his memoir, *Our Share of Night,* published immediately after the war: "If you lived in London, going to the front [in the summer of 1944] presented a unique mental problem. It meant leaving my wife in far more danger, more constant, enveloping danger, than I was likely to face on the Continent. A week before I had seen what was left of seven people splattered into a red jam across the face of a broken building. It was in my mind as I said good-by and went away."

Notwithstanding the onset of V-1 attacks, Cronkite was preoccupied as usual with schemes for bringing Betsy to London. His attitude was a reflection of post-invasion euphoria, which was widespread that summer in civilian and military circles alike. Once the American army broke out from Normandy in mid-July, followed by the landing of a second invasion force in southern France in August, Allied optimism soared. Cronkite was not alone in expecting the imminent collapse of Nazi Germany, which would, of course, bring an end to the V-1 threat to London, and make it possible for Betsy to join him there in safety.

The vital deepwater port of Cherbourg, at the end of the Cotentin peninsula in France, was captured by U.S. forces between June 26 and July 1, 1944. Before surrendering, the Germans had wrecked the harbor facilities, and when Cronkite visited in early August, Allied engineers were hard at work trying to clear debris and reopen the port.

Sunday, Aug. 6, 1944

My darlingest wife:

I've been over to France again this week, spending a couple of days kicking around in Cherbourg and south of there but again failing to get up into the battle area. I went over with six other newsmen and a couple of photographers on a sortie arranged by the ordinance command. We traveled by air both ways with a very high ranking officer included in the party. Everything went perfectly and it was a wonderful trip. We followed the path of the American advance up from Isigny through Carentan and Montebourg to Cherbourg. God, what desolation. It is hard to imagine a town, say the size of Sedalia, completely flattened. The towns just do not exist anymore. And everywhere convoys and the ever-present dust. Goggles like those worn in the desert are essential. The food was good and the sleeping, after "southeast England" and its buzzbombs, was heaven-sent.

When I got back your V-mailer with the questions about what to bring and what to do if you should come over was waiting for me. Unfortunately I am writing this at the office and I find I don't have that letter with me. So I can't go through the questions one-by-one. I'll answer what I can remember of them. First: I'm afraid I have some disappointing news. As you know, I have been harboring a hope that I could perhaps get a few weeks home leave this summer. Well, I finally gathered my nerve and asked [Virgil] Pinkley a few days ago. His answer beat slightly about the bush in that he said he would give it consideration, but actually all of his equivocation simply added up to "no." His point was that [Hugh] Baillie is coming over in a few weeks and he thinks it would be a very bad thing for me to be away when the Great Man is here. I think that is much malarkey, but I couldn't very well tell Pinkley so. With all the action over in Normandy and all the people intimately connected with fast-developing political affairs here, I'm strictly a second-stringer these days and whether or not

I am here is not going to make much difference to Baillie. But that is
Pinkley's answer anyway. And Pinkley went on to say: "Things are devel-
oping too fast, and it would be pretty tough if you were in the States when
we suddenly needed you to go into Amsterdam and get things rolling. It
shouldn't be too long before you are able to get Betsy over here, so I'd
advise you just to sit tight." Well, that would seem to be that. Boiling all
this talk down—and for goodness sakes don't relay this part to Mother—it
looks to me like I am stuck at least for another year or so. In my opin-
ion, chances of home leave are either right now or not again for months
and months. Once Germany collapses we all are going to be so damned
busy over here home leave will be out of the question for some time. That
means that the only answer is for you to come here. Now let's take up that
aspect of the problem. If the [Marcel] Wallenstein letter has not grown too
cold and if you still can work out something with the [Kansas City] Star,
by all means do so. If that fails and you can think of any other angles, play
them. I see no possibility of our being separated for very long at a time
once you got over here. It looks as if I will be remaining here until time to
move to the continent, and when that happens the situation should be so
stabilized that I could immediately take you along . . .

The point is that once you got over here and I moved on into the
continent, you certainly could accompany me as an UP employee if there
should be some temporary ban on civilians. As far as living conditions
go, I'd better repeat my earlier warning that they aren't going to be too
pleasant either here or on the continent for some time to come—perhaps
for years. No one can foresee to what extent rationing will be contin-
ued—and rationing as it exists over here is plenty tough particularly so
in view of the fact that it involves long queues at the butchers, at the
dairy, at the greengrocer, at the drugstore, at the clothing stores. We
probably would live in a flat like the one I'm in now . . . And for that
sort of living we would use up most of our salary and living allowance.
(Although the way things are going right now, I'm just about doing that

*on my own. I hate to be a sissy but I still believe the safety of the present
building is worth the thirty two dollars a week I'm paying for it.)*

*Because of the nature of the job I probably would have to spend a few
occasional nights—that is evenings—at work, but the rest of the time would
be ours and we would have a good time I am sure. Foreign corresponding
on the proper plane involves a lot of protocol and there would be a certain
number of cocktail parties and dinners which would have be reciprocated,
a process calculated to strain the budget and the imagination. The imagination would be strained in figuring out how to get it on the expense account.*

*About clothes: I think it is a little premature to get down to that minute
a plan of campaign, but generally a safe rule would be to cram in all the
clothing you possibly could under whatever baggage allowance you were
forced to work. And, above all, don't bring any old clothes. Bring them as
new as you possibly can, because they may have to last for a long time . . .
Typewriter—yes, bring one along, but not an old one. If we can afford it
when that stage is reached, try to get a new, substantial portable. I now
have this Hermes, which is a lovely little job for emergency use to be carted
around on airplanes when weight is a problem, but which is like owning
a Stutz in Arkansas—nobody has any spare parts. All of this, of course, is
predicated on your coming over before the end of the business. If you don't
come until later, then we will have to change signals, because undoubtedly
the situation will alter somewhat. I love you, honey. Send some fruit juice.*

IN JULY AND AUGUST 1944, Cronkite continued to file dispatches on the air
war. Allied bombers were pounding German cities and industry, focusing
much of their efforts against German oil depots and refineries. That continued to be an important story—because the German war machine would
grind to a halt when its supplies of oil and gasoline ran out. But Americans
back home were anxiously following developments on the beaches and
among the hedgerows of Normandy, and the air war was increasingly

consigned to the inside pages of newspapers. A top-level advisory group sent Gen. Henry Harley "Hap" Arnold a secret report in August 1944, noting, ominously from the perspective of the Air Force brass: "The hot pilot is being supplanted in national esteem by G.I. Joe." From Cronkite's perspective, being the "youthful dean of the air-war writers" was no longer a particularly desirable post within the United Press hierarchy.

Cronkite must have chosen his words carefully in his letter of August 15, 1944, because he wrote it on the eve of what would have been his first assignment covering ground combat, an attempt by American airborne troops to liberate Paris. The airborne veterans of Normandy, the 101st and 82nd Airborne Divisions, were going to jump into Rambouillet Forest and seize the French capital from its German occupiers. As he recalled in *A Reporter's Life,* Cronkite was going to jump as well.

*Troops from the 101st Airborne looking for survivors of a glider crash
following Operation Market Garden, September 17, 1944*

However, two factors suggest that Cronkite's memory may have again proved mistaken. First, while he was familiar with parachutes from his flights on U.S. bombers, most recently on June 6, there is no evidence that he had ever actually jumped from a plane. Parachuting under fire behind enemy lines would be a difficult initiation, and neither the military nor the United Press was eager to add to the list of dead correspondents. The second, and more compelling piece of evidence, is found in this August 15, 1944, letter to Betsy: "We are going to be working with a swell bunch of Americans. Catenhauser, incidentally, is one of their tribe." To circumvent military censorship, Cronkite sometimes used coded references that he knew Betsy would understand. As he had told her in a letter on Monday, May 15, 1944, Robert W. Catenhauser was a glider pilot—which suggests that the reference to Catenhauser's "tribe" signaled to Betsy that Cronkite would be making a glider landing.

Although Cronkite wasn't sure of Catenhauser's fate when he wrote the August 15 letter, the glider pilot had indeed survived the Normandy invasion, and lived to age 96.

Whatever the means, Cronkite was eager to accompany the airborne troops on their mission. He was clearly relieved at the prospect of being freed from his desk job in London, especially when he might gain one of the war's great scoops.

The acronym SHAEF stood for Supreme Headquarters Allied Expeditionary Force, Gen. Dwight D. Eisenhower's headquarters.

Tuesday, August 15, 1944

My darlingest wife:

I'm not writing this from my usual post. I am writing tonight from an airbase somewhere in England. Soon I will be leaving on an assignment that is back down the old groove, something of the type of February,

1943, that you will remember. Well, not exactly like that, so don't try to gather too much from that feeble bit of information. By the time you get this letter, you probably will know all about it. At any rate, I hope so.

What I want to say, though, darling, is that there is considerable danger involved in this job. I don't feel that I am unnecessarily worrying you by reporting that, inasmuch as it will all be over before you ever get this note. You will not have heard from me when the first news breaks, but I hope you are able to read and hear something by me. Bill Boni is the only other American newspaperman who will be on the story. He is with the AP. Our stories will be pooled—will go to all newspapers and press services, at least for the first several days. It is not inconceivable that if all goes well, he and I might share the biggest story out of France yet. It is a great chance—one that I willingly took, indeed jumped at, when [Virgil] Pinkley offered it. As you perhaps have been able to read between the lines of my too frequent letters, I have been in terrible doldrums since D-day, with everyone else in action and my sitting by on the SHAEF desk. Now, at last, I am getting into the show and with a splurge that may prove bigger than any correspondent has had since the original landing.

We are going to be working with a swell bunch of Americans. Catenhauser, incidentally, is one of their tribe, but I haven't run across him yet and don't know that I will. (In fact, I don't know that Catenhauser came out of the original landing okay.) Boni and I came down here to headquarters this afternoon and since then have been loaded down with equipment and drinks, none of which they permit us to pay for. That, incidentally, is okay with me since I suddenly realized I did not have any English money along and was equipped only with two hundred dollars worth of travelers checks.

I don't know how long I will be away from England. The assignment could last from a week to a month or longer, and after that I might be in such a favorable position compared to other correspondents that the office will choose to leave me with this outfit. There is no

certainty about that, however, and the last thing Pinkley told me late
yesterday was that his prime interest still was to get me into Amster-
dam and get things rolling there. So I assume that as soon as this initial
story is over, I'll be returning here to go on to Amsterdam.

I'll write again, honey, just as soon as I can. I hope you will have made
some progress by then in getting over. Meantime, darling, remember that
I love you, very, very much. And tell Judy I love her too. Forever, Walter

---

By THE TIME Betsy received Cronkite's letter of August 15, she had
already been forewarned to ignore its contents.

> WESTERN UNION LONDON VIA COMMERCIAL [TIME
> STAMPED] AUG 21
> BETSY CRONKITE=
> 3920 AGNES KASCITYMO=
>   . . . IGNORE AUGST FIFTEEN VMAILER STOP DANGEROUS
> ASSIGNMENT CANCELLED STOP LOVE=
>   WALTER CRONKITE.=

Cronkite's next letter to Betsy, sent on August 20, 1944, was among
his gloomiest. The rapid advance of Allied armies across France in late
July and early August made the planned airborne operation to capture
Paris unnecessary, and it was abandoned, to Cronkite's great disappointment. Paris would instead be liberated by the combined efforts of Allied
ground forces and the French resistance movement on August 25, 1944.

With the belief that the war would be over by Christmas, American and
British airborne leaders were anxious to support the advance. In August
new airborne missions were repeatedly scheduled and just as regularly canceled, and Cronkite despaired of ever getting into combat. As he told Betsy
in a letter later that year, "I was beginning to look a little foolish around the

office. Four times I dashed in, picked up expense money, left last instructions with various people, and dashed out to the wars in my battle clothes only to return a few days later with the whole thing called off."

One of the missions involved a plan to land a Polish airborne division outside Brussels. That one he was not so sorry to see canceled, as he recalled in *A Reporter's Life:* "The Free Poles were a wild bunch. They were tough and mean and impatient to get back at the Germans—and the Russians, for that matter. Few of them spoke English, and we were going to land among not only German soldiers but French- and Flemish-speaking Belgians. The chances were good that I would be shot by someone in this Babelian hell."

When Cronkite finally landed on the Continent in mid-September, he found himself in the land of his paternal ancestors, Holland.

Louis Gerteis was a former United Press correspondent who went to work for the Office of War Information's foreign news bureau at the start of the war. From the context of the letter, he was clearly an acquaintance of both Cronkite and Betsy—and perhaps not the snappiest of dressers.

———

August 20, 1944

Darlingest:

I have just returned to town after one of the bitterest disappointments of my life. I wrote you Tuesday night telling you that I was about to go on a big assignment. Well, I was. I probably would have been the first American correspondent in Paris, although I might have had to share the honor with Bill Boni of AP. Unfortunately I still can't give you all the details. But I can say that we waited five days for our little show to come off, knowing each day that our chances of going were growing slimmer. Then, finally, Saturday they definitely cancelled the whole plan. So here I am back at the

same old stand in the same old slough of despond which has been grow-
ing deeper and blacker ever since D Day left me standing on the platform
holding the sack.

Things are really in terrible shape now. This assignment had sort of
snapped me out of my doldrums, and with its collapse all my hopes col-
lapsed too. I can't seem to get back into the groove. I don't feel that I
have done a really useful thing for the UP in weeks, and I'm afraid [Virgil]
Pinkley feels that way too. I've been trying to find a little release with social
activity but don't feel any better for that. This expensive flat to elude buzz
bombs as best one can has added another burden which is oppressive. In
a few days I shall have to draft another month's rent of some $130 from
our bank account and that is too damned depressing for words. Part of my
unhappiness stems also from the clothing situation. I had sort of thought a
couple of months ago that I might draft enough money to get a couple of
decent suits, a pair of shoes or so, and other accessories, but now with the
other heavy drain on the bank account I can't do that. And frankly I look
like hell. I'm down to something like 155 pounds. My blue tweed (Bonds—
$22.50) fits me like a hand-me-down. My three-year-old Rothschild brown
job looks like I had worn it every day of those three years and the cuffs are
even frayed. I'm still wearing those Wellington-last Bostonians although the
tops have cracked now and before long I suppose my corns will be show-
ing. In short, I feel that I look like Louis Gerteis only not so fat. My teeth
have gone to hell but I just can't seem to get around to doing anything
about them. You aren't here and the prospect of home leave seems defi-
nitely to have flown out the window in which poverty has crawled. Nuts!

I'm sorry to unload this on you, honey, but—well, there it is. I don't
know whether you have made any headway or not regarding coming
over. As I said earlier, home leave seems definitely out. Things are simply
moving too fast and our manpower situation is too acute for anyone's
release. Unless some miracle occurs, I doubt now that I shall be seeing
the States again for many, many months perhaps stretching beyond a year.

That is plenty gloomy. I want to see you and Mom and the grandfolks
and Judy and bright lights and rest. Maybe I won't mail this. If I do, for-
give me. I love you, honey, Walter

———

CRONKITE NEED NOT have worried about sitting out the remainder of
the war behind a desk in London. His letter of September 15, 1944,
was written two days before the start of the largest airborne operation
in the history of warfare—the off-and-on "assignment" he mentions in
his opening lines. Operation Market Garden, the brainchild of British
Field Marshal Bernard Montgomery, was a combined air ("Market")
and ground ("Garden") attack intended to open up a back route into
Germany by seizing a line of bridges on the north-south highway running across eastern Holland, bypassing the Nazis' vaunted Siegfried
defensive line, then pushing across the Rhine River into the heartland of
industrial Germany.

Even on the eve of a combat assignment, Cronkite continued to fret
about the lack of progress in arranging for Betsy to join him. And about
the state of his wardrobe.

———

September 15, 1944

My darling: I accidentally addressed this to 4007 Kenwood—absent-
minded me!

I'm back here again for another hiatus. That "assignment" I keep
mentioning is an off and on again proposition. I get back Wednesday
from the latest alert and am leaving again tomorrow morning on another.
My morale isn't being helped any by these continual periods of expectant
buoyancy followed almost immediately by complete deflation. Well, per-
haps things will go as scheduled this time.

When I got back your cable was waiting for me. The office could not have communicated it to me because I was at a secret address and sealed in from any contact with the outside world. I called [Marcel] Wallenstein's office just as soon as I got it and learned that he is on the continent somewhere and will not be returning here for some time. I don't think I will be anywhere in the neighborhood where he is at the moment, and it would be hopeless to try to take up the matter by mail now. I'm completely at a loss to understand exactly what is happening back there . . .

What the situation is going to be about getting you over simply as a civilian traveler I haven't the foggiest idea either. It simply is impossible to foresee the various governments' policies on this one, and I suppose we will just have to wait and hope. Your fear that you might arrive here just in time to tell me good-bye as I leave for a visit in the States is, of course, honey, preposterous. No such thing could possibly occur. As a matter of fact, the way things look now, I don't see much chance of home leave for many, many months. Another year under conditions similar to this would not surprise me. Already the confusion of peace is spreading over Europe and it is going to get worse before it gets better. All the world at war was a comparatively easy one to figure out. With half the world at peace and the other half still at war it is going to be tougher . . .

Give my love to all the family and to that little red-haid. Love and hugs, Walter

---

OPERATION MARKET GARDEN played havoc with Cronkite's correspondence, but when news of the Allied airborne invasion of Holland hit American newspapers on the morning of September 17, Betsy must have known that her husband had found the new great war story he had aspired to cover since the previous spring. For nearly three weeks, from September 15 through October 3, Cronkite was unable to send her a letter, so she had to find out about his whereabouts (and survival) from his dispatches from the war's latest front line in eastern Holland. The September 17 airborne assault (the "Market" portion of Operation Market Garden) was undertaken by the U.S. 101st and 82nd Airborne Divisions, the British First Airborne Division, and the Polish Brigade. The 101st Airborne made a parachute and glider landing north of Eindhoven, its immediate objective the seizure of bridges across the Son and Veghel Rivers northwest of the city. Unlike those in Normandy on D-Day, the landings this time took place in daylight and went fairly smoothly, with most parachutists and gliders landing at or near their drop zones.

Cronkite was assigned to a glider with about 14 other men. Their Waco glider put down in a potato patch, a soft landing, although bumpy enough that the soldiers' helmets flew off and rolled on the floor. Cronkite grabbed what he thought was his helmet and headed for the unit's predetermined rendezvous point—a nearby drainage ditch. He was surprised when a soldier called him "Lieutenant" and asked if he was sure of his directions. "I shouted back I wasn't a lieutenant," Cronkite recalled in *A Reporter's Life*. "I was a war correspondent. With a full GI vocabulary of unrepeatable words he advised me, rather strongly, that I was wearing a helmet with an officer's big white stripe down its back."

The rest of the first day went well for the 101st. The paratroopers met only light resistance and seized four out of the five bridges they had been assigned to take. The failure to capture the fifth bridge, blown up by the Germans, would, however, slow the Allied ground advance.

During the bombing of Eindhoven, for which he provided a dramatic account in his September 21 UP dispatch, Cronkite was separated from his companion, CBS reporter Bill Downs. He feared the worst, until he later bumped into Downs in the bar of the Hotel Metropole in Brussels. A few days later, back in Holland, he and Downs found themselves separated from the American soldiers they had been accompanying, and then caught in a hail of mortar and small-arms fire. Huddling together for shelter in a ditch, Downs yelled over the din of the firing, "Hey, just remember, Cronkite, these are the good old days." On another occasion, at nighttime, Cronkite was riding in a jeep with a GI driver when five German tanks came rolling toward them. They pulled off the road, fearing the worst, but when the tanks rolled by, a German soldier, apparently assuming they were all in the same army, called out a friendly greeting. (Or, at least, that's one way Cronkite told the story; in another version, the Germans drove right by them, oblivious to their presence.) If Cronkite felt he had missed the real war up until then, Holland cured him of any lingering regrets.

The 101st and 82nd Airborne remained in position in Holland for the next two months.

The bridge at Arnhem, crossing the Rhine River into Germany, was supposed to be secured by an Allied tank column by the end of the third week of September, but it remained in German hands until it was destroyed by American bombers on October 7. The city of Arnhem would not fall to the Allies until mid-April 1945.

From page 2 of the *Dunkirk* (New York) *Evening Observer,* September 18, 1944:

DUTCHMEN CHEER ALLIED AIRBORNE INVADING ARMY

... United Press War Correspondent Walter Cronkite, who landed with the first glider train, said the sky troops, most of them veterans of the Norman invasion, liberated several towns within an hour after their landing and expected to take their "first big objective" by nightfall.

"Opposition is comparatively light," Cronkite reported in a pooled dispatch from Holland at 4:40 p.m. yesterday. "Half an hour after we had landed the small-arms and mortar fire in our sector had ended and only the distant rumble of battle somewhere to the south— where the Allied armies are advancing toward us—was audible.

"Some of our gliders and some C-47 tow planes went through anti-aircraft fire to reach their landing places, but our dive-bombing Mustangs and our vast aerial support silenced the enemy guns one by one."

From page 6 of the *Billings* (Montana) *Gazette,* September 20, 1944:

WRITER TELLS OF NAZI THRUSTS AGAINST ALLIED AIR-BORNE UNITS

By Walter Cronkite

WITH THE ALLIED AIR-BORNE FORCES IN HOLLAND, September 19—The heavily-reinforced Germans in eastern Holland, facing entrapment between Lieutenant General Lewis H. Brereton's air-borne army and the British advancing from Belgium, opened counterattacks Tuesday morning.

We knew that men, guns and tanks had arrived in the German lines. Throughout Monday night the artillery roared on the perimeter of our own air-borne island.

Steadily the Germans lobbed shells at a river crossing the loss of which would seriously delay the push of the British armor through Holland to our men far behind the enemy lines . . . As I write, the Germans are bringing up their heavy artillery—105-millimeter and 166-millimeter guns and 88-millimeter mortars . . .

From page 15 of the *Lowell* (Massachusetts) *Sun,* September 21, 1944:

EINDHOVEN, HOLLAND, GETS VICIOUS NAZI AIR POUNDING AFTER WELCOMING ALLIES

City "Gets It" While Deliriously Greeting Its American and British Liberators

By Walter Cronkite

For Combined American Press

EINDHOVEN, Holland, Sept. 21 (UP)—This city of 100,000, that 30 minutes before was wildly cheering its American and British liberators, took a vicious pounding last night in a German air raid.

Dutch flags that were brought out of hiding after four years and hung—for 24 gay, carefree hours—today hang in burned tatters on charred poles.

Streets where children danced to the music of an accordionist, where people crowded around American vehicles so thickly that traffic was halted, are now littered with glass, brick, stone and cherished possessions . . .

I was dining with Bill Downs of CBS when he first noticed panicky civilians running toward their homes. We learned that some of the army was ordered out and decided to go to headquarters to verify it. Enroute we picked up Henry Standish, an Australian newspaperman.

The city was almost deserted as we drove through. The Dutch, fearful that the Germans might be returning, had removed their flags and pictures of Queen Wilhelmina from many windows. Most of the American and British troops appeared to have left. Only a few civilians were standing in wonder before their homes. They had discarded the carnival hats and false noses they had been wearing so happily only a few minutes before.

It was a strange feeling and one had a hunch something was about to happen. It did. Just before we reached headquarters a lone German twin-engined bomber swept over, dropping orange yellow and green flares.

We sped toward open country but only got as far as the city park when the first bombers came in. The first bombs landed within 10 feet of us. We lay huddled on the ground while bombs ringed us. At least three more sticks hit home near us. The last bomb showered us with twigs, branches and dirt . . .

Cronkite's first letter to Betsy since the start of Operation Market Garden was sparing in details of his combat experiences. Perhaps he wished to relieve her worries by keeping his time under fire vague. He devoted but a single paragraph to what had happened in Holland. In contrast, he lavished details on the visit to Paris that followed, with a chronology of famous tourist sites visited and a description of fashionably dressed ladies, their parasols, and their dogs.

Joe Grigg was a veteran United Press correspondent who had covered the start of the war from Berlin; after the war he would become the UP Paris bureau manager. Ronald Clark was a United Press correspondent.

———

Tuesday, Oct. 3, 1944

My darlingest wife:

At last at least a brief moment in which to write you although God knows how long it will be before you get this letter. I am now assigned for the duration of the war or, at least, the campaign in Holland, to the British Second Army and most of my mail will go and come through its public relations unit. How much of a delay that is going to mean, I have no idea. All we can do is hope for the best.

By now, I suppose, you know that I made the airborne landing with the Americans in Holland two weeks ago Sunday. There really isn't much more to tell except that which has appeared in the papers. Except that I was scared. Not the landing itself but the twelve days of almost constant shelling and bombing afterward really frightened me for the first time in this war. That I plainly admit and if I can help it I have no intention of ever getting back within range of artillery again. I don't suppose I shall be able to avoid it on some limited occasions, but I intend to keep such operations to the absolute minimum.

I'm absolutely in love with Holland—what I've seen of it, and even the residents of that portion claim that it is the ugliest section of the country. "You must go north, and over toward Amsterdam and The Hague to see the real Holland," they all say. But I like the area around Eindhoven all right. The people are so friendly and, in contrast to so many others with whom I have associated in the last couple of years, so clean and neat. And they are modern. I have seen rural kitchens in Holland that beat the all-electric ones in the General Electric ads. The women are homely as hell but they have such wonderful personalities that they seem to have acquired a certain redeeming ugly beauty. Most of the men are equally unattractive but equally personable.

Friday the airborne story was pretty well told and I drove on down here to Brussels with a couple of Yank correspondents for a little rest. When we got here they decided to go on to Paris, so I figured that after what I had been through, plus all those weeks in London without a day off, I was entitled to that fun too. We left here about noon Friday in this open Volkswaggon (captured German jeep), stopped at a little town down the road for lunch, and had reached the Compèigne forest about thirty miles north of Paris about six o'clock when the damned car broke down. In our haste to get to Paris we had talked our way onto the broad highway that the military police had made a one-way northbound road for convoys—talked our way onto it with a story of having to make a broadcast in Paris. So there we were stranded, going the wrong way on a one-way highway and in the middle of a forest. Hitchhiking south on a north-bound line is pretty hopeless, but I got a ride to the next town where I told the MP's to send a repair car after my pals.

Then I kept on hitchhiking. I reached Paris about ten-thirty, dirty and deadly tired. I didn't even bother to look anyone up that night but collapsed in a Red Cross officer's club at the Hotel Edouard VII on the Avenue de l'Opera. Saturday morning I went to the office to find that Sam Hales was in charge temporarily while Joe Grigg was on business

back in London. I had not had breakfast because it is almost impos-
sible to get a meal through normal commercial channels in Paris and I
had gotten up too late for the Army mess, so Sam took me back to the
Red Cross Rainbow Corner (a beautiful club for enlisted men in the
fancy Hotel de Paris) where we had doughnuts and coffee. We had lunch
at the Hotel Scribe which has been taken over as the newspaperman's
hotel and the headquarters of the public relations people and the wire-
less transmitting offices. They operate a mess and bar for the Press in the
hotel and although for the most part it is limited like all the other allied
messes to army rations, it is not too bad and you don't quite starve to
death if you eat there regularly. I had all the rest of my meals while in
Paris at the Scribe as well as most of my drinks. I continued to stay at
the Edouard VII however. It doesn't make much difference where you
stay—no place has any hot water. There is virtually no fuel in Paris and
it looks like a cold winter for the boys and girls there.

Sam had to work Saturday afternoon. I ran into a Red Cross girl,
Irene Starke, I had known in London, and Bill Downs, former United
Presser in Kansas City (his home town) and now with CBS. There
are no taxis in Paris either, and the few horse-drawn hacks and "velo
taxis" (bicycle-drawn jobs for two) are terribly expensive. So we hired
a horse-drawn hack to take us down the Boulevard Capucines, Boule-
vard Madeleine, Rue Royale to the Place de la Concorde and then up
the Champs Elysees to the Arch de Triomphe. We got out there and
walked back down through some side streets to the Champs Elysees
again where we had a couple of cognacs at a sidewalk café and watched
the Parisians (and American soldiers) parade past. Except for essentials
such as food, heating and transportation, Paris appears unaffected by
war. The women are the most fabulously dressed people I have ever
seen complete with silk stockings, cosmetics (of which there are few in
England), beautiful clothes and insane hats and shoes. And all carry-
ing long, rolled parasols with lace frills or leading dogs as insane as the

*hats. Many dressed like that peddle by on bicycles with their skirts up
to their thighs. Most disturbing!*

*We walked half-way back to the Scribe and finally gave it up and got
a couple of velo taxis. At the Scribe we had drinks and dinner and found
that a lot of the correspondents were planning on taking in the reopening of the Bal Tabarin, home of the famous Can-Can, that night. So we
all went up to Montmarte. The Bal Tabarin turned out to be sort of a
glorified Coney Island dime-a-dance joint but it had two good bands
as hot as anything I've heard in the States, and, of course, the Can-Can
which was a little less than terrific. They are short of many liquors in
Paris but there is plenty of champagne. So that is what we drank.*

*Honey, I had to interrupt this for some work. Now I am back but
must again dash off. Briefly, Sunday I had a wonderful sightseeing trip
over Paris and yesterday morning flew back here to Brussels. [Hugh]
Baillie was here until this morning and I have been very busy with
him. He had a message from [Virgil] Pinkley—the first from anyone I
have seen since the landing—which said in part: "Tell Walt Cronkite
his material simply terrific playedest omniwheres [Pinkley was telling
Cronkite in 'cablese' that his dispatches were widely published] stop
also he's assigned british second army stop clark Wilson mcmillan
Cronkite gave us outstanding superior report exbritish second army airborne operations."*

*I'll write about Sunday in Paris later today. Write me at least for the
time being as follows: "Walter Cronkite, United Press War Correspondent, With Second Army, Care Press Relations Group 5, British Liberation Army, London."*

I love you and miss you terribly. Your—Walter
Tell Miss Judy I love her too.

*P.S. Well, I didn't get this letter mailed in my haste after all. This is
a horrible mess here. I stepped in absolutely cold on the thousand and*

one little jobs that the regular Brussels man, Ronald Clark, handles,
and he took off immediately for three days in London to get some win-
ter clothes. So here I am with the serious difficulty of not knowing the
language or anything about the sources of the news, the transmission
channels, or even the locations and times of the official British army
briefings. Besides for the first time in two years I am out here without a
single close friend around and am terribly, terribly lonely. That will pass,
I assume, when I get back toward the front.

I'm not going to try and tell you the rest of the story about Paris right
here because I want to get this letter back into its envelope and ready to
go when next I get summoned out of this hotel room to another confer-
ence. The place for mailing is miles away and there is no transportation.
Love, Walter

———

THE BRITISH SECOND ARMY, commanded by Lt. Gen. Miles Dempsey,
under the overall command of Field Marshal Bernard Montgomery, had
fought in the Normandy campaign in June and July and then liberated
much of Belgium, including Brussels and Antwerp, in the early days of
September. In Operation Market Garden, Second Army armored units
were unable to push through German defenses in Holland in time to
relieve the airborne forces holding the bridge at Arnhem—the famous
"bridge too far." For the remainder of 1944, the British soldiers fought
to hold and expand their salient on the German flank. Because Cronkite
was charged with reestablishing the United Press presence in the Low
Countries, he was also assigned to cover the Second Army.

From page 2 of the *Wisconsin State Journal,* October 5, 1944:

YANKS REACH COLOGNE PLAIN

. . . United Press Correspondent Walter Cronkite reported from Lieut.
Gen. Sir Miles C. Dempsey's Second Army front that the British struck

out up the Nijmegen-Arnhem road in the Rhine triangle Wednesday
and the initial impact of the attack carried forward a mile . . .

Tom Wolf was a reporter with the Newspaper Enterprise Association
(NEA).

The U.S. Embassy in Brussels was reestablished on September 14,
1944, with Ernest de W. Mayer as chargé d'affaires ad interim.

With Second Army in Holland   Monday, Oct. 9, 1944

My darlingest:

*I'm writing just a note tonight hoping that somehow or other I will
find a way to get it mailed in the near future . . .*

*(This typewriter didn't survive the airborne operation as well as I did.
It has gone a little ockeyed.)*

*Well, as I was saying, Paris was terrific. Sunday we borrowed a cap-
tured German Wasserwaggon (amphibious jeep) that Tom Wolf has been
using for transportation, wangled some gasoline and went for a three-
hour tour of the city. We hit the Arc de Triomphe again, all the way out
to the end of the Champs d'Elysee, over to Notre Dame and the Eiffel
Tower, down the left bank into the Left Bank, back over to the Place
Bastille, and up through Montmarte to the exquisitely lovely Sacre Cour
from which all Paris is laid at your feet. The only disappointment was the
Left Bank which wasn't as Greenwich Village as Greenwich Village.*

*Monday, after buying you and mother a present (That God knows how
I'm going to get back to you), I flew back to Brussels. I spent a horribly
lonely and discouraging week there kicking myself out to the army press
conferences twice a day because I had never learned French and felt like
a damned baby. When you are a newspaperman and can't even read the
daily papers you are in a pretty sorry state. Things did pick up Saturday*

*when I visited the Embassy. I was amazed to find that the charges' [chargé
d'affaires's] secretary was Pat Sussmann who used to room with a girl
with whom Harrison Salisbury went around a little. So she gave me the
grand introduction to Ernest Mayer, the charges, and the remaining two
days of my Brussels stay were swell. I had dinner at the Embassy Saturday
night with the Canadian charges and Winthrop Greene, the U.S. charges
in Luxembourg who was over for a visit . . .*

*We went for a ride after lunch in the Embassy Packard (whose
diplomatic immunity had been zealously guarded by the Germans for
four years) and stopped at the Brussels Country Club for a short walk
around the lovely golf course there. (They have women caddies for
women golfers, incidentally, just in case, I suppose, a little boy caddy
couldn't stand the language—and the chattering.) . . .*

*We are here at the Second British Army press camp and tomorrow plan
to shove on up to the front for a day or so to pick up whatever is available.*

*I had a delightful surprise Friday when a packet of letters arrived from
London, forwarded by this office. There were several from you, one from
mother . . . and most delightfully, one from Eva enclosing some pictures
of you, Judy and Petty (but, darnit, none of Molo—tell her to crowd you
folks out of one of those snaps anyway). I love the one of you in bathing
suit and Judy sitting up even if both of your backs are to the camera. I'm
putting that one in my already crowded billfold. Your hair looks as lovely
as ever, darling. I'd like to run my fingers through it again . . .*

*Now that I finally have gotten your letters about seeing Roberts
I'm sorry I'm not in a position to do anything from this end. Frankly,
honey, I'm wondering how all this is going to work out now anyway. I
don't mean to be discouraging, but after seeing the awful mess in which
Europe is, and now with the added prospect that Holland, where I am to
be for some time, is going to be flooded and the worst off of any—after
seeing all that I'm wondering how advisable it is to subject you to it.
England already is improving and is not going to be so bad. Paris might*

be all right if the ports are opened fairly soon and the railroads are at least partially relieved of military traffic . . . But the Low Countries, Germany and the Balkans—ugh! I really dread to think of the prospects of this winter here and even, perhaps, next winter before things improve enough to make living comfortable. However, we will see in the next month or so how things are going to work out. The only thing I can suggest is that, if you can work a deal to get to London, that is a heluva lot closer to Europe than America. But London might be an awfully lonely place unless we were together there.

I'll try to get this off by the quickest possible means. Tell all the family and little Judy hello for me. Oh, by the way, I got your Sept. 20 v-mailer today and am terribly disappointed that the airborne stuff didn't get a better play out there. I love you, Walter

———

THE FAILURE OF Operation Market Garden to enable the promised Allied breakthrough into Germany brought an end to the summer's "home by Christmas" euphoria, as evidenced by both Cronkite's October 17, 1944, letter to Betsy and his United Press dispatch of the same day. For the first time in the nearly two years he had been overseas, he began to have second thoughts about the idea of bringing her to London.

The letter also had some interesting details about Cronkite's postwar plans, as he conceived them in the waning days of 1944. He planned to be a foreign correspondent for at least "a score of years," expecting the first decade of that "foreign service" to be spent in conditions of dire privation. He also felt himself, still some days short of his 28th birthday, to be displaying the symptoms of "advancing old age."

Only toward the end of the letter, in his description of his encounter with the king, did some of the familiar Cronkite humor show itself. King George VI visited the British Second Army on October 15, 1944, and knighted its commander, Lt. Gen. Miles Dempsey. The press corps attached to the Second Army was driven to Eindhoven airport to meet the king when his plane landed. Tongue in cheek, Cronkite told Betsy that, on the basis of a two-word conversation with the king, "he seems like a great guy. I'll have to get to knowing him better."

Cronkite added more details of his royal audience in *A Reporter's Life*. Field Marshal Montgomery's press aide disapproved of his battle garb, which included pants bloused in combat boots, paratrooper style. The aide ordered Cronkite to don a pair of white gaiters, regulation gear for British soldiers on dress occasions. Citing the Boston Tea Party, Cronkite refused. In the end, he remembered proudly, "I met the King in my good American combat boots."

Somewhere in Holland   Tuesday, Oct. 17, 1944

Hello, darling:

. . . Your August 25 letter was all about what to do in preparation for coming over here and it made me sick to read it and realize that you still are there and I'm still here and that days still slide by without our being together. You ask whether I have changed or not. I imagine I have, honey. An awfully lot has happened in these two years and it would be pretty amazing, I guess, if I hadn't undergone a few alterations. Physically I know I have. For one thing—most obvious, of course—I'm back to the gangling youth you met at KCMO, except that the lines are a little deeper and the circles under the eyes are a little blacker. Then my teeth have gone to hell and I just haven't had time to do anything about them—which is disgraceful. I have stomach aches and back aches and night risings and other little symptoms of advancing old age. And I'm afraid I've lost a lot of my sense of humor. Somehow or other, despite the synthetic attempts at gaiety, things don't seem very funny over here. And that applies even more now that we are in Europe. It is really depressing when you know there

is nowhere to go for a good meal, that there is nowhere to go for a hot bath, that there isn't a room in town that is really warm, that you can't go downtown and buy a pair of shoes or a shirt, that there isn't any laundry because there isn't any gas. God knows how long things are going to be that bad here, but I'm afraid prospects aren't very bright.

I'm frankly extremely pessimistic about the whole thing. I have committed myself now to the foreign service and, at any rate, would not back out because I think financially it is by far the better deal. That means at least a score of years over here and, assuming that we don't have another European war in the near future, that still means at least the first ten aren't going to be particularly pleasant. There is still hope, of course, that Amsterdam will not suffer the fate the Germans seem to have planned for it and things might not be so bad as I have pictured—but I am pessimistic, as I say. Paris, for instance, is lovely and once food, clothing and utilities are available there in decent quantities it will not be bad. But I don't think I'm likely to get very near Paris. I'm praying that I don't get saddled with any part of the Berlin bureau. That will be sheer hell.

Darling, this is sort of a ticklish subject but in all fairness I think I ought to bring it up. Whereas three months ago, even after D-day, I still thought it smart for you to come over as soon as possible and was feeling around for ways of getting that job done, at the moment it looks damned inadvisable to me, and, even if we could work it, I don't see how you could be with me on the Continent for months and months to come. Well, I've been away two years now and the day when I shall be able to come home, even for a visit, or you shall be able to join me permanently, seems as remote as ever. It has worried me a lot that, while my interests have broadened almost faster than I can keep up with them and while I'm constantly circulating among other people and (within some pretty definite restrictions) kicking around the world, you have been living the same, monotonous, sheltered existence there. I love you more than you know for the thought behind it and the constancy it implies, but, honey, these should be pretty good years in anybody's life instead of a sort of enforced spinsterhood and old age.

What I'm getting around to, sweetheart, is that I want you to have a good time. I want you to buy fancy clothes and wear them, I want you to have cocktails with people and go out dancing with them, I want you to travel if you feel like it and go to New York and visit Janey. That money that is piled up there is yours, Betsy. A little nest egg for the eventual European trip is a good idea but don't let it stop your living now. If you travel I want you to go Pullman or fly. Be a little selfish about it if it would help ease the conscience any: remember that while I don't call most of this life over here fun, at least it is different and I'm seeing a lot of country and meeting a lot of people. Don't overdo the thing, my darling, but please have a good time. Really, I worry terribly about it.

Incidentally, while I am at the front I am on a full living account and it ought to be possible for me to repay those few hundred dollars I had to draw while dodging buzz-bombs. So, in the same mail, I am writing the accounting department in London to start sending to you the full weekly check of $90 (less occasional insurance deductions). If I suddenly get transferred back to a population center where I'm on only a limited living allowance and have to dip into my salary, then I'll occasionally draft enough to get by. So within two or three weeks you should start getting $90 a week from New York.

I have gotten one or two congratulatory messages since I got up here on the British front but the front has been so comparatively inactive that there really hasn't been very much doing. The competition is stiff here and it is like a movie version of war reporting to race with Charlie Lynch, the Reuters man, and Roger Greene, the AP man, for the breaks and then the transmission facilities to get the stories out. I'm living with Lynch in a screamingly funny, horribly uncomfortable, semi-blitzed village hotel whose plumbing belches all night and whose roof leaks drop by drop into a big pail at the foot of the bed and which has a swinging iron sign that rattles in the wind like all the artillery in the world opening up against you . . .

Now it can be revealed that I covered part of the King's tour of the Dutch front last week. At one point we exchanged a couple of words. I was standing with other newsmen at the end of a row of troops he was reviewing. He walked right on beyond the last troops and suddenly stopped in front of our ragamuffin group in a wonderful double-take. "What's this?" he said, looking at me. "The press," I answered, quick as a flash and without the slightest suspicion of awe. He nodded, looked again, turned and said something to [Field Marshal Bernard] Montgomery, and walked away. Quite an interview, that was. He seems like a great guy. I'll have to get to knowing him better.

I've heard rumors that there is a traveling American army post office down the road a few miles and I'm going out this afternoon to try to find it so I might get this letter off to you in fairly rapid fashion. As I've said before, I think the fastest way to write me is still by V-mail to APO 413 as per the old address. The office will see that it is forwarded.

Give my love to little Judy and to all the family. Well, that part of my love you think you can spare. Forever, Walter

P.S. Which one of my stories were in the [Kansas City] Star?

FROM PAGE 4 of the *Abilene* (Texas) *Reporter-News*, October 19, 1944:

TROOPS LIKELY TO SPEND CHRISTMAS IN FOXHOLES

By Walter Cronkite

WITH BRITISH SECOND ARMY IN HOLLAND, Oct. 17— (Delayed)—(UP)—We might as well face it; barring a political collapse inside Germany, we won't be out of the foxholes by Christmas.

For a month since the bold air-borne descent on Holland, we have sat on this salient. We have broadened its flanks just enough to protect the lifeline corridor up the middle of it . . .

We have shattered their tanks and artillery all along the way, but what they have left is banked tread to tread and hub to hub along the Siegfried line. We are operating over territory they have held for four years and their guns are ranged in and operated at the very points on which they know we must concentrate.

Then there's the weather. Even if the normal rain and snow come, this country is going to be hell. Already the flat Dutch fields are bogs in which tanks cannot operate. The fighting must be done on the hard roads. And it is against them that the Germans can concentrate their mines, mortars, artillery and men.

Cronkite's letter of November 19, 1944, was one of his longest and most interesting. He began by confessing his fear that Betsy might misinterpret either his silences when he didn't write or his words when he did. And then, in a lengthy section that seems almost as if it were written for the convenience and edification of future biographers, he offered a year-end review of his experiences and emotions in the eventful months of 1944. During the first five months of the year, he wrote, "the air [war] was the big thing, and I was its papa." Since the invasion, however, he felt he had let down his readers and his employer, even during the dramatic days he spent behind enemy lines in Operation Market Garden: "I didn't do any really outstanding stories from what should have been the best assignment I ever had."

Maj. Louis M. "Mel" Schulstad, singled out in Cronkite's letter as a friend with a "screwball" sense of humor, enlisted in the Army Air Corps in 1939, flew 44 combat missions in a B-17 over France and Germany, and was twice awarded the Distinguished Flying Cross for valor. He retired as a colonel after 27 years in the military.

Alfred Wagg was a correspondent for the *Chicago Tribune*.

Bill Walton was a *Time* correspondent; he dropped into Normandy with the paratroopers on D-Day.

"Nightside" was journalist slang for the night shift in a newspaper office—a less desirable employment option than the day shift.

———

Sunday, November 19, 1944

My darling wife:

It has gotten to be nine-thirty in the evening of the day which for a week I have set aside to spend writing to you. And I am just getting started on this letter. The maid permitted me to oversleep this morning and I barely had time to finish a letter to [Virgil] Pinkley before I had to run to meet Ronald Clark, BUP [British United Press] reporter, for lunch. At lunch it developed that Clark had a sore throat and wanted to beg off covering the afternoon military briefing. So this afternoon was lost to me while I handled that. Then I had a date for dinner with Boyd Lewis, UP man down from the Canadian front. So I have just gotten home.

But, despite the delay, I consider this a very important letter. I want to turn over a new leaf, honey. I want to write you daily, if possible, and if anything prevents that, then to fill you in as quickly as possible on the missing days. I have been so depressed lately because I can't be with you and because I have been without you so long, and I feel that the only way I possibly can snap out of it is to be closer to you again. The only way I know to do that is to write. Part of my melancholy, I know, is a feeling of guilt, a feeling that perhaps I have hurt you by not writing oftener. If anything, it is more horrible to hurt you when we are apart for then it seems an almost impossible task to make amends. Just like we can never catch up on the years we have lost, so I can never make amends for the loneliness I've sharpened by not writing. All I can do is beg, darling, and tell you again that I love you so.

I don't know exactly which—if indeed any particular one—of many factors have contributed most to my sudden realization of the meany

I've been. Perhaps it is that for the first time since we have been apart I have been without mail for weeks on end and know, for the first time, how really cruel and horrible that can be. Perhaps, quite candidly, it is a sudden fear that gripped me as soon as I had mailed that letter written at the depth of my gloom; the one in which I urged you to play and have a good-time because we were wasting so many precious years apart. I thought over that letter a long time before I wrote it, and fiddled with it a long time in the writing, and finally thought it was what I wanted it to say. Then, when I had mailed it, I sank even lower in to despond fearing that you might put the wrong interpretation on it. I'm afraid even now of the answer I'm going to get from it. Perhaps another factor is that for the first time in many, many months I've reached some resemblance to permanency and feel that I can keep any pledge to write and can really settle down to a somewhat normal existence.

I thought maybe, if you would like, honey, I'd make this sort of a year-end report to catch up. I'd kind of review the year, where I've been, what I've done, who I've known (as nearly as this horrible memory of mine will know), what I've thought. Would that be all right? But before I get into that, a couple of current matters.

First of all, there is some chance again that Pinkley may act to get you over here. He only hinted at it when I saw him in Paris last week and said he would go into it more fully with me later, but I had to pull out rather suddenly and we didn't get to finish the discussion. He is due up here next week and I plan, of course, to go into the matter in minute detail then . . .

Secondly, Pinkley turned me down again in Paris on my proposal to go home for a short leave, but we left the door open to further negotiations. I hate to shirk a job, particularly at this stage of the game when I have been named to a pretty important post, but dammit, darling, two years without you is too much. (Two days is too much, but it seems that we are destined to deal with years . . .) So I thought that when I see Pinkley here next week I'd put a set of conditions up to him . . . I have been overseas now, in a continuous stretch, longer than any other married man in the company . . . Pinkley's soft-soap answer to me always is the same—that I'm indispensable. I'm getting just a little tired of the line (despite the fact that I pat myself on the back, grin at myself in the mirror, and almost believe it). I think that if my conditions were met and I still were denied the home leave, I'd feel strong enough about it to threaten to quit. I'm awfully homesick for you and Judy and if months more of loneliness stretched before us I think I'd go mad.

Thirdly, by sheerest chance and strangest accident, two Christmas packages for me arrived in Paris while I was there. Of course, they weren't supposed to have gone to Paris but anyway they showed up there at the correspondents' mail room and one of the UP boys spotted them on their way back to the proper APO. So I claimed them the morning that I was about to go out to the Post Exchange and buy a pair of shoes. They looked like shoe boxes so I thought the better part of valor was to open them—and anyway it was just a few days past my birthday and I hadn't had a birthday gift except your sweet telegram. I opened them and found in one the wonderful slippers that I needed so badly, and in the other the Bostonian shoes. I can't tell you yet, for sure, whether the shoes fit. For two months I've been in oversize parachute boots and my feet have spread out a little . . . I feel guilty every time I get a package. All you folks are far too good to me.

Well, about this year: Looking back on it, I guess it was a pretty successful one for me, but I didn't have much fun living it. During the first five months, of course, I had the main story almost every day completely to myself. The air was the big thing, and I was its papa. At its height, just before D-day, I had five and sometimes more men working for me. I sort of city edited the job, writing all the leads and directing my staff out in the field. Virgil has said since that my organization, sense of responsibility, and blah-blah on that one helped him make up his mind to give me the Low Countries for post-war development. My stand-bys were Collie

Small (who is a swell, slightly irresponsible youngster who the Moorheads dearly love and who used to be a sports writer in the States), Bob Rich-ards, Bill Disher. At one time or another Bill Higginbotham and Sam Hales and McGlincy helped me. It seemed a little odd ordering Sam around, but he took it in good spirit and we got along nobly. My only source of real trouble was Phil Ault, a Minnesota boy with plenty on the ball who has battered his way right up to the top in the UP foreign service and for whom I have a lot of respect. He was sitting in the day slot in London and used to have a habit of signing the short overnight cables he would send about RAF night activity. He had some cohorts in New York who put his name on all the day stories on the air war, the great bulk of which I was writing. It took me two months of that shadow boxing before I finally laid down the law to Pinkley and got him to send a definite order to New York that I would be signed around the clock on all air news except the individual, side-bar features that Collie and the others dug up. That job, with the amazing growing of the air forces, kept me pretty well tied to the desk but I managed some out-of-town trips up into lovely sections of England which, unfortunately, because of air forces still based there, I still can't identify. Also I had been over that territory so much in the preceding year that I knew it by heart and it got to be just a tedious grind standing up for hours in crowded train corridors and sticky-handed children paw-ing at my already dirty pants, and then long, cold, bumpy rides in open jeeps, and finally miserable Nissen huts wallowing in the mud and smoky officers' bars where pilots insisted on a drink-for-drink basis. I made a lot of friends, of course, the best of whom usually were non-flying officers like Major Bill Laidlaw, public relations officer for First Bombardment Division, who was a left-banker in Paris for years before the war, writing weighty stuff for Atlantic Monthly and being a Bohemian. He is strictly a delightful screwball with a terrific sense of humor, an insatiable thirst, and an over-active mind that is hard to keep up with. I told him once I thought his brain was on a Pogo stick—and he loves me for the remark, which, I think myself, is pretty good. Then there was Major Clayton Smith, old-time Houston oil man who suddenly found himself a public relations officer for a medium bomber outfit and was swell because he became a father to the youngsters there. He loaned them money, solved their personal problems, arranged their parties, did their Christmas shopping for them, got them out of trouble. There are hosts of others who will come up as we talk it over in the years to come, and I hope you get a chance to meet some of them.

The biggest trouble was the flyers who came to London on "48's"— forty-eight hour passes—and expected me to show them the town and keep up with their drunken "tomorrow we die" sort of entertainment. I still don't like that sort of party and never got mixed up in them, arriving at an early stage at a formula of meeting them for a quick drink before dinner, then perhaps taking them to Sandy's, and then excusing myself to return to work—which was no lie. The only one I ever really went out with was Mel Schulstad, who now is a Major. He is in his early twenties, and came from the group with which I flew over Wilhelmshaven. He is a screwball like the rest but with the kind of sensa humor we both love, and he reminded me of you and home, and that's why I liked him. He had a wonderful little rhyme, recited to gestures when the right moment came. It went: "If you're a droop, you end up in group, and if from there you're canned, it's Bomber Command. Out of the sack, into the flak; out of the flak, into the sack. How now, brown cow." Perhaps it is meaningless to anyone but the air boys, but to them it was a knockout.

I found out only tonight that the only other funny thing I've said all year has gained immortality. I was having dinner tonight with Boyd Lewis, Bill Johnson of Time, and Barney McQuaid of the Chicago Daily News. When I brought up this crack, as I often do, McQuaid leaned over the table and grabbed my hand and said he always wanted to shake hands with the author of that marvelous line. It seems that there is a lecherous little writer who no one likes named Al Wagg. Bill Walton of Time and I were walking down a London street when two horribly ugly Wacs passed up—as ugly as only WACS can be—and immediately after them Wagg, with his tongue fairly hanging out. He barely had time to pipe a hello in his squeaky voice. I said to Walton: "Just a case of Wagg dogging his tail." (Laughter.)

Incidentally, funny thing about Walton. He is one of my favorite people. I met him the first night he hit London just about a year ago and tried to show him a few of the ropes and we got to be pretty close friends although we didn't see a great deal of each other. He jumped with the parachutists D-day and I have seen him here once and in Paris once since then. Scene switches and we meet Al Newman, a very nice guy from Newsweek and used to be one of their top sports men and now is a war correspondent. I've never known Al very well, our paths simply cross-ing in the usual course of events. But a couple of days ago I ran into Al on one of the streets here. He was just passing through on his way back from London to one of the fronts. He then threw in the bomb shell that in his hut near Aachen a few weeks ago he and Bill Walton were having a little chat when Walton's eye suddenly fell on a copy of Chakett, a Chi Phi magazine. And then it all came out—Walton, Newman and I are frater-nity brothers. It seems so strange since I never seem to run into Chi Phi's anywhere and had just given up asking people. Now I'm all fraternity-conscious all over again.

During those months before D-day Jim and I were living at 78 Buck-ingham Gate, the old building by Wellington Barracks where young Guardsmen used to have their bachelor quarters. It wasn't much of a flat but it was convenient and comfortable—that is until Robin Duff, the BBC commentator, got bombed out of his flat and came to stay with us for a few days until he found another. He was there for three months—until the invasion moved both him and Jim out. I was so busy with the air story—working toward the last up to twenty hours a day—that Jim and I didn't get a chance to do much helling around and the little socializing we did do was over the bar at El Vino's, Frank Bauer's little emporium on Fleet street around the corner from the office. We would have an occasional drink in there and talk over things before I went back to the office for another stint. I really love Jim like a brother but the guy is strictly black Irish. Like all those people he has a special fairy sitting on his shoulder whispering wonderful lines in to his ear which he transposes onto paper with all the ease of a man licking a stamp. But sometimes the fairy whispers dark things to him and he goes out and gets fiery, Irish drunk and ends up in a typical saloon brawl. Sometimes he doesn't show up for work, and the office loses faith only to regain it with his next smashable piece. Where he'll end up remains to be seen but there will be no middle ground. He'll either be on top or in the gutter. He went over to Ireland to do the DeValera crisis in March and met there an Irish girl with whom he is much enamored and she may have some effect in straightening him up— but I don't believe much in that sort of reform. Besides, I suspect Bunty [his girl] of harboring the same traits Jim does, and that ain't good.

That, in sort of a slap-dash fashion, brings us up to D-day. That was when my, as well as Hitler's, little world seemed to crumple around my shoulders. There, first of all, was that abortive D-day bomber flight over the invasion coast which I couldn't see because of the clouds and about which I told you. Then, from there on out, the air story took a back seat and it was such a come-down from handling the top story everyday that I didn't seem to ever get back into the swing. Except for the appearance of the flying bombs and the smash play I got on the early stories regarding them, I didn't do a really valuable piece of work for the first three months of invasion. I just sat in London champing at the bit to get to the front but being held back to do the work-horse job that still had to be done on the air story. I was pretty envious of McGlincy and the others in Normandy and pretty unhappy. I was also terribly lonesome living alone and a little upset about being bombed out. I made those two trips to Normandy to do special stories but neither of them made the front-pages. Then in the middle of August Pinkley asked if I'd be interested in the airborne assignment. I, of course, jumped at it. Then for the next month I spent my time shuttling back and forth from London to airborne headquarters as they set up one after another airborne show only to have Patton's or Dempsey's men move so fast that the parachute and glider landing was not needed. The biggest disappointment of them all was the first one which had us scheduled to land on the outskirts and take Paris. That would have been a great show. I was beginning to look a little foolish around the office. Four times I dashed in, picked up expense money, left last instructions with various people, and dashed out to the wars in my battle clothes only to return a few days later with the whole thing called off.

The rest of it you know. I didn't do any really outstanding stories from what should have been the best assignment I ever had. It was just a good workmanlike job with no flashes of brilliance. I think everyone, including Cronkite, was a little disappointed but communications, plus the fact that I was scared to death most of the time, had something to do with it. Even so I got some nice cables and Baillie and Pinkley sent along congratulations. Then a couple of weeks ago I got a little certificate from the commanding general of the airborne division saying that I had made a glider landing in the presence of the enemy and was hereby a glider pin which looks a little like a pilot's wings and which I proudly wear.

I stayed with the airborne troops until the first of October, went to Paris for a couple of days' leave, returned to Brussels to fill in for Clark for a week, then back to Brussels to begin the job of organizing our Low Countries bureaus and services for both the incoming and outgoing services. I took off that few days last week to go to Paris and am now back here settling down for the long grind until it is time to shove on toward Rotterdam, The Hague, and Amsterdam. Or until I get to come home.

I'm living now with Dave Anderson, 39-year-old New York Times correspondent who is sort of a pretty-boy social butterfly and strictly an old maid around the house. We have been living together a week and I don't know that I'm going to make a go of it. He is at the opposite end of the scale in every respect from McGlincy.

The flat, however, is wonderful. It is owned by American Jews who fled when the Germans came, and for four years was occupied by the Nazis. It is strictly modern (although without heat or hot water, of course), on the fourth floor of a fancy apartment building on a fashionable drive at the top of a hill overlooking a wide stretch of the city. It has a big living room, dining room, little alcove with desk and bookcase, and, off of a long corridor, three bedrooms. The maid, who was here eight months before the war and stayed throughout the German occupation, has the back bedroom. It is only about twenty minutes from the center of town by tram, and only ten minutes from the main government quarter and the spot where we have to file our copy. My principal problem now is to find office space for the UP, get some furniture somewhere, locate an English-speaking staff, etcetera. I'm really beginning to feel the executive burdens, complicated all the more by my lack of language. For a newspaperman that is a terrifying handicap. I can't even read the papers to find out what is going on, I can't make appointments by telephone, I can't dicker for office space. It is the one thing that might defeat me in this job and then, as Norma Chaney seems so confident of, I might have to come traipsing back out to Kansas City to run the nightside. No, I don't really think that will happen. If language does defeat me here, there are plenty of other good spots with the UP where such a handicap won't matter.

I like it here, though, being the big fish in the little pond. As UP manager for the Low Countries I find I garner a lot of respect. The American ambassador likes me and I have open sesame to his precincts. Tomorrow night his first secretary (MALE!) is coming here for dinner, and things go swimming along that league. Once this war is over, you and I ought to have a lot of fun in this supposedly gay international set. That is the day I'm living for. That is what will make all this worthwhile.

That is pretty much of once-over-lightly treatment. It won't ever be possible to just sit down and recite the events of these years, honey. They will just have to come out in driblets as one thing leads to another and reminds me of something else. But I'll try to be a better boy in the weeks to come before we are together again and keep you up to date, day to day.

The important thing, always, is for you to remember that I love you. You must know that. That is one flame that has never gone out. And tell little Judy I love her too. Just because I don't mention her in each of my letters isn't any sign that she isn't as constantly in my thoughts as you yourself. How I'd like to run my fingers through the hair of those two red-haids again! Tell the folks, mine and yours, that I love them too, and thank them for me for their swell packages and their letters. It is nice to know you aren't forgotten.

Forever and ever, my sweetheart.

I love you, Walter

———

As BUREAU CHIEF for the United Press in Brussels, Cronkite found his days filled with bureaucratic chores and social obligations.

Morris Swanoepoel held a position with the Belgian national radio network.

———

Monday, Nov. 20, 1944

My dearest Betsy:

It is now 6:35 p.m. It is raining cats and dogs outside, as it has been all day, but today it is not so cold and we have scrounged a little coal to keep at least this one front room livably warm. In twenty-five minutes Ernest Mayer, the legation first secretary, is due along for dinner and I have to get my face washed and my hair combed and fingernails cleaned. There isn't any question of dressing since all I have here still is this filthy British battle dress. Mayer is a wonderful guy with the look of the career diplomat but a strange aversion to red-tape.

I have had a bitch of a day and am tres tired, as we say here. Dave [Anderson] ran across some English-speaking lad who is a friend of one of his social contacts here and who wants to work for the Americans, so we had him in this morning for an interview as a possible office-boy, translator, and messenger. He seemed like a good boy so we decided to hire him . . . Then I was on my way up to SHAEF to try to arrange some way of speeding up my mail to you and vice-versa when I ran into Major George Hargreaves who spent two months at Fort Leavenworth and won't stop talking about the Hotel Phillips officers' club—a subject close to my heart, all right (namely, you) but which gets a little boring from dear old George. We went up to the Belgium information office and there George introduced me to one Oscar Hellstrom, a fabulous character out of whose clutches I wasn't able to wiggle (and I'll admit I didn't struggle very hard) until three o'clock when I had an appointment at the radio station. Oscar is now a member of the SHAEF mission to the Netherlands and is going to turn out to be a hell of a valuable contact. Already today, in my first three hours with him, I had lunch with M. and Mme. Fernand de Nefvre, veddy, veddy social artists and interior decorators, and an hour with the head of the Belgian Red Cross. Then it turns out that Oscar himself is a multi-millionaire and superbigwig politician from Seattle. He is a close friend of FDR's and has one of those rare sets of cuff links that the prexy passed out to his closest advisers some ten years ago or so and which the Republicans have never ceased talking about. Then out to the radio station for a two-hour conference with Morris Swanoepoel trying to get them to monitor our newscasts from London and New York so I can get some sort of service rolling here. Well, that the day. Boring, isn't it? But through it all, I love you.

In his November 22, 1944, letter, Cronkite reported on roommate trouble and colleague trouble.

Frank Barhydt was an old Cronkite friend—what he meant by "Barhydting my soup in their faces" can only be imagined.

————

Wednesday, Nov. 22, 1944

My darling

I didn't get to write last night, frankly because for the first time I had a chance to go out and have a drink with Dave [Anderson] and it looked to me like a small talk over a bar was pretty essential at that point to a continued amicable sharing of this apartment. We had dinner about seven-thirty and finished, in best continental fashion, about nine-thirty, whereafter he suggested a trip across the street to investigate the Chez Elysee club. I took him up on it and it wasn't until twelve o'clock (despite an eleven o'clock curfew existing here) that we got home. The drinks helped clear the air a little bit but today he returned to his old role of grandma and he began complaining that someone had rearranged his file of newspapers, and I hit the ceiling again. All in all, it isn't too happy an association and, if the flat weren't so damned comfortable, I'm sure it wouldn't last very long.

I'm also having troubles in the office, so to speak. Richard McMillan, as you undoubtedly know, is one of the BUP [British United Press], and consequently the UP, top-notchers, but he also is the biggest prima donna of the bunch. Unfortunately he is on one of the fronts nominally under my control. But Mac, of course, is under no one's control—not even Pinkley's or Fisher's—because that is Mac's nature. Yesterday he all of a sudden appeared here with the announcement that he was going to take it easy for a couple of weeks and that he intended "sending young Clark up to the front for a spell." Well, there is a cardinal rule that no one leaves a front, or any other assignment for that matter, without first informing the office. This is one of the cases where the rule was pretty important, because it happens that Clark is seriously ill with flu. Luckily Boyd Lewis was in from the comparatively quiet Canadian front and I was able to send him up in Mac's place . . .

Yesterday we had a little sunshine which sort of brightened things up but today it has turned beastly again. (Speaking of things turning beastly—Noel Coward is in town in an ENSA—British USO—show but it looks as if I'm going to be too damned busy to see it.) There really hasn't been a thing of interest in the last 48 hours, just dull business negotiations. Oh, yes, two of Dave's British pals came for dinner tonight and we had no sooner seated ourselves than one mentioned some mutual friend with the comment that "he was in school at Harrow with me." . . .

"Oh, I beg your pardon, old chap, he was with me at Eton," said the second secretary of the British Embassy. "By jove, egad, but really he was with me at Harrow, you know," replied the RAF type. Honestly word for word, that went on for a good ten-minutes during which I was doing my best to keep from Barhydting my soup into their faces.

Which, for some reason or other, reminds me that I bought a wonderful English-language volume in Paris "banned in United States and Great Britain." It is privately printed and called "Some Limericks." It has, unexpurgated, all the dirty limericks all the little boys in the world have ever heard, each followed with a perfectly dead-pan explanation of them. I started to say "for example" there and quote one in best "censored quotations" style, but I find even that is impossible. Just one of those post-war projects, I guess.

Last night on Dave and my roamings we stumbled into a wonderful little bar up at the corner whose Dutch owner used to play the trap drums in some European jive outfit. Come to think of it, I guess that falls simply under "incidental intelligence." . . .

Give my love to little Judy and to all the family. I love you, honey. Forever, Walter

WARD COLWELL WAS Kansas City bureau manager for the United Press in the 1930s. "Working the nightside," i.e., the night shift, was Cronkite's favorite expression for a reporting job from hell.

Belgium was in a state of acute political crisis in November 1944, as the conservative politicians associated with the government-in-exile vied for power against members of the Belgian resistance, many of them Communists and Socialists. Cronkite felt that the Associated Press was doing a far better job than the United Press in reporting the story.

Hubert Pierlot was the leader of the Belgium government-in-exile during World War II.

November 28, 1944

My darlingest wife:

This is being written under conditions almost as uncomfortable as a fox hole, but I'm determined to get at least a note off to you today. Right now I'm sitting in the cold, ground-floor press room of the Army public relations division with my fingers so cold they hurt when I hit the keys. I'm sitting here as a dripping failure. As you undoubtedly know, we had violence Saturday afternoon at our regular week-end Communist-Resistance-Socialist demonstration and since then the government has been tottering again. The story is now about seventy-two hours old, and so far UP has done nothing but trail badly with hopelessly inadequate coverage. I could almost have put that line in quotes and cited the messages from New York and London. Some small element may have been played by bad breaks but mostly it was lack of organization on my part and I'm pretty downhearted about it all. I'm absolutely overwhelmed with work—trying to hire a staff, trying to rent an office, trying to get a car, trying to get communication facilities, trying to get contracts with a dozen publishers, trying to cover the government, trying to keep under control the two primadonnas who

BUP has working on this front, trying to keep from getting thrown out of here because I'm still playing one set of army credentials against another set of civilian credentials in order to stay. All this with no transportation at all, virtually no telephone because I can't handle the language.

But I shouldn't be relaying all my problems to you. By the time we are together again they will all be ironed out and I'll be running a couple of well-established bureaus or working the nightside in Kansas City under Ward Colwell. Ah, well.

I'm sorry I haven't been able to keep my promise of a daily note, or at least semi-daily note. I think it has now been about four or five days since my last V-mailer, but, honey, there really just isn't the time for five minutes in front of the typewriter. Right now I'm waiting for a piece of copy to be censored and taking this moment to be with you. Jim McGlincy came up from Paris Saturday to see his Irish girl, who now is in these parts as a voluntary field worker for the Catholic Women's League. (Loud, cynical laughter.) But I have hardly had a chance to see him or talk to him except for a couple of drinks. He is going back today and I had planned to meet him at the Canterbury Hotel for lunch but, as usual, I have been tied up again and suppose I have by now missed him. It is now 1:30 and I don't know when I'll get away from this horrible place. Then at three [Belgian prime minister Hubert] Pierlot speaks to the Chamber. Which, reminds me, that is what I want to do—speak to the Chamber. The urinal here, incidentally, is named "Adamant." I'm thinking of collecting urinal names but I can't figure out what sort of book to get to keep them in.

I got a letter from Molo yesterday with a picture of you, Betty and Molo and some clippings. Tell her how very much I appreciate it, and that I will send along a Maple Leaf right away. I liked the picture. You all look healthy enough, even with the legs removed.

I must go now, darling. I'll write more later. I love you, you know. Forever, Walter

AT THE END of November 1944, little fighting was taking place on the Belgian front, and Cronkite was preoccupied with the problems of getting his United Press bureau up and running. At least he had turkey and cranberry sauce for Thanksgiving dinner.

Sir Hughe Montgomery Knatchbull-Hugessen was a veteran British diplomat (he had been part of the British delegation at the Versailles peace negotiations in 1919). In 1937, as British ambassador to China, his car had been machine-gunned by a Japanese plane, leaving him severely wounded. In 1944 he was appointed ambassador extraordinary and plenipotentiary to Belgium.

———

Friday, Dec. 1. 1944

My darlingest:

It has been a heluva week and it isn't over yet but most of the shouting has died down now and we at least are maintaining a semblance of keeping the old UP head out of water. I've suffered considerable damage to prestige and reputation during these recent days when it seemed everything was going wrong but I suppose it isn't too late to recover and, as Heinie Hoch used to say in his New Year's Day sermon, "We must look forward not backward." I got one message from Buenos Aires saying we were "superior" on the Belgian crisis, which, of course, shocked everyone in London and New York, to say nothing of Brussels where we all knew we had taken the beating of our lives. All we could figure here was that both Reuters and AP must have just forgotten to file the Belgian story that night. And a routine log which [Harrison] Salisbury (who now is foreign editor, by the way) sends every day to all foreign bureaus, said yesterday that we broke even on the crisis that day and among our play was a front-pager in the Kansas City Star. Good old Hess! I imagine he knew that I felt pretty bad about the thing and thought it would cheer me up to let me know that the old hometown sheet used UP on Belgium anyway.

I have had to cancel most of the business-social engagements on the calendar this week, and haven't had a chance even to write you a long enough letter to tell you of the interesting events of last week. The only thing I managed this week was to keep a cocktail date at the very snooty, strictly stag Automobile Club where I secured an officer's membership. It is the place to take cabinet ministers, industrialists, etcetera. Last week the social events really got rolling Wednesday afternoon when I had teas with Count Barbason of Luxembourg who wants me to stay in one of his chateaus when I get to his country. Thursday night the American embassy had a little dinner for the dozen or so high American officers here and a few newsmen as a thanksgiving feast and we had real turkey and cranberry sauce and little imitation pumpkin pies. I got all tangled up with dinner in a long discussion with Sir [Hughe Montgomery] Knatchbull-Hugessen, the British ambassador, about middle and Far-Eastern problems about which, of course, I know nothing and he, having served as ambassador in Ankara and Something-or-other in Chungking, knew all about. Friday night I had dinner at Baron Marengees washed-out mansion. Another guest was a distinguished-looking gent who knew he had met me somewhere previously just as I was certain that I had met him. It was an impressive discussion while he suggested "Shepherd's, Cairo," and I said I'd never been there but I'd been in West Africa. He suggested Rio and I said I'd never been there, but what about London or Paris. It was amazing until we decided it was outside a Brussels building when I was looking for a flat. I love you, Walter

---

THE THIRD ANNIVERSARY of Pearl Harbor passed unmentioned in Cronkite's December 7, 1944, letter. Instead, he was preoccupied with postwar dreams.

Thursday morning, December 7, 1944

My darlingest wife:

I'm afraid this is just going to be a note. It is now 11:20 a.m. and I must shave and get to a meeting with Foreign Minister [Paul-Henri] Spaak at twelve o'clock. Thank goodness, however, my flat is only ten minutes from the foreign office.

I haven't been able to write since late last week when [Virgil] Pinkley suddenly came swooping down on me. We had four really busy but wonderful days. It was a constant round of conferences with publishers, communication experts, government officials, luncheons and dinners. Or else it was weighty conferences just between the two of us with much letter writing and calculating. Well, the result is that Pinkley seems to feel I am doing all right. He plans to announce next Monday or a few days after my appointment as manager for Belgium, Holland and Luxembourg. (My cards here will read "Director for etc."—impressive, eh?) And, best of all, just out of the blue he says he is telling New York to raise the old salary another ten bucks a week effective the first of the year! So, honey, we have cracked the three-figure mark per week which really isn't too bad, I guess. And, in addition, I'll get a commission on all business in my three countries.

I don't think Pinkley figures on keeping us here too long after the war. That is, I think he has other, even bigger things in mind for me if I deliver on this one, and that means that after a year or two in these parts we might be shifting toward the Balkans or, perhaps, even elsewhere in Europe. Anyway, the expense account is practically unlimited (within a few obvious bounds, that is) and the living is gracious, and it is expected that to live in the manner to which a United Press manager should be accustomed abroad with the entertaining of cabinet ministers, ambassadors and the like, you should have a couple of servants. The job is a *terrible worry, a heluva lot of work, but it is beginning to look like the game is worth the candle.*

Darling, I'm not too sure whether it has really happened or not, but Virgil says he has written Earl Johnson (Vice-president and general news manager) in New York to get in touch with you about possibly coming over for the UP. For goodness sakes, if he does write, don't be timid . . . I adore you, Walter

---

IN HIS LETTER of December 10, 1944, Cronkite reminded Betsy that in two days it would be December 12, the anniversary of the last time they had seen each other.

Larry LeSueur was one of the original "Murrow Boys," joining CBS Radio in 1939, covering the London Blitz, and landing with the invasion forces on Utah Beach on D-Day.

The Barthe-Delvilles and the Metzes were wealthy Brussels families.

A drastic coal shortage left many Europeans (and Americans in Europe) shivering during the bitterly cold winter of 1944–45.

Sunday, Dec. 10, 1944

My darlingest wife:

It is ten o'clock of a miserable night. The wind is ripping the rain into little drops the size of pinheads but with the sting of the other end of the pin. Last trams run here now at ten o' clock to conserve electricity and I left the British Officers' Club just in time to catch the final edition. I had dinner and a couple of drinks there with Larry LeSueur, the CBS joe with whom we had dinner that night at Al (Fireside) Schnet's. He has just come up to this sector to replace Bill Downs who is resting or having trouble with the boss, or something that requires his presence in London. I've had a pretty busy day, even for a Sunday. I was up at eight and out by nine chasing down a couple of stories on a meeting here of Allied medical officers, but never got either story. At one I had lunch at the Press hotel, at two-thirty I was picking up my mail at the British army press headquarters, including a letter from you sent regular mail to the London office October 27, at three I was back at home tidying up, at four I was at the Barthe-Delville's for tea, at five-thirty I was the Metz' for tea, and at seven-thirty I met Larry at the club . . .

The officers' club here isn't bad—if you like khaki and the English. I don't like khaki, and I'll tell you the rest when I see you. The British traditionally kick their service people around and rarely furnish them decent living, eating or recreating facilities. But this spot is really okay. It formerly was the building reserved only for State cocktail parties, dances and similar receptions . . . Lot of tear-drop chandeliers, elevated picture-frame sort of orchestra platform, large horseshoe bar, and all the other stuff it takes. The only thing it lacks to make it like other continental casinos is the woman attendant in the men's room. Honestly! Every bar, every night club has one. Usually she is an old grey-haired doll, but occasionally they pop up with something around a fellow's own age and then it is just a little embarrassing. She trots around and sweeps the old cigarette butts into the dustpan, right out from under your feet with complete unconcern. I figure that is worth a tip. Frequently the gents and ladies are side-by-side and you wait for some gal to powder her nose before you can wash your hands and adjust your tie. Strange business.

Things have gone to hell here at the flat. Our ration, which we get from the Army, has been cut; we aren't getting any more coal, and the lamp on the desk has gone blooey. Of all these the coal is the most serious problem. Did I ever tell you how we got our coal? Well, Paula, our maid, lives in our back bed room and also in sin. In the latter case, the affaire d'amour is a gent who works for the Post Office. He takes the usual satchel to work every morning as if he had along his work clothes.

But __his__ satchel is empty. During the day he pinches coal, piece by piece, until at the end of the day the satchel is full. So we have been having a nightly fire in our stove in the living room and living with some degree of comfort. Either he has lost his job or Paula has lost her love. At any rate, there hasn't been any coal for the last four days and I have been living in my fur-lined flying clothes and still freezing to death. Tomorrow [Dave] Anderson and I are going to have to do a little dealing in the black market where we, if we are lucky, should be able to get a ton for about $150. The food situation is not serious and even with half-rations we will have plenty for ourselves but not enough to entertain. That would be all right too if I had had a little advance notice. But I have invited Morris Swanoepoel of the national radio station for Wednesday and John Harrison of the Embassy for Thursday. If I take them to a black market restaurant—the only kind open—it means $30 or $40 a throw. But that is something for the UP to worry about.

Well, darling, Tuesday is the second anniversary of Black Saturday. I should never forgive myself if I hadn't had these two years' experience but they have been lonely. The hope now is, of course, that we will be together again soon. Then we'll start doing a heap of living to makeup lost time. We at least have a well-to-do, comfortable existence ahead. And I love you. Forever and ever, Walter

———

WHILE CRONKITE WAS preparing to drive from Brussels to Antwerp on December 15, 1944, a quarter of a million German troops were moving into position to launch the offensive the following day that became known as the Battle of the Bulge. The Germans hoped to capture Antwerp, dividing the Allied forces in western Europe and forcing the Americans and British to sue for peace. The attack came as a complete surprise to the soldiers posted along a thin defensive line in the Ardennes Forest in Belgium, and panic spread among the outnumbered Americans. But the stubborn resistance of some U.S. forces, most famously the 101st Airborne soldiers sent to the key crossroads town of Bastogne, slowed the attackers. Gen. George S. Patton's Third Army drove relentlessly northward from France to come to the relief of Bastogne's defenders and other beleaguered Americans in Belgium. In addition, when the weather cleared after Christmas, Allied airpower decimated the German forces. Hitler's last desperate gamble to stave off defeat proved to be a costly failure.

———

Friday, Dec. 15, 1944

My darlingest:

Just another quickie. It is 12:15 and I have a few minutes before running to lunch. I'm beset with difficulties these days and my wonder is growing greater that this should be called a satisfactory way of making a living. Maybe I'm not cut out for executive responsibilities but the headaches attached to this job seem sometimes to be simply overwhelming. They have now shipped Henry Tosti Russell from London to help me for a few weeks. Tosti is the fiftyish son of the one-time manager of the Boston Opera House. He remembers Caruso dawdling him on his knee. Tosti is a prima donna of the first order although he could be of great help with his linguistic ability. But, no! Tosti hit town yesterday morning and immediately launched into a long harangue about working conditions, how they did not suit him at all, and etcetera. Now I have to try to pacify him as well as get my own work done. Oh, hell. This afternoon I'm going up to Antwerp on a little combination news and business trip. Dave Anderson, this New York Times character with whom I live, has wangled for himself, and for my occasional use, a car so we are going up in that. It is only a forty-five minute drive or so, and I haven't been yet. Besides it is a very nice day for a change. At least it is at the moment—by the time I've finished this letter it probably will be raining the usual cats and dogs. Speaking of dogs, you know they really do harness dogs under small dairy carts and other such contrivances around here. When you get down to the logic of it, there certainly is no reason why a dog shouldn't work for its living as well as we do, but nevertheless it somehow seems a little cruel to see those pups panting their lungs out under a heavy cart. (For goodness sakes, don't repeat that part about "logic" to that cocktail lounge lizard of ours. I'd never hear the end of it.)

I had to leave this letter to make that run up to Antwerp. Dave was ready sooner than I thought. But we didn't quite get there. Indeed, we barely got out of town on the three-lane highway. Some American OWI [Office of War Information] guy who was sitting in the backseat with the chauffeur (Dave wanted to drive) had just said that you wouldn't have a ghost of a chance of missing one of the trees that lines the road in case of a blowout. Then there it is in front of us. A Belgian driver weaving all over the damned road because he had gotten into a slightly tight squeeze with a jeep. Dave then got slightly rattled and simply piled us into one of the trees. It really wasn't bad except that with my hard head I managed to do what Libby-Owens-Ford claims to have been unable to do with elephant rifles at twenty paces, baseballs from the bat of Babe Ruth at ten paces, and Third avenue subway workers with sledgehammers at one pace. I shattered a shatterproof windshield. But no harm done. I love you, honey.

CRONKITE LEARNED OF the German attack on the night of December 16, when he was awakened by a phone call from the UP office in Paris asking if he had heard news of fighting in Belgium and suggesting he check the story with General Montgomery's headquarters. Shortly afterward, United Press correspondent John Frankish showed up at his apartment. Frankish, who had been covering the U.S. First Army, which took the brunt of the initial German attack, "was dirty, unshaven, obviously tired and considerably shaken," Cronkite recalled in his memoir. "He had reached Brussels after being caught in a maelstrom of American men and vehicles fleeing the front in a disorganized retreat." Frankish wrote a dispatch about his experience that Cronkite tried, unsuccessfully, to get through military censors, and then headed back to the front. He was killed six days later by a German bomb.

After first traveling to Paris to help coordinate coverage of the unfolding story, Cronkite headed for the front on Christmas Eve. He made his base a hotel in Luxembourg City, where he returned every night to file his dispatches. General Patton's Third Army had wheeled northward, and Cronkite reported on its race to relieve the defenders of Bastogne. An Army driver took him close to the front lines—close enough to come under fire. His days were full of dangerous and potentially fatal encounters; his nights included "a bottle of champagne, a hot bath and a warm bed," indulgences for which, he later reported, he felt fortunate rather than guilty.

From page 13 of the *Dunkirk* (New York) *Evening Observer,* December 23, 1944:

CIVILIANS CHEER AGAIN AS COLUMNS MOVE UP TO FRONT
By Walter Cronkite

SOMEWHERE IN FRANCE, December 23—(UP)—In these tiny villages along the Franco-Belgian border, where the war came and went so quickly only four months ago, little knots of civilians gathered again at the crossroads . . . Today they were cheering again and giving little waves and smiles of assurance as the trucks roared by, going now into combat to keep the war from coming back to their worn stone door steps and to these wooden-shoed, bereted and worried civilians . . .

Half-tracks and tanks set up a terrible clatter as they ground over the cobblestones in the narrow streets of these ancient villages and filled every house with the stench of heated engines and overheated oil . . .

It takes more than a uniform and a cheery wave to get by American military police road patrols. My pocket is becoming worn from reaching for credentials.

There was even one rumor that the Germans had gone so far as to give [their] disguised troops packages of American cigarets.

One MP, mindful of the recent cigaret shortage, said:

"If we got any guys in American uniforms with American cigarets, we'll know they're spies. That's one slipup old Rundstedt has made."

From the front page of the (Reno) *Nevada State Journal,* December 27, 1944:

HALF OF GERMANS' VEHICLES SMASHED

By Walter Cronkite

United Press War Correspondent

NINTH U.S. AIRFORCE ADVANCED HEADQUARTERS, Dec. 26. (UP)—More than half of the tanks, armored vehicles and motor transport with which the Germans roared back into Belgium 11 days ago have been destroyed by Ninth Airforce fighter-bombers alone in 36 hours of perfect weather . . .

Tonight 1500 square miles of territory overrun by Field Marsh Karl von Rundstedt's counter-offensive were littered with burned out hulks of armor which were his reserves on which he had counted to turn the tide of battle.

The area was rapidly taking on the same graveyard appearance of Normandy in the days before the race for the German borders began . . .

In his letter of December 27, 1944, Cronkite marked their third Christmas spent apart. As had been the case when he wrote to her after Operation Market Garden, Cronkite provided few details of the Battle of the Bulge, still raging a few score miles away. Instead he told her about the peaceful holiday he had spent in his comfortable hotel in

Luxembourg. His companions that Christmas were a glittering crew of American journalists. Ernest Hemingway was, of course, Ernest Hemingway. Martha Gellhorn was a veteran foreign correspondent and, since 1940, Hemingway's wife. (They would divorce in 1945.) Leland Stowe was a Pulitzer Prize–winning American foreign correspondent. Gordon and Betty Gaskill were American journalists; Gordon had landed on Omaha Beach on D-Day. Desaree Boss cannot be identified.

On December 26, the day before he wrote to Betsy, elements of General Patton's Fourth Armored Division broke through German lines to relieve the siege of Bastogne. Cronkite was at a forward command post south of the city the next morning when news came of the breakthrough. Just then Gen. Maxwell Taylor, the commander of the 101st Airborne, showed up, having rushed back from Washington, where he had gone for meetings before the battle began. After consulting with the local commander and checking his map, he climbed back into his jeep. Cronkite was standing nearby. The two men had known each other from Operation Market Garden, and Taylor decided to do the correspondent a favor. "Cronkite," he said, "I'm going to Bastogne. Do you want to come?"

Cronkite, whose "bitterest disappointment" four months earlier had been the cancellation of the airborne assault on Paris he had been assigned to cover, had seen a lot of war in the meantime in Holland and in Belgium. He had survived enemy bombs, cannon fire, and mortar shells. He had seen German tanks rumbling down roads right in front of him. And his priorities, as a result, had shifted. He recalled General Taylor's offer in *A Reporter's Life*:

"The story would have been great—first correspondent into Bastogne." But, as he explained to Taylor, he had no way to get a story out of Bastogne, so there was no point in his going. He could be more effective reporting on the battle from where he was. "That's the excuse I gave to Taylor, and tried to explain to myself. But I knew the truth—and I suspect he did: Taylor's drive to Bastogne could well have been a suicide mission.

A lot of glory, perhaps, for a career officer; simply a sad footnote for a war correspondent."

A slightly different version of this encounter appears in John S. D. Eisenhower's *The Bitter Woods: The Battle of the Bulge*. Eisenhower, the son of Gen. Dwight D. Eisenhower, fought in the Battle of the Bulge. According to his version, Taylor's offer of a seat in his jeep was tendered not just to Cronkite but to three other correspondents as well: Joseph Driscoll of the *New York Herald Tribune,* Norman Clark of the *London News Chronicle,* and Cornelius Ryan of the *London Daily Telegraph* (later famed as the author of *The Longest Day* and *A Bridge Too Far*). In Eisenhower's account, "Cornelius Ryan spoke for the group: 'No volunteers today, General.' . . . None of them expected to see the General alive again."

Either way, instead of being the first correspondent in Bastogne, Cronkite got to write a letter to Betsy.

———

Wednesday, December 27, 1944

My darlingest:

Well, my best resolutions about writing collapsed as once again it became a war of movement for me. With the German breakthrough I was ordered back to war corresponding, at least temporarily, and since last Wednesday I have been on the go. Wednesday I got a hurry-up call to go to Paris and, must admit, looked forward rather gleefully to spending the Christmas holiday there. But the original intention for me to help out down there on our busy continental desk collapsed almost before I arrived and Sunday, Christmas Eve to some, I was on my way to the front. I have been here four days now working like a dog but not doing particularly well at it. I'm just a little bitter in that I feel that my presence in this particular sector is unnecessary since both Collie Small and Bob Richards are here, but tomorrow I'm moving on to another area where the hunting may be better. Both Small and Richards can write my sort of stuff better than I can—and that ain't good for the old morale. Incidentally, Collie I'm afraid won't be with us much longer. He has developed faster than any man I ever know in the last four months. Satevepost [Saturday Evening Post] is really ga-ga over him. He has sold them a couple more stories and now they are about to put him on the staff. And if he doesn't take that he is going with NBC for two or three times what UP pays. Lucky lad.

I'm sorry I didn't get to write a Christmas day letter to you. It was an awfully lonely Christmas—the worst ever, I think. I must admit that the surroundings weren't too unpleasant, but the fact that I was alone again without you made it almost unbearable. I was in Luxembourg Christmas day and that little principality is just as lovely as the postcards. It was a perfectly clean, sunlit day and driving through the mountains with the old-world villages perched on their sides, all covered like a picture postcard in the snow, was lovely. Christmas night I was back here at these particular digs for a big turkey dinner in a very nice, modern, warm hotel. Ernest Hemingway, Martha Gellhorn, Leland Stowe, Desaree Boss, Gordon and Betty Gaskill, Collie and a few others were here. We had some eggnog and everyone but old hard-working Cronkite, who had a fistful of mediocre stories to do, got pretty well pied. I had a few drinks and filed my last story about midnight after which I was so tired I just collapsed into bed.

There is some pretty good news to report from my short stay in Paris—but I must emphasize I'm not putting too much hope in it until it all goes through. The idea is that [Virgil] Pinkley has finally been sold on the fact that those of us with more than two years service abroad certainly need home leave. He is trying to work out with New York a rotation scheme whereby sometime between February and April, [Sam] Hales, Cronkite, [Bob] Musel, [Jim] McGlincy and [Doug] Werner will get home for a few weeks. It, however, depends on his ability to get reinforcements from New York, which may be very, very difficult. Hales probably will *be first to go since it seems that Eleanor is in bad shape again. (Keep that one under your hat—I don't know whether I'm supposed to know it or not.) I'll of course let you know just as soon as I hear anymore.*

Notes in passing: Christmas day I thought more than once about Etta shedding a tear that Christmas day in 1941. And when we asked her what the matter was she said: "Because this may be our last Christmas together in a long time." I love you, darling. Walter

---

WESTERN UNION   LONDON VIA COMMERCIAL 23=   [DATE STAMPED] DEC 27

BETSY CRONKITE=

3920 AGNES (KANSASCITYMO)=

   DARLINGEST MERRY XMAS YOU JUDY ALL FAMILY STOP MAY THIS BE LAST LONELY ONE LIFELONG STOP LOVE FOREVER=

   WALTER CRONKITE.

Bill Shadel was one of the "Murrow Boys" with CBS Radio. He reported on the D-Day landings and later, with Murrow, on the liberation of Buchenwald concentration camp. After the war he served as a television anchorman for *ABC News*.

Friday, Jan. 3, 1944 [1945]

My darling wife:

   I have just returned from a long, terribly cold, horribly tiring trip from Brussels but I want to get a note off to you. If these lids get too heavy and these arm muscles just cease to function I may have to mail it off before I finish the page.

I went to Brussels to get my warm field clothes. I think I told you that I left there to spend Christmas week-end in Paris with only my dress clothes and, since being rushed out of Paris to the break-through front, have been covering the war in them. I finally managed to wangle a jeep for the Brussels trip, and now I have my long underwear, boots, gloves and fur-lined leather flying clothes which will do a little to alleviate the zero weather here. Good old Sally Stronoch, the aged secretary in London, a couple of months ago finally got around to send part of my luggage over to Brussels. I cursed her roundly at the time because I thought she had sent the wrong pieces—they included miscellaneous items like the flying clothes for which it seemed I would have no earthly use for. And now I'm singing her praises. Hallelujah! I'm now about the most warmly dressed correspondent among the scribblers here who doll themselves up in the damndest assortment in an attempt to keep warm on these long open jeep rides to the front.

I took Lt. Frisbee, a censor, up with me as a driving companion. We had to go up by way of Longwy, Sedan, Charleville and Charletan because the German bulge has the direct road from Luxembourg out. It takes about seven hours and that isn't any fun on these mountainous, often fog-bound icy roads, particularly in an open jeep into which the freezing wind and sleet bite like a million needles. But it is beautiful. Some day, in mid-winter, we must take that drive (in a heated car). Beautiful mountains, trees budding with ice drops, villages clinging precariously on side of hills. A veritable fairyland, to coin a phrase.

A wonderful thing happened to me the other day on the front. I've taken this frozen drive up to a village outside Bastogne with a driver and Bill Shadel of CBS. We're standing there huddling against a wrecked building when a Piper Cub artillery observation plane putts over and this seedy GI next to me says "Hey, I wouldn't do that for nuthin'. That's dangerous." I think this is a good story so get a couple more quotes from the GI, then his name and address, and finally ask, "What sort of outfit is this you're with in this town—infantry, armored or what?" "Oh, me," he says, "I'm with psychological warfare—public relations. I'm a driver. Wherever you correspondents want to go, I'll drive you there." He was just our driver, that was all. Give everybody my love, honey, keeping plenty for yourself.

IN *A REPORTER'S LIFE*, Cronkite told another, similar story about interviewing a GI who turned out to be his driver:

> On one of the early days after I joined the Third Army press camp we were caught briefly in a firefight in a Belgian hamlet south of Bastogne. We piled out of the jeep and I ducked into a doorway. There was a GI there, and every once in a while he'd lean out and take a potshot with his carbine at the Germans down the block.
>
> Ever the reporter, I shouted: "What's your name? What's your hometown?"
>
> He shouted the answers back over his shoulder, keeping a wary eye out the door.
>
> "And what's your unit?" I asked.
>
> Now he turned and gave me a long look.
>
> "Hell, Mr. Cronkite," he said, "I'm your driver."

It could have been two different drivers, two different days in villages outside Bastogne. Or memory could be up to its old tricks.

From page 5 of the *Daily Courier* of Connellsville, Pennsylvania, January 5, 1945:

BASTOGNE LIKENED TO NAZI GETTYSBURG

By Robert Musel and Walter Cronkite

ADVANCED NINTH AIR FORCE HEADQUARTERS, Jan 5.—

Bastogne may well prove to be a Germany "Gettysburg"—representing the high tide of the enemy's ability to wage offensive war in the period between D-day and the end of hostilities.

But whatever fate awaits the Nazi war machine, it is now obvious that Marshal Karl Von Rundstedt's brilliantly-conceived breakthrough into Belgium gained time—and time was one objective at least . . . But every German attack henceforth should be weaker unless the Germans have undisclosed reserves—and that seemed improbable . . .

From the front page of the *Hayward* (California) *Review,* January 19, 1945:

SHAEF REVEALS ARDENNES COST U.S. 55,421
By Walter Cronkite

PARIS, (UP)—Supreme Allied headquarters today placed the cost of the German Ardennes offensive at 55,421 Allied casualties but said 17 German divisions had been smashed or battled battered and that the Nazis had failed "seriously" to affect Allied plans and preparations for future operations.

The official Allied report on the German counteroffensive said that the operation was conceived by Adolf Hitler and Field Marshal Karl Von Rundstedt, "both of whom are equally responsible for its failure."

The attack, said SHAEF, cost the Germans 120,000 men of whom 80,000 were killed or wounded and 40,000 taken prisoner . . .

Cronkite had been thrilled to visit Paris for the first time. But the city in the winter of 1944–45 was shorn of its appeal by the fuel shortage: Even the cancan dancers "had goose-pimples."

Herb Caen, an Army Air Force officer during the war, would return to the *San Francisco Chronicle* and resume his column, which over the years turned him into one of the city's best-known and beloved citizens. His friend Cronkite was a featured guest at San Francisco's Herb Caen Day celebration in 1996, attended by 75,000 people. Caen died the following year.

January 26, 1945

Yesterday was your birthday and I spent most of the day wishing I could be dancing it away with you at some fancy spot somewhere . . .

I unintentionally spent a week in Paris. I flew down in a Piper Cub from Luxembourg Tuesday afternoon to check on some business intending to come back either Wednesday morning or Thursday. But, as it always seems to do in those cases, the weather closed in. Brucker, my pilot, and I made one stab at getting away Friday but the wind was so high it just whipped our Cub into tight spirals and we gave up. When I got back to Le Bourget that afternoon Boyd Lewis suggested I sit in at SHAEF and help him for a couple of days . . . I did that until Sunday and the weather was still closed in. I finally gave up the plane and took a jeep from Paris back here to Luxembourg. When I got back here you could have chopped me up and put me in cocktails. Now I'm planning to leave here today or early tomorrow and return to Brussels where I expect to remain until ordered to a front for temporary duty.

I didn't have much fun in Paris this trip. To save fuel they have closed all the night clubs and none of the theaters or restaurants are heated. I had dinner one night with [Jim] McGlincy and lunch one afternoon with him in the Escargot which seems to be mentioned in most of the guide books. One evening Collie Small, Lt. Herb Caen (who used to be a columnist on the San Francisco Chronicle), Sam and I went to the Casino de Paris which was the original home grounds of Mistinguette, Chevalier, De Lys, and many others, but right now it stinks. Sitting there huddled in our overcoats we almost froze to death. And all the girls had goose-pimples. You really couldn't blame them. More later . . . Walter

NO LETTERS SURVIVE from Cronkite to Betsy for February. An American and British counteroffensive in January rolled back German advances in Belgium, and Cronkite covered the attacks by Ninth Air Force fighters that decimated the retreating Germans. By the start of February the line between the Allies and the Nazis had been restored to the positions of mid-December 1944. On March 7, U.S. soldiers captured the last remaining bridge across the Rhine River, at Remagen, Germany, and rushed soldiers across. On March 23, the British crossed the Rhine north of the Ruhr, fulfilling the long-delayed offensive planned for Operation Market Garden. The Red Army was closing in on Berlin from the east, only a few score miles from the city. By the end of March 1945, everyone knew that the Thousand Year Reich that Hitler had established in March 1933 would not live out its 13th year.

But Cronkite did not cover the renewed Allied advance. Suddenly, he was given the opportunity by his employers at the United Press to take his long-delayed home leave, and he arrived in New York sometime in the first week in March. No letters to Betsy chronicle this event. Instead,

Walter, Betsy, and cocker spaniel Judy photographed during their
long-awaited reunion, March 1945

the only surviving written record of the visit comes from two stray clippings preserved in the Cronkite family papers, both from Kansas City newspapers in 1945: One women's page society news account rather breathlessly recounts Betsy's reunion in New York City with her husband. The second article covers a public speech that Cronkite gave in Kansas City, probably on March 15, on the prospects for postwar peace.

Walter Cronkite with his father, Walter Leland, Sr., and Betsy, April 1945

According to the society page story, Betsy made a "sudden departure," following an all-night packing session with her mother-in-law. In tones of gushing enthusiasm that no doubt reflected her genuine excitement, but also reflected the conventions of society page reporting, Betsy told a reporter that she and her husband "tried to cram in enough fun in three weeks in New York to make up for the 28 months since [they'd] been together, Betsy continued:

> We saw "Oklahoma," "Harvey," "The Hasty Heart" and "The Seven Lively Arts" with Bea Lillie, Bert Lahr, et cetera. We danced to Tommy and Jimmy Dorsey, Leo Reisman and at the Waldorf Wedgewood Room, the Café Rouge, the Astor Roof and several little places in Greenwich Village. And so many chocolate sodas were consumed that when Walter weighed in for his return plane trip, he had gained back almost 15 of the 40 pounds lost in the European Theatre! We celebrated our fifth wedding anniversary with gardenias and a lot of festivity.

The Cronkite wedding anniversary was on March 30, so the "three weeks" in New York were apparently broken into several segments, for by mid-March the happy couple was back home in Missouri. The March 16 clipping describing Cronkite's talk on the postwar world noted, "Airplane travel took Cronkite from a frigid German town less than two weeks ago."

While in Missouri they visited Cronkite's mother, and also his father and stepmother—and photographs taken on the latter occasion help document the happy Cronkite reunion. And, of course, Cronkite also got to see his other "favorite redhead," Judy the cocker spaniel. Finally, "on a bright April morning," in Washington, D.C., according to the society page account quoting Betsy, "Walter left. And I got a cablegram two days later when I flew home that he had already arrived safely somewhere in Europe." The story also noted, "Mrs. Walter Cronkite, Jr., the former Betsy Maxwell, plans to join her War Correspondent husband sometime this summer in Holland."

Cronkite's next letter to Betsy was written on April 10, 1945, from London, where he was temporarily delayed en route to Brussels. He had evidently taken orders prior to his trip home for goods then hard to come by in Europe—hence the girdles, tennis balls, lipsticks, and so forth that he delivered to friends in London.

Bert Brandt was a photographer for Planet/Acme, the United Press picture wire service, who had covered the D-Day landings. Ned Roberts and Bill Higginbotham were UP correspondents. Joan Twelftrees was a British UP correspondent.

———

Tuesday, April 10, 1945

Well, it is Tuesday and I'm still here in London . . . I'm afraid that by now you are back in Kansas City but I do hope that you stayed to take a look around Washington, or perhaps returned by way of New York and saw [Jim] McGlincy. Everyone here thinks he must have arrived in the States just about the time I left. I'm terribly sorry we missed him.

I've delivered the tennis balls, lipstick and girdles and found everyone but Ned Roberts, who, needless to say, got the balls, about as unappreciative as you'd expect these people to be. After I wrote you Sunday, I called Helvi Rintals, the Flemish girl, and told her I had brought the girdle and would leave it at the office for her to pick up. (I still thought I was leaving for Brussels Monday, at that point). She invited me instead to a regular Sunday open house given by one Countess Norborough, a Hungarian refugee intellectual who apparently uses the same cocktail recipe as Earl. It was the darnedest Grand Hotel you ever saw. We counted nine nationalities represented. Lady Iris O'Malley (honest!), Lord Louis Mountbatten's sister who has been going around with a

negro rhumba band-leader much to the embarrassment of the Royal
Family, was there, as was some British naval commander who spoke
nine languages including two Chinese dialects and Japanese, a smooth
Hungarian who did native dances with Countess Norborough, some gal
in the French Ministry of Information at whose wedding DeGaulle was
best man, an American lieutenant-colonel in the railway transport service
who went around slapping on the back and guffawing in the faces of the
continentals in the best Babbit style. The old gal served some Spam and
Hungarian cookies around nine and we all got away about ten which
suited me perfectly because I was still pretty tired from the trip.

Yesterday I took girdle II to the office for Joan Twelftrees and the
lipstick to Joan Mayers at the public relations office. They both nodded a
polite thanks and that was that. I saw Twelftrees again last night, getting
sucked into taking her to the Cocoanut Grove, a Regent Street nightclub.
I went to Sandy's for dinner with Bill Higginbotham and there ran into
Frank Harris, European head of RCA, his date, and Ray Porter of NBC.
They had the nightclub bug and I was so lonely and depressed that they
didn't have to twist my arm very hard to lure me along. Well, to make a
long story short, Frank's date's roommate is Twelftrees and since Joan was
working until eleven the suggestion naturally followed like day the night
that we gather her up. Then Porter decided he'd pick up one Miss Peart of
NBC who also was working late.

So we went to the C.G. where Harris, the belligerent Irish type, kept
getting into arguments with doormen, waiters, busboys, singers, guests.
We killed a bottle of twelve-dollar Scotch and half a bottle of eleven-
dollar gin and naturally everyone got tight but—guess who? I don't think
I had over three drinks all evening. Porter got absolutely stiff. Remember
how [Frank] Barhydt actually got 'cockeyed' at the MU-KU game? Well,
Porter was so stiff he looked like Frankenstein in movement. He insisted
on riding home in the baggage compartment of the taxi, out in the fresh
air alongside the driver. I finally turned in about four A.M. . . .

I find that I forgot a rather important item I was asked to get for
Paul Eve, a heluva nice Australian who works for BUP. He wanted 3
or 4 white, button-down if possible, shirts, 15 1/2, 33. Do you suppose
you could get them and send them, civilian mail, direct to him at British
United Press? Let me know when you do and I'll tell Paul that they are
on the way, then I can collect whatever they cost from him . . . Walter

———

ON MAY 5, 1945, Field Marshal Bernard Montgomery accepted the surrender of the German army forces in western Holland, as well as those
in northwestern Germany and Denmark. The complete surrender of the
remaining German forces came two days later, May 7, and V-E Day was
officially observed on May 8. In Holland, the disarming of the German
army took several days to complete, during which armed clashes erupted
between the soldiers of the Wehrmacht and Dutch resistance units. Not
until May 8 did elements of the First Canadian Infantry Division enter
Amsterdam, occupied since 1940, to the wild acclaim of Dutch citizens.

Reporters were supposed to enter Amsterdam behind the column of
Canadian soldiers assigned to secure the city, but Cronkite and a Canadian reporter set out in an open command car by back roads and got
there first. As a result, they bore the brunt of Dutch rejoicing and were
pelted with tulips.

Cronkite made his way to the United Press office in the city, which had
been shut down five years earlier. Three Dutch UP employees proudly
presented him with the teletype machine they had disassembled and hid-
den in their basements during the entire war. Before the summer was
over, the UP would be back in business in Amsterdam.

Cronkite's letter of May 20, 1945, was his first surviving letter written from peacetime Europe. He had been shuttling between Amsterdam and Brussels since V-E Day. The privations of war were still all too
evident in newly liberated Amsterdam. The previous winter would go

down in Dutch memory as the "hunger winter," for the Germans had cut off food shipments to the western cities in retaliation for Dutch support of the Allied armies in eastern Holland. Thousands of city dwellers had starved as a result.

———

May 20, 1945

This has been a hectic week in which, again, I haven't had a chance to write you although I have been thinking of you . . . The real reason I haven't had the time is that my day ends abruptly now at 9:30. There still is no electricity in the Netherlands and once the sun goes down all activity ceases. I haven't yet been able to get a carbide or kerosene lamp for my room.

I returned to Holland Monday with Collie Small . . . We got into Amsterdam late Monday and checked into the Park Hotel where they were holding a room for me. Wednesday and again Friday I had to make short trips to The Hague attempting to arrange communications, and Thursday I had to make a run to Utrecht, site of the Canadian Press Camp, to replenish our dwindling rations and gasoline. A great deal of my time during the week has been taken with frantic efforts to get an automobile without which I'm hamstrung here. I still have not succeeded and yesterday morning the Brussels vehicle had to return with Collie and Mickey. Now I'm stranded.

Tonight I'm at Utrecht. I had to come down here this afternoon in order to get transportation to cover a big victory parade at the Hague tomorrow. I hope to get a ride back to Amsterdam tomorrow afternoon, and then I'm stuck again.

To make matters worse, Saturday afternoon I was unceremoniously kicked out of the Park. The Canadian Army requisitioned it as a billet for service women. I have now moved into the much nicer Krasnopoldky which is on what is called "the dam" (it isn't), a sort of large plaza flanked on one side by the old Royal Palace. It is only three blocks from the office, however. I am really almost sick from eating the terrible tinned bully beef and other rations which I have to draw from the press camp and have cooked by the hotel staff. There is absolutely no food in this part of Holland. It is impossible to tell you how bad things are. I have seen several persons faint in the streets from hunger. A prominent newspaper publisher whom I invited to meet me downtown said he could come but he couldn't bring his wife. "Her feet are swollen too badly," he said, "no food, you know." The people are walking skeletons. Their eyes bulge from shrinking sockets and their skins are bleached of natural color. I find it sickening to sit across a desk and talk business with many of them . . . Walter

———

WITH THE END of the war, Cronkite began to report on the rebuilding of a war-ravaged continent.

From page 11 of the *Tucson* (Arizona) *Daily Citizen,* June 12, 1945:

DUTCH SCORING FAST COMEBACK BUT LIFE HARD
Raggedness and Hunger are Everywhere After Years of Nazi Rule
By Walter Cronkite

AMSTERDAM, June 25. (UP)—The Dutch people are coming back to something near normal perhaps faster than any other on the continent. But the mark of five years' German occupation still is deep and the job of rehabilitation has barely begun.

Everywhere is hunger and raggedness and the thousand and one harassments of survival in a country where electricity, coal, gas, soap and every conceivable "necessity" are strictly rationed or non-existent.

Food is coming into the country regularly and the calory count of the average diet has risen from last April's low of 400 to about 2,000 calories daily.

But most of the food is canned goods shipped in by Allied military authorities. Fresh meat, milk, and cheese are almost unknown . . .

In his letter of June 12, 1945, Cronkite reported on progress in the Low Countries. The Brussels UP operation was up and running, using teletype communications; Amsterdam had yet to be linked to the wire service network.

Food remained scarce, but Cronkite was happy to report a new addition to his wardrobe—a dashing, short-waisted "Eisenhower suit," better known as the Ike jacket, which was modeled on the British battle jacket.

———

June 12, 1945

This letter is going regular mail because I have run out of v-mail blanks and can get no more until I return to The Hague where there are a few Americans. Incidentally, I hear from London that a lot of the air mail from there is reaching New York in three days now. If that is true, things certainly are looking up.

But I hope we won't have to depend on mail much longer. I cabled Virgil [Pinkley] to inform you what progress was being made in getting you over. I trust by now he has been in touch with you and things are being worked out. Meanwhile I assume you are taking the very necessary shots.

I'm afraid there isn't much to report from here. Things have been going along in a deadly dull rut for me. Doeppner and I have signed one paper and are on the verge with a couple of others. Last Friday

we went down to Rotterdam to lay our proposition before an old cli-
ent there, and tomorrow we return for his answer. I'm keeping my
fingers crossed. Meanwhile, I'm working full speed on the annoying
office routine and communications. Incidentally, Sam Hales has done
a terrific job in Brussels and has almost got us set up there with a
leased teleprinter line to Paris, which is one of the great feats of the
age, considering the terrible disruption in which all European commu-
nications are. I have got teleprinters in our office here—another major
feat—but as yet there are no lines to connect us with anybody so they
are useless . . .

There is absolutely no social life here because the usually hospitable
Dutch have nothing to offer at the moment. Barrows and I take all our
meals in the hotel, with our Army canned rations. It is unbelievable how
sick we have gotten of Spam and terrible British sausage with an occa-
sional tin of sardines and the inevitable beans. We get virtually no greens
and no fruit or milk of any description. We have had two or three bowls
of lettuce in the last month—at $1.20 per serving.

Did I tell you that, when I made the last run to Brussels, I bought
in the U.S. Officer's Store there an "Eisenhower suit." It is the latest
thing for the well-dressed man in the XTO. You probably have seen the
general in his. He designed it, and a Paris manufacturer makes it so if
anyone happens to ask you, tell them I get my clothes in Paris. It is made
of a fine green material that holds a press and resists spots like nobody's
business, and is cut in the natty style of a sort of lounge jacket. Great
stuff, unseen in any other theater of war. Or peace.

By the way, it seems more like a pre-war than a post-war era here.
Everyone talks about, and worries about, what the Russians are going to
do. I hope it is a bogey, and suspect strongly that it is simply the hang-
over of a lot of well-planted German propaganda.

A recent party resulted in a connection through which I have obtained
from the seized German property pool a 1939 Hudson convertible. Now,

if I can keep the damned thing running—because there are no parts avail-
able—and can get some sort of military permission to retain it, I have
a car. The military permit is going to be difficult. Other correspondents
have seized their own cars only to have them taken away later by the
military. But because of my definite commitments for post-war duties
here, I may be able to cling to it. It is almost essential for the job at hand,
because there will be no possibility of getting a civilian car here for per-
haps two or three years.

I am now looking for a flat for us here, but hope that it will be possible
to delay a decision on that pending your arrival. If we have a certain means
of communications, perhaps we can get a house somewhere on one of the
quiet canals on the outskirts. There are some really lovely ones out there,
and before the war they weren't too expensive. Of course there are terrible
black market prices in all commodities now, and I imagine the same thing
applies to furnished flats or houses.

Love to the family and Judy too. Walter

———

CRONKITE'S LAST SURVIVING letter to Betsy from Europe, written on
June 26, 1945, is concerned, not at all surprisingly, with plans for her to
join him there. Following this letter, he began to communicate with her
via the much faster and newly available medium of wire service cable.

———

June 26, 1945

Don't use civilian addresses yet. That mail is being long delayed. I cabled
you today to resume mailing to: c/o PRO HQ UK Base, APO#413, U.S.
Army, c/o Postmaster, New York; instead of to Major Cutting. That is
because the SHAEF Mission Netherlands is likely to fold up any day
now. I also cabled that you should apply for visas to both Netherlands

*and Belgium, but, failing to get those, should ask for one for London.
The latter is likely to be much simpler, and once we get you that far we
can get you on over here in comparatively short order by one hook or
another crook. At least we'll be in the same hemisphere.*

*I'm all right for clothing at the moment and package delivery is so
uncertain that perhaps you had better hold onto my sweat shirt, extra
shoes, etc., for the moment. But please keep on sending food, canned
fruit, tobacco, cigarettes, cigars, vitamin pills, and the like.*

*Regarding wives joining their occupation troop husbands: Every
Army source here has been denying that story for months, and there was
a recent story in Stars & Stripes that the House of Representatives had
even frowned on the idea. As I get it, only State Department wives are
going to be permitted now, and even then it depends on the conditions in
the country to which they are going, and the attitude of the government
there. For instance, because of difficult living conditions here, most of
the American Embassy personnel at The Hague are bringing their wives
only as far as London for the moment. This would not apply, however,
to Belgium, and probably not in our case anyway because we would be
living in Amsterdam instead of the Hague . . . Suggest you bring plenty
of warm clothes: damn few summer ones on account of that's how it is
here—top coats most of the year around for gals, winter suits for men
. . . Keep plugging that old French . . . Walter*

ON JULY 19, 1945, Betsy Cronkite wrote to her mother-in-law, Helen
Cronkite, to bring her up-to-date on plans to join her husband in Europe:

---

*. . . I haven't done anything interesting to tell you about, except study
French and try to break in a new gal at my office, which is harder than you
think. I got a cablegram from Walter last night, in cablese, quote:*

KANSAS CITY   NEW YORK

MANUFACTURERS OF
FINE GREETING CARDS
GRAND AVENUE AND McGEE AT TWENTY-FIFTH
KANSAS CITY, MISSOURI
July 19,1945

Dear Helen:

It's so hard to phone from work that I thought I'd just
drop this "get-well note" instead. Last night Norma Chaney
was here for one night and we had dinner with some of the
old gang(Rex worked with Walter and was one of his best friends,
you may remember,in U.P.)so I didn't get to the hospital til
after visiting hours,too late to see you at all.

I haven't done anything interesting to tell you about,
except study French and try to break in a new gal at my
office,which is harder than you'd think. I got a cablegram
from Walter last night which said,in cablese,quote:

"Although been traveling wherefore unreceived recent
letters just returned London presonally handle with British
vise. Stop. Now seems likely issuable within month. Stop.
Peck says cably can furnish transportation within week after
visa issued. Stop. Will mean getting you as far England
whereafter utmost get you rest way. Stop. Keep fingers
crossed. Stop."

So it sounds as if I'll be en route ere long. Got a
thousand things to do,dullish chores which take weeks,like:
repairing of watch and camera,making a hat or two,fitting
slacks and evening clothes,remaking fur coats,and buying
numerous warm things for the coming cold winter. I'll be
off work as of tomorrow,ready to buckle down and finish
taking the last of my shots,then shop like mad and have
Mother make some stuff,if I ever find material.

I want her to make a plaid taffeta evening blouse
I thought up,with gloves to match,both with sequins out-
lining the pattern here and there--to wear with my black
skirt,should I need same. Much confusion thinking up 175
pounds of clothes which will last me!

No other word from Walter or anyone. Etta will be
here the rest of the week and I haven't seen her since
Sunday so am in the doghouse,currently. Marjorie Davis,
one of my dearest chums,is leaving for Mexico day after
tomorrow for six weeks or more,so I won't see her again;
and so want to get by there to pay a last call....I'll no
doubt talk to you on the phone later - can't call from here
very well,as you know. Love to the grandfolks and you. Tell
Mrs.Ludy hello for me.....Seein' ya!

Love,

Betsy

Letter from Betsy Cronkite to her mother-in-law, Helen Cronkite,
describing plans to join her husband in Europe

"Although been traveling wherefore unreceived recent letters just returned London personally handle with British visa. Stop. Now seems likely issuable within month. Stop. Peck says cably can furnish transportation within week after visa issued. Stop. Will mean getting you as far England wherafter utmost get you rest way. Stop. Keep fingers crossed. Stop."

So it sounds as if I'll be en route ere long . . . Seein' ya!

Love, Betsy

CRONKITE'S DISPATCHES DWINDLED over the summer of 1945, as he took on greater managerial responsibility as chief of the United Press's Brussels bureau. He was in the Brussels office on August 6, 1945, when he learned of the bombing of Hiroshima. Japan's surrender followed soon after, ending World War II. Probably around mid-September, Betsy joined him in Europe, a story whose final episodes can be patched together from this letter to his mother and grandparents, sent from Brussels in December 1945.

Brussels

December 14, 1945

Dearest Mom and Grandfolks:

Well, at last, a letter from your wandering son and Grandson. It has been a long time since I've written but that seems to be the curse of the Cronkites. Believe me, the lack of letters is no inclination that I am not thinking of you most of the time, but rather that there just seems to be so few hours in the day and so few minutes in the hours.

Lately I have been working from about eight in the morning until ten and ten-thirty at night. I have at last obtained another American to work in the

Brussels office also, but he has had no newspaper experience and for awhile at least he takes more of my time than he pays back.

Business has just been so-so. I don't get to do much reporting or writing these days because I have to spend most of my time trying to sell the United Press service to the Belgian newspapers, and supervise similar operations in the Netherlands. Thank goodness most of our pre-war staff returned to the United Press in Amsterdam and I don't have to wet-nurse them along as I do the Brussels staff.

Because I prefer to report and write rather than sell, I am hoping for a new assignment soon after the first of the year. I don't know what it will be yet. I would like to go to Moscow for six months or so but there doesn't seem to be very much chance of that. [Virgil] Pinkley, the vice president for Europe, has mentioned, however, that he might send me to Moscow for a few months and then to Vienna to handle the Balkan countries. But Pinkley talks a lot of plans that never materialize so I'm not counting too many unhatched chickens. I hope that if I do go to those countries Betsy will be able to go along but there is no certainty that she would be permitted to. The Russians are very tough about issuing visas, and Vienna still is technically a military zone—which means only accredited war correspondents are permitted there.

There is also some very, very slim chance that I might be returning to the States. The New York office has asked a couple of times—informally—if I wouldn't like to come back to the cable desk there. Frankly I don't know whether I would or not. There is a lot to be said for living in New York, but then there is still a lot to see and a very interesting story to write from over here . . .

Of course I was terribly happy to have Betsy come over. As you undoubtedly have heard from her letters, I met her on the ship at Plymouth, England. We had about ten days in London during which I had a lot of fun introducing her to all my war-time friends—at least those of them who are still around.

We *went on over to Paris on the boat-train, landing at the war-famous port of Dieppe. We were only in Paris a few hours between trains, but we later were to return there for nearly a week's stay, including my birthday . . .*

It is funny how Betsy and I are almost exactly retracing my steps of one year ago. Her first view of Paris was on September 30 (as I remember) which was exactly one year after my first view of the city. Her next trip to Paris, when she was able to stay longer, was on November 1, which was just one year after my second trip. Now she will be going to Luxembourg almost exactly one year after I first went there . . .

With all my love, forever,

Walter

Walter and Betsy Cronkite in Brussels, Belgium, December 1945

MEMORIES OF THE WAR, 1946-2009

★ ★ ★ ★ ★ ★ ★

In August 1963, CBS anchorman Walter Cronkite and former President Dwight D. Eisenhower spent six days together in England and France filming a CBS News special report to mark the next year's 20th anniversary of the D-Day landings. The 90-minute special, titled *D-Day Plus 20 Years*, aired on CBS on the evening of June 6, 1964, and attracted millions of viewers. *Time* magazine's response was typical of the rave reviews that greeted the program's broadcast:

> Never before in history has such an immediate and permanent record been made of a general returning to the field of a great battle and describing it in his own words, while film archives supplied scenes of the actual warfare. It was something to see.

The CBS special report included segments with Cronkite and Eisenhower revisiting famous scenes associated with D-Day, including Portsmouth (the English port from which the invasion flotilla embarked)

Walter Cronkite and former President Dwight D. Eisenhower at the American
military cemetery above Omaha Beach, Normandy, France, August 1963

and the Normandy beaches where the landings took place. The two
men, both native Midwesterners, were obviously at ease in each other's
company. Cronkite respectfully addressed the former Supreme Commander of the Allied Expeditionary Force in Europe as "General,"
while Eisenhower addressed the former United Press correspondent
familiarly as "Walter."

The program's final scene depicted Cronkite and Eisenhower con-
versing in the field of white crosses in the St. Laurent American military
cemetery at Colleville-sur-Mer, on the bluff above Omaha Beach. At one
point in their unscripted conversation, Eisenhower looked at Cronkite
and said, "You know, Walter, I come here and the thought that over-
whelms me is all the joy that Mamie and I get from our grandchildren.
I look at these graves out here and I just can't help but think of all the
families in America that don't have the joy of grandchildren."

Walter Cronkite and his wife, Betsy, did go on in the aftermath of the war to know the joy of children and grandchildren. Cronkite also experienced the satisfactions of professional success and public affection. But memories of the war in which he first established his reputation as a journalist were never far away for him. Cronkite, indeed, played a significant role in shaping the popular national memory of World War II for those who lived through the war as well as for their children and grandchildren.

When peace came in 1945, Cronkite was not yet 29 years old. He fully expected he would make his career in the decades to come as a print journalist for the United Press. Writing to his mother and grandparents from Brussels on December 14, 1945, he contemplated his options—perhaps heading up the UP bureau in Moscow or Vienna, or returning to New York to take charge of the international cable desk. "There is a lot to be said for living in New York," he wrote, "but then there is still a lot to see and a very interesting story to write from over here." As it turned out, he got to tell those interesting stories from Europe for the next few years, and this time, fortunately, with Betsy as his companion. In January 1946 Cronkite moved to Nuremberg, Germany, to cover the trials of the top Nazi leaders; Betsy joined him there in May. That summer they traveled on to Moscow, where Cronkite headed up the UP bureau for the next two years. When Betsy, by then age 32, became pregnant in 1948 with their first child, Nancy, the Cronkites decided to return to the United States. Two more children followed over the next several years, daughter Kathy and son Walter (Chip).

With a growing family, Cronkite was no longer willing to put up with UP's notoriously stingy pay scale and made the switch to more lucrative positions in broadcast journalism, at first as the Washington, D.C., correspondent for a group of ten midwestern radio networks. Following the outbreak of the Korean War in June 1950, Cronkite switched to CBS Radio, with the expectation that he would be sent to Korea as a war correspondent. Edward R. Murrow, who had failed to recruit him as one of the "Murrow Boys" in London during the war, was instrumental in bringing him to CBS in 1950.

That summer Cronkite's career took a dramatic new turn when he was asked to make an appearance on CBS's brand-new television station in Washington, WTOP, and give a chalkboard-illustrated talk about the Korean War. The origins of electronic television date back to the late 1920s, and by the Second World War there were stations in five American cities that were broadcasting to a tiny audience of television viewers. Commercial television did not emerge as a significant competitor to the newspaper and radio industry until 1947. By the following year, the Big Three television networks—the Columbia Broadcasting System (CBS), the National Broadcasting Company (NBC), and the American Broadcasting Company (ABC)—were all on the air with regular programming, including daily 15-minute news broadcasts on CBS and NBC. The number of television sets in use jumped from fewer than 10,000 in 1946 to more than ten million a half decade later.

Cronkite still hoped to be sent to Korea as a radio correspondent, but one thing led to another, and soon he was delivering the entire daily 15-minute news broadcast for WTOP. He was both the reporter and what would soon be described as the "anchorman" of the news program (the term "anchorman" was occasionally used to describe newsmen before Cronkite joined CBS, but it first gained widespread currency when applied to Cronkite's role in reporting from the Republican National Convention in Chicago in 1952.)

Cronkite projected a naturally reassuring screen presence, at one and the same time plainspoken and authoritative, a man of the people and a man of the world. He could effortlessly ad-lib commentary if need be, and his Midwest-inflected baritone usually conveyed the excitement of events without carrying any hint of personal emotional involvement (those few occasions in later years when he did display emotion on-screen immediately took on iconic status in the folklore of television journalism). There was certainly a good deal of craft involved in his nightly performance before the camera, but unlike some celebrity newsmen, his screen persona was not at significant odds with his character off-camera. At his memorial service in 2009, fellow CBS newsman Bob Schieffer recalled that when Cronkite was approached on the street by strangers asking to talk about something he had said on-screen, "he was never rude, he wanted to talk about the news." "Right from the beginning," Cronkite told interviewer Don Carleton many years later, "I took the attitude that I was talking to one person when I was in front of the camera," rather than thousands or millions of viewers. "It was always on a one-on-one basis." In time, he matured into the avuncular "Uncle Walter," a familiar and welcome presence in millions of American homes.

In addition to anchoring CBS's coverage of national political conventions, Cronkite became host of the network's *Morning Show* in 1954. Although that turned out to be a short-lived assignment, it was the occasion for Cronkite's move from Washington to New York City, his home for the rest of his life. In 1961 he succeeded Edward R. Murrow as senior CBS correspondent, and in 1962 he became anchorman and managing editor of *CBS Evening News*. The dramatic events of the early 1960s, including cold war confrontations over Berlin and Cuba, and the rise of the civil rights movement, suggested to network executives the need for extended news coverage, and in 1963 Cronkite oversaw the expansion of the *CBS Evening News* broadcast to a half hour, an innovation soon copied by the other television networks.

Cronkite remained as anchorman of *CBS Evening News* for the next 18 years, during which he reported on such major stories as the assassination of President John F. Kennedy, the Vietnam War, the race to the moon, the Watergate crisis, and the Iran hostage crisis, famously closing each show with the line "And that's the way it is." In the process he became, as a 1972 poll recorded, "the most trusted man in America."

Beginning in the 1950s, along with his established on-screen roles as reporter and anchorman, Cronkite was the host of a number of popular television series and special broadcasts that introduced CBS viewers to the history of their country and the world. CBS was in some ways the original (and superior) "history channel," with Cronkite as the preferred narrator for all things historically consequential. From 1953 to 1957, Cronkite hosted the series *You Are There*. Produced by CBS's entertainment division, each episode of the Sunday evening program featured real CBS news correspondents "reporting" on dramatized historic events as if they were breaking news. As host, Cronkite opened the show by providing the appropriate historic setting, and he capped each week with the line "And all things are as they were then, except you are there."

Many episodes were devoted to events in the pre-film era, such as the assassination of Julius Caesar, the Boston Tea Party, and Gen. Robert F. Lee's surrender at Appomattox, but the series also included a fair share of re-created moments from World War II—from Pearl Harbor to the surrender of Wake Island to the liberation of Paris.

In 1956–57 Cronkite hosted a series titled *Air Power*, which focused mostly on the Second World War and was inspired by the success of NBC's documentary series on World War II naval warfare, *Victory at Sea*. Cronkite revisited some of the stories he had reported on during the war in episodes like "Schweinfurt" and "Target Ploesti."

After *Air Power* ran its course, Cronkite narrated his most popular CBS documentary series, *The Twentieth Century*, several hundred episodes of which were broadcast Sunday evenings between 1957 and 1967. Some *Twentieth Century* episodes were written by Andy Rooney, Cronkite's old comrade from the "Writing Sixty-Ninth." As with the *You Are There* series, *The Twentieth Century* covered varied topics, but the

Second World War accounted for about a quarter of the shows, including episodes devoted to Winston Churchill's wartime leadership, D-Day, Gen. George S. Patton and the Third Army, the capture of the Remagen Bridge, the Battle of the Bulge, and the atomic bombing of Hiroshima.

Scenes from the You Are There *series, which ran from 1953 to 1957. The show re-created great moments in history, including many from World War II.*

There is no question about Cronkite's personal favorite among the historical programs with which he was involved over the years. As he wrote in *A Reporter's Life:*

> The 1963 trip to England and Normandy with Ike to prepare a documentary on the 20th anniversary of D-Day was sheer delight—a lot of hard work but sheer delight.

Mamie Eisenhower and Betsy Cronkite accompanied their husbands on the trip. At one point, on Omaha Beach, CBS executive producer Fred Friendly set up a sequence where Cronkite and Eisenhower were to drive slowly along the beach in a jeep, with Eisenhower providing commentary on the desperate battle that had taken place there. The idea at first was for Cronkite to drive the jeep, "but then," as Cronkite recalled, "it occurred to Fred that it was Eisenhower who was showing me the area and that he should be driving." So they switched places. The result, visible in the segment when it aired, made for a jerky ride.

> Watching this drama unfold from a little knoll behind the beach were Mamie Eisenhower and Betsy. Mamie gasped and reached over for Betsy's hand. "Betsy, your Walter has never been in greater danger. Ike hasn't driven in thirty years, and he wasn't any good at it then."

Although Eisenhower had been back to the Normandy beaches several times since the end of World War II for commemorative events, Cronkite realized that this trip was the first time Eisenhower had been there without having his views constricted by crowds of onlookers and officials:

> Ike stood in a German bunker, looking out to the English Channel through a gun slit, and he said he couldn't imagine what those Germans

thought that morning, looking out there at the Allied armada. He was really dumbfounded by the sheer cliff at Pointe du Hoc. He said to me, "How could we have ordered those soldiers to climb this thing?"

And as he recalled the chaos and bloodshed of the early hours of June 6, 1944, Eisenhower saluted the common soldiers who made the difference in the day's outcome:

> It had to be the local commanders, the platoon leaders and the squad leaders. That was not a general's battle after all. We'd all done all the planning. We'd thought we'd made the best plan that would save the most lives and get the most benefit out of it, but they were the people who had to do the job, and we must never forget that. It was just the G.I. and his platoon, and company, and squad leaders.

For Cronkite, as for most Americans in the postwar era, World War II had become a touchstone of national pride and sense of mission. The United States had not sought war, but when war was forced upon it in 1941, the nation had risen to the occasion, and its citizen-soldiers had prevailed in battle on two fronts against the forces of aggression and fanaticism.

Even as Cronkite and Eisenhower filmed their anniversary report in Normandy, another and very different war involving young Americans was escalating on the opposite side of the world. On September 2, 1963, the night that CBS Evening News moved to its new half-hour format, the program featured Cronkite's interview with President John F. Kennedy at the family compound at Hyannis Port on Cape Cod. They touched on a number of topics, but the interview is best remembered for Kennedy's comments on the Vietnam War, which had not been going well over the past year. The President took the opportunity to put a little distance between the United States and the increasingly unpopular government of its ally, South Vietnam, led by President Ngo Dinh Diem:

CRONKITE: Mr. President, the only hot war we've got running at the moment is of course the one in Vietnam, and we have our difficulties here, quite obviously.

PRESIDENT KENNEDY: I don't think that unless a greater effort is made by the [South Vietnamese] Government to win popular support that the war can be won out there. In the final analysis, it is their war. They are the ones who have to win it or lose it. We can help them, we can give them equipment, we can send our men out there as advisers, but they have to win it—the people of Vietnam—against the Communists. We are prepared to continue to assist them, but I don't think that the war can be won unless the people support the effort, and, in my opinion, in the last 2 months the Government has gotten out of touch with the people.

The repressions against the Buddhists, we felt, were very unwise. Now all we can do is to make it very clear that we don't think this is the way to win. It is my hope that this will become increasingly obvious to the Government, that they will take steps to try to bring back popular support for this very essential struggle.

Less than three months later, both Kennedy and Diem were dead, one of a lone assassin's bullet, the other of a military coup covertly encouraged by the United States. Cronkite made several trips to Vietnam as a reporter over the next few years, interviewing generals and ordinary GIs and flying on missions over enemy territory in bombers, just as he had in World War II, and also in that new weapon of aerial warfare, the helicopter. Initially a supporter of the war, Cronkite listened to the doubts expressed by younger CBS colleagues reporting from the field.

By 1965 he had developed serious misgivings about the wisdom and morality of America's war in Vietnam, viewing the events, characteristically, through the prism of his memories of World War II. It "seems to this observer," he wrote in his memoir,

> that in those early post–World War II years we had squandered one of the greatest reservoirs of good-will any nation ever had. We let the admiration and hopes of the world's people and their leaders drain away through the huge cracks in our idealism. All in the name of self-interest and military expediency.

Cronkite's doubts came to a head in January and February 1968. The Communists' Tet Offensive, launched on January 30, 1968, with near-simultaneous assaults on hundreds of South Vietnam's cities and towns, including the capital city of Saigon, dispelled years of optimistic predictions by U.S. military spokesmen that the "light at the end of the tunnel" was in view in the Vietnam War. The offensive dragged on for four bloody weeks before subsiding, and Cronkite went to Vietnam for a firsthand look. While there, he had a conversation with Gen. Creighton B. Abrams, who was second in command of the U.S. military effort in Vietnam (and who would shortly replace the commanding general, William Westmoreland). Cronkite had last met Abrams during the Battle of the Bulge, when Abrams was a young officer commanding a tank battalion, the tip of General Patton's Third Army as it rushed to the relief of Bastogne in December 1944. Cronkite found Abrams "remarkably candid in admitting that the Tet attack had come as a surprise and the serious extent of the damage, in casualties, material and morale." General Westmoreland, in contrast, was proclaiming Tet an American victory—and asking for an additional 206,000 servicemen, to join the half million or so already in Vietnam, to finish the job. Cronkite was unpersuaded.

On his return he broadcast a CBS special report on the Tet Offensive on February 27, 1968, titled *Report From Vietnam: Who, What, When, Where, Why?*, that closed with the most famous editorial comments in American broadcast journalism:

> To say that we are closer to victory today is to believe, in the face of the evidence, the optimists who have been wrong in the past . . . It is increasingly clear to this reporter that the only rational way out, then, will be to negotiate, not as victors, but as an honorable people who lived up to their pledge to defend democracy, and did the best they could.

Cronkite's public image, based as it was not only on his nightly screen presence as news anchorman but also on his association with popular memories of the "good war" of 1941–45, provided him with the moral authority to deliver such unvarnished criticisms of the war his country was fighting in Vietnam. Few other public figures in that time and place would have been able to do the same without provoking a furious counterreaction. "That's it," President Lyndon Johnson's aides reported him as saying after he heard Cronkite's remarks. "If I've lost Cronkite, I've lost the country." A little less than a month later, on March 31, 1968, Johnson announced that he was suspending most bombing missions against North Vietnam, that he would seek to open peace negotiations with the Communists, and that he would not seek reelection. The war ground on for another seven years, but under another President, who kept promising that his goal was to wind down the war, and without any resumption of public faith in ultimate and unconditional victory.

Walter Cronkite remained anchorman of the *CBS Evening News* until his retirement in 1981. He returned to the *CBS Evening News* in June 1984 to commemorate the 40th anniversary of D-Day, and he offered commentary on National Public Radio in June 2004 to mark its 60th anniversary.

He also continued to narrate specials on the war for the Public Broadcasting System and other networks. In 1996 he published *A Reporter's Life,* providing new insights and information about his wartime experiences, as well as his subsequent career.

Walter Cronkite reporting from South Vietnam on the Tet Offensive,
February 1968

Betsy Cronkite died on March 15, 2005. Her death fell two weeks before the anniversary of the day, 60 years earlier in March 1945, when a young United Press correspondent returned home on leave from Europe and was reunited with his wife after 28 months of separation. Cronkite outlived the woman he addressed in his wartime letters as "Darlingest wife," and to whom he was married for six decades, by a little over four years. He passed away on July 17, 2009.

—MAURICE ISSERMAN

AFTERWORD

★ ★ ★ ★ ★ ★ ★

After the happy couple was finally reunited in Europe, my grandfather was able to fulfill his promise to show Betsy all the places he had written about in his letters. From Belgium, where he worked to restore the United Press offices in the Lowlands, they took trips through the battle-scarred countryside to Paris, just as they had dreamed about for the past two and a half years. She was eventually credentialed as a foreign correspondent, and she helped him cover the Nuremberg trials. Then they headed to Moscow for UP. What they had hoped would be a three-month adventure turned into a two-year slog. While he constantly battled Soviet censorship, she worked at the American embassy so that they could have access to better rations. At least the monotony and the cold were broken up by frequent parties, including several with novelist John Steinbeck.

After they came home to have their first child (my aunt Nancy always wished they had waited, so she could have "Moscow" on her passport instead of "Kansas City"), they made their way to Washington, D.C. He joined CBS not as a "Murrow Boy" but as a journalist doing a little bit of everything in the early days of television.

His career was long and tremendously successful. And the same could be said of his marriage to Betsy. They raised two daughters in D.C. as he shuttled back and forth to New York. They moved to New York for good in 1957 and had their third and final child: my father, Chip. Now they were back in the city where they had said goodbye to each other in December of 1942, down at the old Maritime Building. I wonder if they ever returned to that building and had a drink for old times' sake. They must have thought back to the dangerous ocean passages during the war when, later in life, they took cruises, even though the ships were fancier and my grandfather was often mobbed by fans. Now when he had to go off on assignment, they had to be parted for only a few days instead of years.

Gifted in his profession, my grandfather established many of the standards in the then brand-new field of television news, mostly by hewing to the old-fashioned wire service rules he had mastered in the Midwest and Europe: Be fast, be accurate, be hard-hitting, be objective. He was also blessed in his family and personal life, building on the strong relationships he had formed in World War II. Andy Rooney remained a lifelong best friend, and Jim McGlincy remained a friend in need.

As a boy, I revered my grandfather, and now as a young journalist, I aspire to follow in his footsteps. When he was my age, the Germans had just invaded Poland, the United States was two years from entering the war, and my grandparents weren't even married yet. As I look around at my colleagues at CBS News, where I now work, I hope to learn from them as they had learned from him. One of the veterans around here, Steven Besner, director of *Face the Nation*, said that he came to CBS in 1964. By that time, my grandfather had been working here for almost 15 years.

Everywhere I see the high standards for television news that he set during his years as anchor. Early on he recognized the importance of

Walter Cronkite IV takes a driving lesson from his grandfather on Martha's Vineyard, 2004.

the medium, and he helped television journalism grow. My grandfather brought the no-nonsense, straight-news mentality of the United Press to his broadcasts. He even disliked people referring to the *Evening News* as "the show," always insisting on the term "the broadcast."

Nothing was as sacred to him as the importance of objective journalism in a democracy. He refused to register for a political party and tried to never insert his opinions into his broadcasts. Although he famously voiced his concerns about the Vietnam War in 1968, saying that he believed the U.S. authorities were misleading the American people and that the war was locked in a stalemate, for the rest of his life he agonized about whether that had been the right thing to do.

Part of the reason is that my grandfather remained an ardent patriot throughout his life. Every single morning during those summers on Martha's Vineyard, even when he was in his nineties, he would hobble out to haul up a huge American flag on the tall flagpole in front of his house. (Of course, given his competitive spirit, he aimed to have the tallest flagpole with the biggest flag in the neighborhood.) At dusk he would hobble back out and take down the flag. He taught us grandchildren how to fold it properly. A mini-scandal erupted in the household when we found out that when the grandchildren weren't visiting, he would simply put it away neatly at night rather than go through the full triangular fold.

It can't be overestimated how important Betsy was in his life. She kept him real, true to his roots and his best instincts. She kept him grounded and never allowed him to float away on the ego bubble that his television celebrity threatened to inflate. He was lucky to have found a partner who always made sure that he focused his efforts on being the

Betsy Cronkite with her young grandson Walter on Martha's Vineyard

best that he could in his career, not on shallow show business values. When my grandfather's celebrity forced him to travel by private limo, my grandmother made a point of always traveling in New York by public bus—and made sure everyone knew it. Even when she was an old lady, her purse always jingled with bus tokens.

Ironically, the ties that bound them in their 60 happy years together after World War II were forged during those lonely years of separation. Throughout all his letters to Betsy runs the theme of desperately wanting what he could not have, and when they finally came together, he was determined never to let her go again. So from those years of deprivation and terrible loss, Walter and Betsy Cronkite found renewed life once again—standing side by side.

The letters to Betsy collected in this book show not only the importance of WWII to the figure he became but also the importance of this loving and enduring marriage.

—WALTER CRONKITE IV

TIME LINE FOR WALTER CRONKITE 1916-2009

1916 Walter Leland Cronkite, Jr., is born in St. Joseph, Missouri, on November 4.

1932 Wins journalism competition in high school and writes for and delivers the *Houston Post* during summer break.

1933 Attends the University of Texas at Austin while juggling jobs with the *Houston Press* and the Scripps-Howard News Service.

1935 Drops out of college to pursue journalism full time.

1935–37 Works as a news and sports radio announcer in Kansas City and Oklahoma City; a United Press correspondent in Austin, Kansas City, and El Paso; and a public relations executive for Braniff Airways.

1936 Meets and begins courtship of Betsy Maxwell while working at Kansas City, Missouri, radio station KCMO.

1939 Joins the United Press news service.

1940 Marries Betsy Maxwell on March 30.

1942 Accredited as a war correspondent.

1942 Covers the battle of the North Atlantic and the invasion of North Africa. Leaves New York and wife Betsy Cronkite in early December, en route by convoy to United Kingdom.

1943 Covers air war from London and flies on a bombing mission over Germany.

1944 Flies in a bomber over Normandy on D-Day, is caught in a buzz bomb attack in London, lands in a glider with 101st Airborne in Operation Market Garden, and covers the Battle of the Bulge.

1945–46 Covers the Allied victory in western Europe and the Nuremberg trials. Betsy Cronkite finally joins him in Europe.

1946–48 Is head of the United Press bureau in Moscow.

1950 Becomes a CBS News correspondent.

1962–81 Is anchor and managing editor of *The CBS Evening News With Walter Cronkite*.

2005 Betsy Cronkite dies on March 15, at age 89.

2009 Walter Cronkite dies on July 17, at age 92.

ACKNOWLEDGMENTS

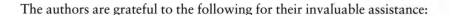

The authors are grateful to the following for their invaluable assistance:

Tom Brokaw, for sharing his thoughts on Walter Cronkite's wartime reporting.

Chip Cronkite and Deborah Rush Cronkite, for sharing photos and memories of Chip's father and mother, Walter and Betsy Cronkite.

Don Carleton, executive director, along with the staff of the Dolph Briscoe Center for American History at the University of Texas at Austin, for stewardship of the Walter Cronkite Papers and assistance to visiting researchers.

Linda Mason, Senior Vice President, Standards and Special Projects, CBS News, who graciously opened the CBS archives and who also allowed a certain CBS News associate producer to work on an outside project.

Doug Brinkley, author of *Cronkite,* for his insight and encouragement on this project.

Tim Gay, author of *Assignment to Hell: The War Against Nazi Germany With Correspondents Walter Cronkite, Andy Rooney, A. J. Liebling, Homer Bigart, and Hal Boyle* (2012), for generously sharing the fruits of his research.

Reid Larson, research librarian at Hamilton College, for assistance on many matters, including tracking down Walter Cronkite's wartime dispatches for the United Press.

Patrick Reynolds, Dean of Faculty at Hamilton College, for providing financial assistance for rights acquisition.

Carl Mehler, Director of Maps at National Geographic, for creating the map for this book.

Lisa Thomas, our hardworking editor at National Geographic.

SELECT BIBLIOGRAPHY

Baillie, Hugh. *High Tension: The Recollections of Hugh Baillie*. New York: Harper and Brothers, 1959.

Beattie, Edward William. *Diary of a Kriegie*. New York: Thomas Y. Crowell Company, 1946.

Brinkley, Douglas. *Cronkite*. New York: Harper, 2012.

Calder, Angus. *The People's War: Britain, 1939–1945*. New York: Pantheon, 1969.

Cronkite, Walter. *A Reporter's Life*. New York: A. A. Knopf, 1996.

Cronkite, Walter, and Don Carleton. *Conversations With Cronkite*. Austin: Dolph Briscoe Center for American History, University of Texas, 2010.

Edwards, Bob. *Edward R. Murrow and the Birth of Broadcast Journalism*. Hoboken, N.J.: John Wiley and Sons, 2004.

Eisenhower, John S. D. *The Bitter Woods: The Battle of the Bulge*. New York: Da Capo Press, 1995.

Gay, Timothy M. *Assignment to Hell: The War Against Nazi Germany With Correspondents Walter Cronkite, Andy Rooney, A. J. Liebling, Homer Bigart, and Hal Boyle*. New York: New American Library, 2012.

Harnett, Richard M., and Billy G. Ferguson. *Unipress: United Press International, Covering the 20th Century*. Golden, Colo.: Fulcrum Publishing, 2003.

Longmate, Norman. *The G.I.'s: The Americans in Britain, 1942–1945*. New York: Charles Scribner's Sons, 1975.

———. *How We Lived Then: A History of Every Day Life During the Second World War*. London: Hutchinson and Co., 1971.

Middleton, Drew. *Our Share of the Night: A Personal Narrative of the War Years*. New York: Viking Press, 1946.

Reynolds, David. *Rich Relations: The American Occupation of Britain, 1942–1945*. New York: Random House, 1995.

Riess, Curt, ed. *They Were There: The Story of World War II and How It Came About, by America's Foremost Correspondents*. New York: G. P. Putnam's Sons, 1944.

Rooney, Andy. *My War*. New York: Public Affairs, 2002.

Salisbury, Harrison. *A Journey for Our Times: A Memoir*. New York: Carroll and Graf, 1984.

Severeid, Eric. *Not So Wild a Dream*. New York: Atheneum, 1976.

Snyder, Louis L., ed. *Masterpieces of War Reporting: The Great Moments of World War II*. New York: Julian Messner, 1962.

Sorel, Nancy Caldwell. *The Women Who Wrote the War*. New York: Arcade Publishing, 1999.

Stenbuck, Jack, ed. *Typewriter Battalion: Dramatic Front-Line Dispatches From World War II*. New York: William Morrow and Company, 1995.

Wade, Betsy, ed. *Forward Positions: The War Correspondence of Homer Bigart*. Fayetteville: University of Arkansas Press, 1992.

Illustrations Credits

All photographs courtesy of Chip Cronkite unless otherwise noted:

xiv, Dolph Briscoe Center for American History, University of Texas at Austin; xxxiv, Walter Cronkite IV; 12, WW2 Signal Corps Photograph Collection/Courtesy United States Army Military History Institute; 16, United Press International; 46, Dolph Briscoe Center for American History, University of Texas at Austin; 53, Dolph Briscoe Center for American History, University of Texas at Austin; 70, United Press International; 145, Dolph Briscoe Center for American History, University of Texas at Austin; 203, WW2 Signal Corps Photograph Collection/Courtesy United States Army Military History Institute; 215, WW2 Signal Corps Photograph Collection/Courtesy United States Army Military History Institute; 290, CBS/Landov; 295, CBS/Landov; 301, CBS/Landov; 305, Walter Cronkite IV; 306, Walter Cronkite IV.

INDEX